DORLING KINDE
—HANDBOO

DOG

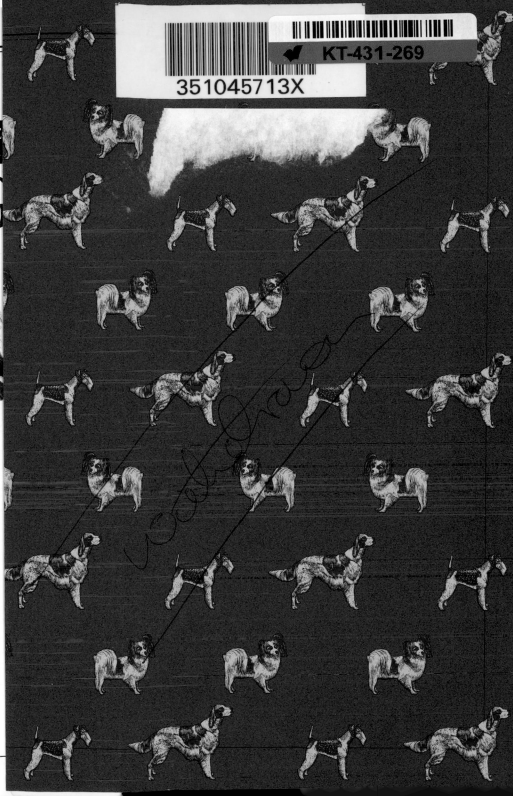

DORLING KINDERSLEY
──HANDBOOKS──

DOGS

DAVID ALDERTON

Photography by
TRACY MORGAN

A Dorling Kindersley Book

Dorling Kindersley

LONDON, NEW YORK, AUCKLAND, DELHI, JOHANNESBURG,
MUNICH, PARIS and SYDNEY

DK www.dk.com

Project Editor Damien Moore
Art Editors Vicki James, Shaun Mc Nally
Series Editor Jonathan Metcalf
Series Art Editor Spencer Holbrook
Production Controller Caroline Webber

First published in Great Britain in 1993
Reprinted with corrections in 2000
by Dorling Kindersley Limited,
9 Henrietta Street, London WC2E 8PS
10 9 8 7 6 5 4 3 2

Copyright © 1993
Dorling Kindersley Limited, London
Text Copyright © 1993 David Alderton

A CIP catalogue record for this book is available
from the British Library

ISBN 0-7513-2751-4

Computer page make-up by
Damien Moore

Text film output by
The Right Type, Great Britain

Reproduced by Colourscan, Singapore

Printed and bound by
Kyodo Printing Co., Singapore

CONTENTS

INTRODUCTION • 6
Author's Introduction 6
How This Book Works 9
The Dog Family 10
Domestic Dog Groups 12
What is a Dog? 14
Coat Types 16
Senses and Instincts 18
Puppies 20
Choosing a Dog 22
Pet Care 24
Showing Your Dog 26
Dog Identification Key 28

COMPANION DOGS 38
GUNDOGS 60
HERDING DOGS 105
HOUNDS 138
TERRIERS 206
WORKING DOGS 231

Dog Credits 296
Useful Addresses 298
Glossary 299
Index 300
Acknowledgments 304

AUTHOR'S INTRODUCTION

Despite the variety of shapes and sizes in today's domestic dog breeds, all are directly related to the Grey Wolf. The process of domestication began more than 12,000 years ago, probably in disparate regions in the northern hemisphere, at a time when wolves had a far wider distribution than they do today. The early semi-wild dogs were probably kept for herding and guarding stock, rather than as companions.

ARCHAEOLOGICAL evidence has now revealed that marked distinctions in the sizes of domestic dogs had already become apparent over 9,000 years ago, even in dogs living in the same region. This trend seems to have gathered momentum, with the characteristic build of many of today's breeds being established by Roman times. By this stage in their history, dogs were being kept largely for the same purposes as they are today: hunting; working with livestock; guarding property; and acting

ANCIENT GODS
Dating from about 200BC, this mummified dog was prepared by the Egyptians to resemble the jackal-god, Anubis.

as companions. Highly selective breeding and natural adaptation to various climatic conditions led to the emergence of countless new forms of dog through the Middle Ages. By the 1800s many of the highly intelligent and specialized gundog breeds known today had evolved.

BREED STANDARDS

In the past, many dogs may have been similar in general appearance to the way they are today, but they were not then classified in specific breeds. The most significant change in this respect occurred very recently in canine history.

As dog shows became fashionable in the late 19th century, the need arose for specific criteria against which individual dogs could be compared and judged. Enthusiasts in Great Britain grouped together in 1873 to form what became known as the Kennel Club. This led directly to the establishment of stud books and set standards for certain dog breeds. It also set basic rules for shows. Similar organizations followed in other

OFF TO THE HUNT
This medieval hunting scene depicts a distinctly greyhound-type breed in pursuit of its quarry. Leaner, sleeker dogs were better adapted for speed.

EARLY FOXHOUND
Many hounds have been developed to pursue a particular quarry; foxhounds are bred to have the pace, stamina, and tenacity needed for fox hunting.

purpose of this book is to serve as a guide to identifying these breeds, whether worldwide or local. Official recognition of breeds, however, depends largely on the individual countries and organizations. Breed standards often differ slightly between countries, as do the regulations concerning ear cropping and tail docking.

Wherever possible, and with the co-operation of top breeders in countries throughout the world, this book includes illustrations of top class examples of the dogs as representatives of their breeds.

countries: the American Kennel Club was formed in 1884, and its Canadian counterpart in 1888.

BREED RECOGNITION

Nowadays, certain breeds, such as the German Shepherd Dog, have become popular throughout the world. Others, however, such as the American coonhounds, remain far more localized, perhaps even restricted to one specific region of a single country. The main

CHARLES CRUFT
The founder of the famous Crufts dog show started his career as a dog food salesman.

EARLY SHOW
Great Danes come under scrutiny at the 1933 Crufts dog show (below).

SHOWING

Not all opportunities to show a dog are dependent on the animal's adherence to breed standards. Nor are they as demanding, on dogs or owners, as championship shows such as Crufts. Open shows follow the same format as the championship shows, but they are considerably shorter: the best-of-breed winners compete for the best-in-show award. For dogs and owners new to showing, these can prove to be excellent venues at which to learn what is expected by judges.

Field trials (to put gundogs through their paces) and sheepdog trials are specialized events. At sheepdog trials, a dog herds a flock over a preset course into an enclosure. Points are given for speed and concentration, and penalties incurred for barking and

AGILITY EVENTS

At an agility event, both pure-bred and mongrel dogs are judged on their competence in negotiating obstacles and obeying verbal commands.

nipping when dogs grow impatient. The teamwork between man and dog displayed at these events is perhaps the most striking example of the progress that has been made since man and wolf embarked on their curious alliance over 12,000 years ago.

TOP DOG
The winner's cup or rosette is not only a reward for a good performance on the day – it is the culmination of months of dedicated hard work.

HOW THIS BOOK WORKS

FOLLOWING the Introduction and the Identification Key, the main breed section of the book is divided into six dog groups: companion dogs, gundogs, herding dogs, hounds, terriers, and working dogs. The breeds are ordered according to country of origin, ranging worldwide from the USA to Australia. The annotated example below shows how a typical entry is organized.

name of country where breed was originally developed •

function for which breed was originally developed •

approximate date of • breed's origin

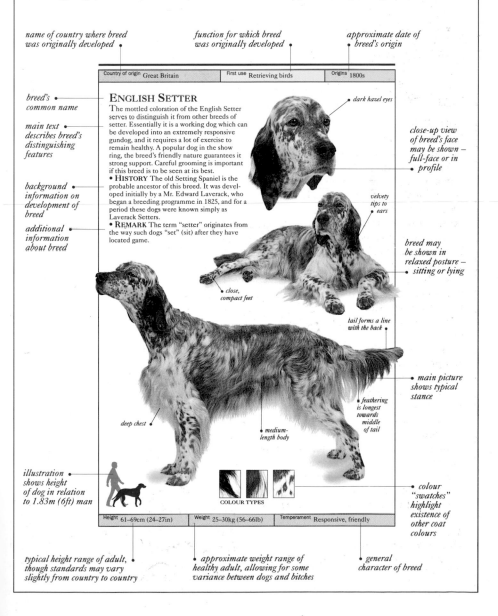

breed's • common name

| Country of origin | Great Britain | First use | Retrieving birds | Origins | 1800s |

ENGLISH SETTER

dark hazel eyes

The mottled coloration of the English Setter serves to distinguish it from other breeds of setter. Essentially it is a working dog which can be developed into an extremely responsive gundog, and it requires a lot of exercise to remain healthy. A popular dog in the show ring, the breed's friendly nature guarantees it strong support. Careful grooming is important if this breed is to be seen at its best.
• HISTORY The old Setting Spaniel is the probable ancestor of this breed. It was developed initially by a Mr. Edward Laverack, who began a breeding programme in 1825, and for a period these dogs were known simply as Laverack Setters.
• REMARK The term "setter" originates from the way such dogs "set" (sit) after they have located game.

main text • describes breed's distinguishing features

background • information on development of breed

additional • information about breed

close-up view of breed's face may be shown – full-face or in • profile

velvety tips to ears

breed may be shown in relaxed posture – sitting or lying

close, compact feet

tail forms a line with the back •

main picture shows typical stance

feathering is longest towards middle of tail

deep chest •

medium-length body

illustration • shows height of dog in relation to 1.83m (6ft) man

COLOUR TYPES

colour "swatches" highlight existence of other coat colours

| Height | 61–69cm (24–27in) | Weight | 25–30kg (56–66lb) | Temperament | Responsive, friendly |

typical height range of adult, though standards may vary slightly from country to country

approximate weight range of healthy adult, allowing for some variance between dogs and bitches

general character of breed

THE DOG FAMILY

THE EARLIEST MEMBERS of the Canidae family, which comprises all living dogs, jackals, and foxes, can be traced back some 30 million years. Today there are 13 genera and 37 recognized species of these carnivores spread all over the world, although the distribution of some, such as the Grey Wolf (*Canis lupus*), has contracted greatly in recent times. Other species, such as the Red Fox (*Vulpes vulpes*), have adapted to urban living and their range is now much wider. All modern domestic dogs (*Canis familiaris*) are descended from the Grey Wolf and still retain much of the wolf's instincts. Wolves have the same social instinct that

OTHER GENERA

SPECIES
Arctic Fox *(Alopex lagopus)*
Bat-eared Fox *(Otocyon megalotis)*
Dhole *(Cuon alpinus)*
African Wild Dog *(Lycaon pictus)*
Maned Wolf *(Chrysocyon brachyurus)*
Raccoon Dog *(Nyctereutes procyonoides)*
Bush Dog *(Speothos venaticus)*
Small-eared Dog *(Atelocynus microtis)*
Crab-eating Fox *(Cerdocyon thous)*

GENUS *CANIS*

SPECIES
Grey Wolf *(C. lupus)*
Red Wolf *(C. rufus)*
Coyote *(C. latrans)*
Golden Jackal *(C. aureus)*
Simien Jackal *(C. simensis)*
Silver-backed Jackal *(C. mesomelas)*
Side-striped Jackal *(C. adustus)*
Dingo *(C. dingo)*
Domestic Dog *(C. familiaris)*

AFRICAN WILD DOG
A hunter of the African plains, the African Wild Dog lives in family groups. Its numbers have fallen dramatically in recent years, so that the species is now considered endangered.

DOMESTIC DOG
There are now more than 300 different breeds of domestic dog, but they are not recognized by zoologists as separate species. All are grouped under the heading of *Canis familiaris*.

GREY WOLF
Known to have evolved about 300,000 years ago, the highly social Grey Wolf is the largest wild dog. It is a fearless hunter but wary of humans, by whom is has been persecuted for centuries.

dogs display in their loyalty towards their masters; they have the territorial instinct exploited in guard dogs; and they have the hunting instinct refined in gundogs, hounds, and terriers. The Grey Wolf even has the herding instinct – one of the pack specializes in isolating a victim from its herd by using similar skills to a sheepdog.

DINGO

For many years dingoes were thought to be wild dogs. They are now known to be feral – that is, domestic dogs that have reverted to living wild.

CANIDAE

GENUS VULPES

GENUS DUSICYON

SPECIES
Red Fox *(V. vulpes)*
Grey Fox *(V. cinereoargenteus)*
Island Grey Fox *(V. littoralis)*
Swift Fox *(V. velox)*
Fennec Fox *(V. zerda)*
Indian Fox *(V. bengalensis)*
Blanford's Fox *(V. cana)*
Cape Fox *(V. chama)*
Corsac Fox *(V. corsac)*
Tibetan Sand Fox *(V. ferrilata)*
Pale Fox *(V. pallida)*
Kit Fox *(V. macrotis)*
Rüppell's Fox *(V. rueppelli)*

SPECIES
Chilla *(D. griseus)*
Colpeo Fox *(D. culpaeus)*
Small-eared Fox *(D. microtis)*
Pampas Fox *(D. gymnocercus)*
Sechura Fox *(D. sechurae)*
Hoary Fox *(D. vetulus)*

RED FOX
This highly adaptable canid has adjusted well to urban living, emerging at night from its den to feed on garbage. Apart from the domestic dog, it is the most widely distributed member of the family.

CHILLA
As with wild dogs in other parts of the world, the Chilla, or South American Fox, has been hunted for its fur, and this has had an adverse effect on some populations. In comparison with other canids little is known about South American foxes.

DOMESTIC DOG GROUPS

DOMESTIC DOGS may be classified in many different ways, but the fundamental means of separating breeds is on the basis of their function. Although many breeds are now kept as pets, irrespective of their origins, most were first used to carry out specific tasks, such as herding, hunting, and guarding. Their temperament, physique, and behaviour have developed accordingly. For the purposes of this book, six major categorizations have been employed.

GUNDOGS

Bred to work closely with people on a one-to-one basis, gundogs are characterized by their responsive, biddable natures, and high intelligence. The gundog category includes spaniels, setters, retrievers, poodles, and pointers. Many gundogs have multiple uses: they can track the game, indicate the target for the hunter, and retrieve the game if it is shot.

COMPANION DOGS

The idea of keeping dogs as pets was popularized by the royal courts, where dogs have been fashionable for centuries. Companion dogs are generally characterized by small size and gentle nature.

WORKING DOGS

Around the world, dogs have been trained for a wide variety of specific tasks, including pulling sledges across snow and ice. In many countries they are employed to guard property and livestock; in others they are little more than livestock themselves, and have been traditionally used to provide food and fur.

HERDING DOGS

This is an ancient category, dogs having been employed to control the movements of livestock for many centuries. They are most commonly used to herd sheep and cattle, but have also been used to control deer, and even chickens. A good sheepdog is said to possess an "eye" with which it fixes the sheep, persuading them to move with the minimum of disturbance. The development of herding dogs has tended to be localized, which is reflected in the diversity of such breeds today. They are active, intelligent dogs with some of the more distinctive coats.

HOUNDS

This is probably the most ancient category of dog, bred to pursue game. It includes the fastest members of the dog family: the elegant sight hounds, such as the Saluki and the Greyhound. But other hounds, such as the Bloodhound, have been bred for stamina, and these, mostly short-coated, breeds will relentlessly pursue their quarry by scent rather than sight.

TERRIERS

These working breeds, whose development has been centred in Great Britain during the last 100 years, are small but tenacious. Bold and fearless by nature, they are also highly inquisitive. They make first-class rodent-killers, and their small size allows them to "go to earth" in pursuit of quarry, such as foxes, driving them out to be chased by hounds. They make personable companions and enjoy exploring their surroundings.

WHAT IS A DOG?

Aᴸᴸ ᴅᴏɢs are primarily carnivorous, with teeth especially adapted for eating meat and gnawing bones. As they were originally hunters, dogs are equipped with acute senses for detecting prey, and have very powerful muscles, allowing them to run at a great pace, with bursts of speed when necessary. All canids walk on their toes (rather than on the soles of their feet like bears), which allows them greater agility – often an important factor when they are tackling prey much larger than themselves. Dogs also evolved the ability to work together in a pack, thus overcoming the problem of hunting larger animals.

MALTESE DOG SKELETON

WOLF SKELETON

DOWN TO THE BONE

The skeletons of most canids, from the Grey Wolf to the smallest lap dog, are strikingly similar in shape, but natural evolution and man's selective breeding have resulted in some distinctive differences, primarily in the length of limbs and the skull shape. Usually, limb bones are long in relation to the height of the animal.

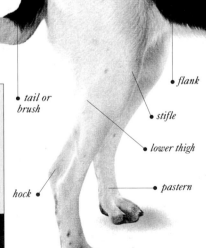

loin

croup

flank

tail or brush

stifle

lower thigh

hock

pastern

hindfoot

CROPPING AND DOCKING

cropped ears

docked tail

Cropping ears to make them erect is a common practice in many countries, but illegal in the UK. In breeds where it is traditional, tail docking is usually carried out soon after birth. It seems to cause little pain, but has become controversial. There is no standard length for a docked tail; in some breeds more is left intact than in others.

SKULL SHAPE

The difference between the tiny, rounded (brachycephalic) skull of the selectively bred Japanese Chin, and the elongate (dolichocephalic) skull of its ancestor, the Grey Wolf, illustrates the extent of man's influence on the development of the domestic dog.

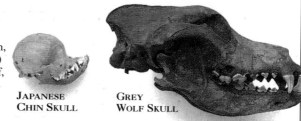

JAPANESE CHIN SKULL

GREY WOLF SKULL

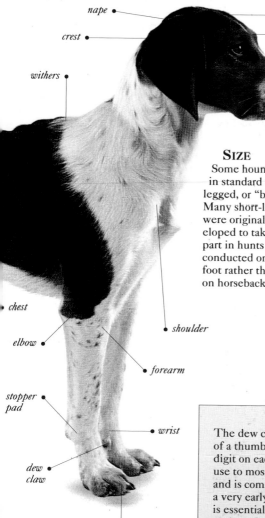

nape

crest

withers

skull

stop

muzzle

SIZE

Some hounds occur in standard and short-legged, or "basset", forms. Many short-legged forms were originally developed to take part in hunts conducted on foot rather than on horseback.

SHORT-LEGGED FORM

STANDARD FORM

chest

elbow

stopper pad

shoulder

forearm

wrist

dew claw

forefoot

DEW CLAWS

The dew claw (equivalent of a thumb) is the innermost digit on each foot. It is of no use to most domestic dogs, and is commonly removed at a very early age. However, it is essential for some breeds, such as the Puffin Dog, as it aids mobility in rough terrain.

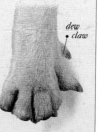

dew claw

COAT TYPES

A DOG'S COAT is comprised of two basic types of hair: the longer, outer, guard hairs, which are fairly coarse in texture; and the softer secondary hairs that make up the undercoat, and through which the guard hairs protrude. Variations on this basic pattern do occur, however, and not all breeds have both types of hair. A dog's coat is an important feature in its development: dogs bred in cold climates are likely to have dense coats; hunting dogs tend to have short, sleek coats; and terriers are often bred with wiry coats for protection against the elements.

CARE CONSIDERATIONS

The type of coat is an important consideration when choosing a dog. As a guide, those with short, smooth coats, such as Dalmatians, are easiest to care for, needing little more than a polish with a hound glove and an occasional bath. In contrast, dogs with wiry coats, such as Schnauzers, must be regularly combed. For show purposes, their coat must be stripped and plucked about once every three months; pets can be clipped about every two months and excess hair trimmed from around the eyes and ears. Breeds with longer coats, such as the Rough Collie, need daily grooming to prevent the coat from becoming matted. Many breeds will benefit from a bath every three months or so, both to keep their coat clean and to reduce their doggy odour. Excessive bathing is not recommended, however.

DESERT DWELLER
Its short coat allows this young Dingo to tolerate the Australian desert sun.

LONG-HAIRED COAT

WIRE-HAIRED COAT

SMOOTH COAT

COLOUR TYPES

Whereas some breeds occur in just a single colour form, in other cases a much wider range of combinations exists. The colour panels accompanying the breed entries in this book serve to give a general indication of some alternative colour types for each particular breed. The panels themselves are not exact colour replicas, but reflect major colour groupings, as set out below. In the case of patterned varieties, precise distribution of the colours may be laid down in the breed standard. Not all colours in a particular breed may be recognized for exhibition purposes.

LIVER
Includes reddish brown, sable, and cinnamon shades.

BLACK BRINDLE
Includes "pepper and salt", a grey/black combination.

CREAM
Includes white, and light shades such as ivory, blond, and lemon.

BLUE MOTTLED WITH TAN
Includes blue and brindle, and bluish black and tan.

TAN AND WHITE
A colour combination seen in many breeds of hound.

RED/TAN
Includes red, red-fawn, tawny, rich chestnut, orange roan, chestnut roan.

BLACK AND WHITE
Includes black or brindle markings with white.

BLACK
Some breeds are pure black, but may become grey around the muzzle with age.

BLUE
Includes merle (blue-grey), and speckled blue (with black).

BLACK, TAN, AND WHITE
Otherwise known as tricolour.

GOLD AND WHITE
Includes white with lemon, gold, or orange spots.

DARK BROWN
Includes mahogany and blackish brown.

GREY
Includes all shades from silvery to blue-black grey, and grey or black brindle.

RED BRINDLE
Includes orange or mahogany brindle.

BLACK AND TAN
Clearly defined colours which result in good contrast.

LIVER AND TAN
A combination of two reddish shades.

FUR COLOURS
A black and a yellow Labrador. There is also a liver-coloured variety.

GOLD
Includes russet gold, fawn, apricot, wheaten, and tawny.

LIVER AND WHITE
A coloration often associated with gundog breeds.

CHESTNUT RED AND WHITE
Includes combinations of white with orange, fawn, red, chestnut.

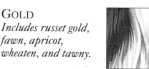

SENSES AND INSTINCTS

SINCE THE PROCESS of domestication first began, selective breeding over 4,000 generations or more has changed the physical appearance of some dogs almost beyond recognition. But even the tiny Chihuahua (see p.41) still displays many of the behavioural characteristics of its ancestor, the wolf. Like the wolf, the domestic dog communicates by means of calls and body language, its ears and tail being especially expressive, and it retains the same strong social instincts.

SENSITIVE EARS

HEARING
Dogs generally have a very acute sense of hearing, and are able to hear sounds that are too high-pitched for human beings. This greater hearing range assists dogs in tracking down their quarry, and in communicating with each other. Recently, dogs have been used to help deaf people, some being trained to indicate such sounds as a ringing telephone.

COMMUNICATION
Wolves keep in touch with each other by howling, a means of communication well developed in northern spitz breeds, which work in groups. Pack hounds tracking a scent may also bay, which is useful to the hunter when the dog is not visible.

ON THE SCENT

SENDING A MESSAGE

KEEN EYESIGHT

SIGHT
The position of the eyes, towards the sides of the head, gives dogs a wider field of vision than human beings, making them more aware of their environment. Dogs also have better vision at dusk because the cells in the retina, where the image is focused, respond well to low light. However, colour vision is limited.

SMELL
The keen sense of smell common to all dogs is most fully developed in breeds such as the Bloodhound, which uses it to track quarry. Dogs rely on the nose, as well as Jacobson's Organ in the mouth, to detect scent particles.

SCENT MARKING

Dog urine contains highly individual chemical scent markers, or pheromones. A male will convey the boundaries of his territory to other dogs by using urine as a marker. After puberty, male dogs spray urine by lifting their leg, rather than squatting like a bitch, in order to hit a target such as a tree or a post. They may also scratch the ground, leaving a scent from the sweat glands between their toes. There is a distinct difference in scent marking between the sexes, and male dogs urinate perhaps three times more frequently than bitches.

IDENTIFYING A STRANGER

AGGRESSION

Male dogs meeting in antagonistic situations carry out a well-defined series of gestures, indicating submission (below), or threatening aggression without actually attacking their opponent. The dog stands upright, tail erect, raising its hackles (the hairs along its back). The neck extends forwards and the mouth opens into a snarl.

READY TO FIGHT

SUBMISSION

If a dog wants to submit, it will probably crouch down, with its tail between its legs and its ears down. In some cases it may run off, with the dominant dog in pursuit. Alternatively, it may roll over on to its back, like a puppy, and may urinate a little if it has no easy means of retreat. A submissive dog is not likely to be attacked.

OFFERING NO DEFENCE

COMPANIONSHIP

Despite their need to establish a "pecking order", dogs are social by nature and generally get on well together. Dogs bred as companions tend to be less noisy than hounds, since barking is not considered a desirable trait where dogs are living in close proximity to people. A companion dog will wag its tail and open its mouth slightly in greeting when a member of the family returns home.

FAITHFUL FRIEND

PUPPIES

MOST PEOPLE prefer to own a dog from a puppy, so that they can train it themselves. A puppy will settle more rapidly into unfamiliar surroundings than older individuals, and is unlikely to display the behavioural problems that can be encountered in adult dogs. Even so, it is important to realize that some disruption and damage in the home is likely to follow its acquisition. Carpets, for example, may be soiled or chewed, and puppies may bark or yelp a great deal when first left on their own. This calls for tolerance on the part of owners. Sensible training and adequate attention to the puppy's needs should reduce such problems to a minimum. Dogs are creatures of routine, and will soon learn to respond as required.

GOLDEN
RETRIEVER
AND PUPS

THE BREEDING PERIOD

Domestic bitches (female dogs) usually have two periods of "heat" each year, whereas wild bitches come into season only once during this time. Both wild and domestic dogs have a gestation period of about two months before the litter is born. The offspring, known as pups or cubs, are helpless at birth, and are suckled and cleaned by their mother until they start to be weaned on to solid food at about four to six weeks old.

HEALTHY PUPS

Young dogs tend to play vigorously and then sleep for long periods. This is not a sign of ill-health. Similarly, in a new home, a pup will be less active than an adult dog. Key health indicators to look for are a good appetite, and firm motions with no trace of blood. The skin is normally loose, but watch for a pot-bellied appearance, which could indicate worms. Deworming is a vital process for the pup's continued good health. Your vet will be able to advise you on essential vaccinations.

PLAYFUL
PATTERDALES

THE DEVELOPING PUP

The coat of a pup may be less profuse than its mother's (as in the example of the Old English Sheepdog, shown right), but the distribution of markings is unlikely to change as the pup matures.

By the time it is six months old, the pup should be house-trained. It should also be walking readily on a leash and can soon be allowed to exercise freely. Choose a quiet spot away from roads, and away from distractions such as other dogs or farm animals. If the dog runs off, do not chase it, because it is likely to see this as a game. Instead, stand still and call it back. It should return after its enthusiasm for its new-found freedom wears off.

OLD ENGLISH
SHEEPDOG AND PUP

SHAR PEI PUP   COCKER SPANIEL PUP

RELATIVE SIZES

All young puppies, no matter what their breed, are of a relatively similar size at birth. Only later do the larger breeds, like the Shar pei (far left) start to grow at a faster rate than the smaller breeds, like the Cocker Spaniel (near left). Avoid exercising young dogs too strenuously, especially the larger breeds, because this puts stresses on their frame. It is better just to give them daily walks, with the opportunity to run free if they wish.

TOWARDS ADULTHOOD

Changes become apparent as pups grow older. In certain breeds, such as the German Shepherd Dog, the ears will start to become erect. In a few cases this does not happen, but generally the ears should have started to lift by the time the puppy is approaching six months old. In breeds in which pups are noticeably paler at birth than the adult dogs (as in the case of the Australian Cattle Dog, shown right), coat coloration is also likely to have darkened by six months. Other characteristics, such as eye colour, may also be more adult-like by this age.

AUSTRALIAN
CATTLE DOG
AND PUP

CHOOSING A DOG

WHEN CHOOSING A DOG the potential owner is influenced by a number of factors, such as health, appearance, and character, but the size of the adult dog is generally the chief concern. However, size can often be deceptive, as some large dogs, such as the Greyhound, can be much less active in the home than smaller breeds. Unfortunately, the more dogs are kept as companions the more their origins become obscured, though the instincts that first shaped their development often remain largely intact. Too many people choose a dog on the basis of its appearance alone without giving adequate consideration to the breed's ancestry, which is a factor that affects both its character and behaviour.

SMALL IS BEAUTIFUL

Toy dogs such as the Papillon have a built-in advantage over larger breeds – their appetite is smaller and so they are less expensive to feed. They are quite easy to train and tend to be keen to please their owners. They thrive on affection and are usually good with children. However, it does not always follow that small dogs need less space; many small dogs, especially terriers, are very active and like nothing better than to run loose in open country.

PAPILLON

BEAGLE

HOUNDS

Some smaller hounds, such as the Beagle, have much to recommend them as pets, often having short, easy-care coats and lively, active natures. All scent hounds can be difficult to train, however, and will be reluctant to return to their owners if they pick up a scent. Pack dogs by nature, they can be greedy eaters.

SPANIELS

Gundogs were developed to have a close rapport with their owners, and breeds such as the English Springer Spaniel make admirable house companions, provided they have plenty of opportunity to exercise and plenty of time devoted to their needs. Grooming is a must, and particular attention should be paid to the heavy, pendulous ears, or they may become a source of problems in later life. Infections in the ears are common in spaniel breeds. One simple precaution is to invest in a very deep food bowl. The ears should then hang down outside the bowl, where they are less likely to become soiled by food.

ENGLISH SPRINGER SPANIEL

POINTS TO CHECK

backbone not prominent

coat free from lice or fleas

clear ears

eyes clear and free from discharge

clean anal area

pup should walk and run freely

pot belly may indicate worms

check for presence of dew claws

CHOOSING A PUP

Having decided on the breed, you may be able to obtain a puppy locally. Breeders can be traced through the dog magazines or via the national kennel club. The cost of pups varies depending on their pedigree and the relative rarity of the breed. Pups are generally fully weaned and ready for their new home at about nine weeks old. Arrange for a veterinary check-up as soon as possible to ensure that the pup is in good health. However, not everybody wants, or can afford to buy, a pedigree dog and, in terms of companionship, mongrels (dogs of mixed breed) can be delightful pets. But remember that it may be hard to determine the ultimate size of a mongrel.

DOBERMANN

GREAT DANE

GUARD DOGS

Breeds suitable for guard work, such as the Dobermann, have recently undergone a surge in popularity. However, many guard dogs retain strong working instincts and are dominant by nature. Consequently, they require firm training from a very early age if they are not to become a liability as they grow older.

THE BIGGER THE BETTER

The size of dogs such as the Great Dane can be off-putting. But size is no reliable indicator of a dog's temperament, for this is a gentle, largely placid breed. There are certainly drawbacks in keeping an animal of this size: feeding costs are considerable, and they need plenty of living space.

PET CARE

A VARIETY OF EQUIPMENT is needed for grooming, feeding, and exercising a dog. However, it is important to choose the right equipment for your particular choice of breed, as requirements differ somewhat. Choosing the right equipment for the right stage in your dog's life will save you unnecessary trouble and expense. It may be better to defer the purchase of a bed, for instance, until the teething phase has passed, at around nine months of age. A cardboard box will do until then. Otherwise, your expensive purchase may be damaged beyond repair.

GROOMING AND COAT CARE

Regular grooming is vital from an early age, not only to keep the dog's coat in good condition, but also to accustom it to the procedure, which the dog will then readily accept throughout its life. Some breeds require more coat care than others, depending on the quality of the hair, the length of the coat, and the lifestyle of the dog. Regular grooming sessions are a perfect opportunity for you to check for any health problems your dog may be experiencing, such as rashes, hair loss, sores or wounds, or any lumps or swellings that may need attention from a veterinarian. If you intend to show your dog, these sessions will also accustom the animal to being handled.

COMBS AND BRUSHES

double-headed brush for finishing off

wire comb for untangling

flea comb

BRUSHING
Regular brushing to remove tangles and snags is the first step to keeping your dog's coat in good condition. You will have better access to all of the coat if you can persuade the dog to remain standing throughout this process.

SLEEPING QUARTERS
Encouraging a dog to use its own sleeping quarters from an early age will deter it from sleeping on your bed or using the sofa and chairs as a substitute.

DOG BEDS
When you decide that the purchase of a bed is in order, make sure that it is fully washable, for this is the site where fleas typically deposit their eggs. By cleaning the bed on a regular basis, you may be able to spare yourself an explosive epidemic of these troublesome parasites. If you are buying a bed for a young dog, make sure that it is sufficiently large to accommodate the dog comfortably once it is fully grown.

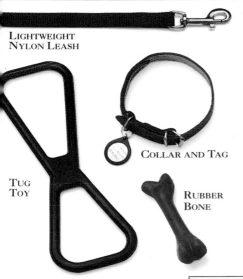

LIGHTWEIGHT
NYLON LEASH

COLLAR AND TAG

TUG
TOY

RUBBER
BONE

COLLARS, LEASHES, AND TOYS

Pups from six to seven weeks old should be introduced to wearing a collar. Proper training of all dogs must include learning to walk calmly on a collar and leash with their owner. A leather collar can be unbuckled and made longer as your dog grows. Adjust it so that it fits loosely, but is not so slack that the dog can pull its head free of it. In case your dog wanders, be sure to attach a tag to the collar stating your address and telephone number.

Dogs, even when fully grown, enjoy play, and your pet store should have a wide range of suitable toys. Play sessions are not only fun for the dog, they also represent good exercise. Tug toys and rubber bones help to keep the dog's teeth in good condition, but avoid small items that pups may swallow.

CERAMIC
BOWL

STAINLESS-STEEL
BOWL

NUTRITIONAL CARE

Food and water bowls should be made from a material that can be properly cleaned. Replace ceramic bowls once they are chipped or cracked, for such defects are sites where bacteria may breed.

Try not to vary the puppy's diet at first, even if you intend to change from canned to dry food, for example, at a later stage. This should help to minimize the likelihood of any digestive upsets. If you decide to use a feeding supplement, be sure to follow the manufacturer's instructions carefully, because overdosing may well prove harmful.

HEALTH CARE

TEETH CARE

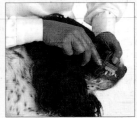

You can now buy specially made toothpaste and brushes for your dog. These will help to ensure healthy teeth and gums throughout its life.

GIVING MEDICINE

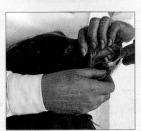

If your dog is co-operative you should be able to administer medicine orally using a spoon. If not, use a syringe. Give it slowly or the dog is likely to spit it out.

EAR CLEANING

Remove dead hair with your fingers, use a dropper to put oily cleanser into the ear canal, massage the base of the ear to spread it, then clear oil or wax at the surface with cotton wool. Never poke into the ear canal.

SHOWING YOUR DOG

MANY OWNERS of pure-bred dogs are great show enthusiasts and travel considerable distances in the hope of success in the show ring. For the vast majority of participants, however, there are no financial rewards for all their hard work. This is one arena where the amateur still reigns supreme, with people taking part simply because they enjoy the opportunity to show their dogs, meet other people who have similar interests, and share in the excitement as the final winners are chosen. For information on shows, consult the specialist dog press.

BATH TIME
For the show dog, a bath is the first stage of preparation for the ring. Place the bath in a draught-free spot, and use warm water and shampoo formulated for dogs. Hold the dog's head up so that water runs away from its eyes and nose. Thoroughly rinse out the shampoo, towel dry, and, for long-haired breeds, use a hairdryer before brushing.

HAIRDRYER
Use a low-heat setting only.

CLIPPING
With some breeds of dog, such as the poodle (left), the coat must be clipped to conform to the breed standard for show purposes. The traditional show clip for the poodle is either the English Lion Clip or the Continental Lion Clip. Dogs under one year of age may be shown in the "puppy clip". For non-show dogs, a less stylized, more easy-going coat shape is the "lamb clip".

CONTINENTAL LION CLIP

ENGLISH LION CLIP

KEEPING CLEAN
With a long-haired dog, you may have to go to considerable lengths to keep it clean and tangle-free after it has been bathed in the run-up to its appearance in front of the judges. Here (right), a Yorkshire Terrier has been bathed and had its hair tied up until show time. Its marvellous, flowing, full-length coat is then revealed, with just a single bow remaining.

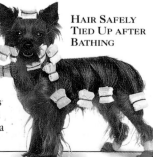

HAIR SAFELY TIED UP AFTER BATHING

COMBED AND READY

THE BIG DAY

The show ring is the culmination of much hard work by the owners. A good show dog is trained to display itself to best advantage in front of the judge. A calm disposition is essential, for the dog must tolerate close examination and handling by a stranger, and it must ignore the unsettling presence of the

A DOG SHOW IN PROGRESS

A class of Afghan Hounds and their handlers wait anxiously for the verdict of the judge.

other dogs. In turn, a judge needs a thorough knowledge of the official breed standards in order to assess the dog's demeanour, stance, presence, movement, and temperament.

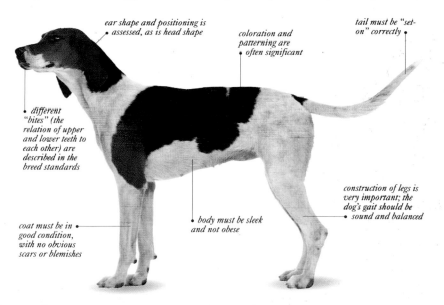

ear shape and positioning is assessed, as is head shape

coloration and patterning are often significant

tail must be "set-on" correctly

different "bites" (the relation of upper and lower teeth to each other) are described in the breed standards

construction of legs is very important; the dog's gait should be sound and balanced

coat must be in good condition, with no obvious scars or blemishes

body must be sleek and not obese

BREED STANDARDS

The breed standard in every country where a breed is recognized usually specifies such things as the height and weight of the dog; the proportions of the body with reference to specific body parts; coloration; and the appearance and texture of the coat, ears, tail, eyes, and feet. Typical faults that count against a dog are also listed at the end of the standard.

DOG IDENTIFICATION KEY

THE SYSTEM OF IDENTIFICATION used here assumes no prior knowledge of dog character or function, but offers instead a method of recognition based on noting key physical characteristics, as defined below and opposite. On the following pages (pp.30–37), all the breeds in the book are separated into groups, first by size (small, medium, or large), then by head shape (round, long, or square), ear type (long, erect, or short), and finally by coat type (short, long, or wiry). At the end of this trail appears a typical dog of that type (e.g., small, round-headed, long-eared, and short-coated), together with the page numbers on which all breeds with similar features appear.

In a few cases, a breed may appear in more than one group.

SIZE
This is the most evident feature that separates breeds. Three categories are used – small, medium, and large – and they refer to the highest point of the shoulder (the withers). This is also the measure for show purposes, and is the figure given in the actual breed entries.

HEAD SHAPE
This is obviously a less precise feature than height, but, again, the breeds have been divided into three broad categories: round-headed, long-headed, and square-headed. Round-headed breeds tend to be short-nosed; long-headed breeds have long noses, which may taper; square-headed breeds often have relatively short, muscular jaws.

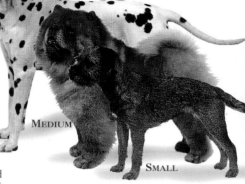

LARGE

MEDIUM

SMALL

SIZE VARIANTS
The sizes shown are: large, over 61cm (24in); medium, 46–61cm (18–24in); and small, under 46cm (18in).

SQUARE HEAD

LONG HEAD

ROUNDED HEAD

HEAD SHAPE
This can give an indication of the dog's ancestry. Sight hounds, like the Greyhound, typically have a long muzzle. Breeds originally bred for fighting tend to have a short, squarish muzzle.

LONG EARS

EAR SHAPE AND LENGTH

The shape and length of a dog's ears vary considerably. Erect ears trap sound waves most effectively, but in hounds that rely on their sense of smell to locate quarry, the ears tend to hang down. By obscuring the ear canal with the flap, the sensitive inner part of the ear is protected when the hounds are pursuing quarry through vegetation, and this also reduces the risk of seeds or thorns falling into the ear. Short ears allow dogs to go to ground more easily, and are particularly encouraged in terrier breeds.

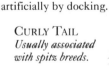

SHORT EARS

CROPPING
The appearance of a dog's ears can be altered by cropping, which is still practised in some countries. The breeds in this identification key are grouped on the basis of their natural ear shape and position.

ERECT EARS

COATS

Another significant feature that can help to identify a dog is its coat type. Coats can be divided into short- or long-haired, on the basis of their length, while the third category, wire-haired, is distinguished by texture. Some breeds, such as the Dachshunds, have been developed in all three coat types, while others may occur in both short- and long-haired forms, although one type often tends to predominate today.

TAILS

Tails show considerable variation in length and shape, but recognition of the various types is not essential for breed identification. Tails can be altered artificially by docking.

CURLY TAIL
Usually associated with spitz breeds.

SHORT HAIR
Creates a smooth, sleek appearance, with the hair tight against the skin.

LONG TAIL
Used as a means of communication; enables a dog to be seen in undergrowth.

LONG HAIR
Usually combines with a dense undercoat to give weatherproofing.

FEATHERED TAIL
Formed by longer hair on lower tail surface. Associated with setters and other gundogs.

WIRE HAIR
A harsh and dense type often found on breeds working in undergrowth.

DOCKED TAIL
Mainly carried out on terriers, this procedure creates a short, erect tail.

BREEDS GROUPED BY KEY CHARACTERISTICS

SMALL DOGS

THIS GROUP INCLUDES all breeds under 46 centimetres (18in) in height. Once you have established that the dog belongs to this category, you should identify the head shape (see p.28), followed by the ear and coat type. You will then be able to locate a breed of that physical type in one of the bands below or on pages 32 to 33,

ROUND-HEADED

	SHORT-HAIRED	LONG-HAIRED	WIRE-HAIRED
LONG-EARED	 Beagle *146(b)*	 Tibetan Terrier *55(b)* OTHERS *38, 40(b), 43(b), 46(b), 49, 51(t), 52, 53(b), 55(t), 56(t & b), 57(b), 58, 59(b), 60, 63*	 Dandie Dinmont Terrier *213(t)*

LONG-HEADED

	SHORT-HAIRED		LONG-HAIRED
LONG-EARED	 Basset Hound *146(t)*	 Italian Greyhound *50* OTHERS *40(t), 43(t), 47(b), 48, 50, 59(t), 146(b), 155(t), 158–59, 173(t & b), 175, 186(b), 187, 209(b)*	 Cesky Terrier *230(b)*
ERECT-EARED	SHORT-HAIRED  Miniature Bull Terrier *212(t)*	 English Toy Terrier *210(t)* OTHERS *42, 54, 107(b), 111(t), 111(b), 132(t), 197, 206, 210(b), 246(t), 249(b), 291(b)*	LONG-HAIRED  German Spitz: Mittel *44(b)* OTHERS *39(t), 44(t), 45(t & b), 51(b), 57(t), 132(b), 221(t), 225*

where there will also be page references for all similar breeds featured in the book. "Small" dogs include the so-called toy breeds, and many terriers. Their size makes them popular as companions today, although some were quite localized in former years. Some terriers share a common ancestry, and may resemble each other, whereas true companion dogs show a much wider variation in appearance.

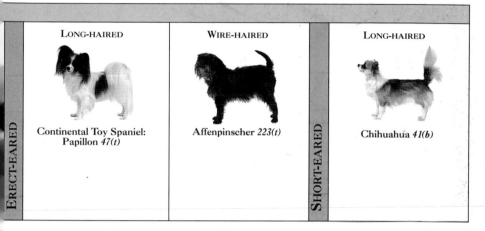

ERECT-EARED

LONG-HAIRED

Continental Toy Spaniel:
Papillon 47(t)

WIRE-HAIRED

Affenpinscher 223(t)

SHORT-EARED

LONG-HAIRED

Chihuahua 41(b)

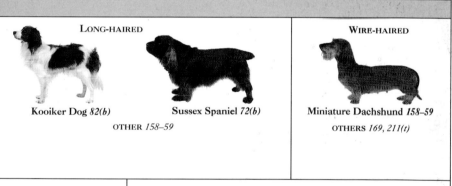

LONG-HAIRED

Kooiker Dog 82(b)   Sussex Spaniel 72(b)

OTHER 158–59

WIRE-HAIRED

Miniature Dachshund 158–59

OTHERS 169, 211(t)

LONG-HAIRED

Shetland Sheepdog 109(b)

WIRE-HAIRED

Australian Terrier 220(b)

Podengo Portugueso
Pequeno 197

OTHERS 211(b), 217(t), 225

SMALL, LONG-HEADED DOGS *continued*

SHORT-EARED

SHORT-HAIRED

Parson Jack Russell
Terrier *215(t)*

Japanese Terrier *292(t)*

OTHERS *218(t), 221(b), 222, 223(b), 228(b)*

Smooth Fox Terrier *216(t)*

SQUARE-HEADED

ERECT-EARED

SHORT-HAIRED	LONG-HAIRED	WIRE-HAIRED

Boston Terrier *208(b)*

OTHER *263(t)*

Skye Terrier *217(b)*

OTHER *219*

Cairn Terrier *213(b)*

OTHER *218(b)*

MEDIUM-SIZED DOGS

THIS GROUP INCLUDES all breeds between 41 and 61 centimetres (18–24in) in height. Once you have established that the dog belongs to this category, you should identify the head shape (see p.28), followed by the ear and coat type. You will then be able to locate a breed of that physical type below or on

ROUND-HEADED

LONG-EARED

SHORT-HAIRED	LONG-HAIRED

Labrador *69*

OTHER *136*

Polish Lowland Sheepdog *123(t)*

OTHERS *66(b), 67(t), 95, 106,
123(b), 136, 266*

WIRE-HAIRED

Wire Fox Terrier *215(b)*

Lakeland Terrier *214(t)*

Welsh Terrier *216(b)*

OTHERS *214(b), 215(t), 221(b), 224, 228(t)*

SHORT-HAIRED	WIRE-HAIRED

Pug *53*

OTHERS *39(b), 212(b)*

Sealyham Terrier *220(t)*

OTHER *229*

pages 34 to 37, where there will also be page references for all similar breeds featured in the book.

Many common breeds are medium sized, including various gundogs, sheepdogs, and hounds, though others remain localized, even within their country of origin. Nevertheless, rare-breed shows are gradually introducing many of them to a wider audience.

LONG-HAIRED

Chow Chow *288*

LONG-HAIRED

Briard *116–117*

MEDIUM-SIZED, LONG-HEADED DOGS *continued*

LONG-EARED

SHORT-HAIRED

Weimaraner 76–77

OTHERS *61, 62, 67(b), 70–71, 72(t), 74, 79, 82(t), 87, 88–89, 90, 91, 92(t), 93, 98, 101, 102, 103, 104, 120–21,*

138, 139(t & b), 140, 141, 142–43, 144, 145, 147, 151(b), 152, 153, 154(t & b), 155(b), 156, 157, 160(t & b), 161, 164, 165, 166–67, 168, 170–71, 174, 178, 180, 182, 183, 184–85, 188, 189(t), 190, 191, 195, 199, 201, 205, 230(t & b), 272, 274, 279, 280(t), 284(t)

LONG-HAIRE

Afghan Hound 2

OTHERS *64, 65, 66 68, 73, 75, 76–77, 80 83(t & b), 84, 86,*

ERECT-EARED

SHORT-HAIRED

Pharoah Hound 193

Sarloos Wolfhound 125

OTHERS *109(t), 112, 113, 115, 119, 129, 192(b), 194, 198, 204, 233(b), 234–35, 239(t), 245(t & b), 246(b), 247(t & b), 248, 249(t), 281, 284(b), 285(t & b), 286, 287, 290, 292(b)*

LONG-HAIR

Keeshond 46(t)

OTHERS *108, 114(t & b), 124, 126, 128*

SHORT-EARED

SHORT-HAIRED

Sloughi 203

Chinook 233(t)

OTHERS *107(t), 150, 151(t), 186(t), 196*

Irish Red and White Setter *85*

OTHERS *96, 103, 105, 110, 134(t & b), 135, 137, 149, 275, 280(t), 267, 270–71, 295*

WIRE-HAIRED

WIRE-HAIRED

Spinone *100*

Briquet Griffon Vendéen *177(t)*

OTHERS *78, 97(t & b), 99, 122, 165, 176, 177(b), 179, 180, 181, 189(b), 192(t)*

Berger de Picard *118*

OTHERS *239(b), 243, 262, 268*

WIRE-HAIRED

Laekenois *127*

Podengo Portugueso: Medio *198*

OTHERS *194, 226*

LONG-HAIRED

Soft-coated Wheaten Terrier *227*

Border Collie *107(t)*

WIRE-HAIRED

Airedale Terrier *209(t)*

MEDIUM-SIZED, SQUARE-HEADED DOGS *continued*

LONG-EARED

SHORT-HAIRED

Dogue de Bordeaux *263(b)*

OTHERS *238, 242, 260, 273, 280(b), 293*

LONG-HAIRED

Bouvier des Flandres *130–31*

OTHERS *133(b), 273*

LARGE DOGS

THIS GROUP INCLUDES all breeds over 61 centimetres (24in) in height. Once you have established that the dog belongs to this category, you should identify the head shape (see p.28), followed by the ear and coat type. You will then be able to

LONG-HEADED

LONG-EARED

SHORT-HAIRED

Great Dane *252–53*

OTHERS *243, 283, 291(b)*

LONG-HAIRED

Pyrenean Mastiff *278*

OTHERS *200, 258–59, 261, 264–65, 282*

SQUARE-HEADED

LONG-EARED

SHORT-HAIRED

Neopolitan Mastiff *276–77*

Mastiff *236–37*

ERECT-EARED

LONG-HAIRED

Pumi *133(b)*

SHORT-EARED

SHORT-HAIRED

Boxer *255(t)*

OTHERS *207, 208(t), 231, 232, 289, 294*

locate a breed of that physical type in one of the bands below, where there will also be page references for all similar breeds featured in the book.

As might be expected, these breeds are relatively few in number, though some can trace their ancestry back to the oldest forms of the domestic dog.

WIRE-HAIRED

Irish Wolfhound *162–63*

SHORT-EARED

WIRE-HAIRED

Deerhound *148*

SHORT-EARED

LONG-HAIRED

Landseer *256–57*

Newfoundland *240–41*

COMPANION DOGS

BRED ESSENTIALLY AS PETS and not as working dogs, companion dogs appear in a wide variety of shapes and sizes. They are often simply scaled-down versions of much larger dogs, but some, such as the Chihuahua (see p.41), were created specifically as companions, with no hint of a working ancestry. Others, like the Bulldog (see p.39) and the Basenji (see p.59), were developed from former working stock.

Companion dogs are typically loyal and affectionate by nature, but concerns have been expressed regarding the constitution of some members of this group. A hindlimb weakness centred on the knees (called luxating patellas) is one type of problem found in some companion breeds. However, by careful selection of adult breeding stock, breeders are continually seeking to eliminate such weaknesses.

Country of origin USA	First use Companion	Origins 1972

KYI LEO

One of the newest breeds to enter the dog world, the Kyi Leo is a small, solidly built animal with a profuse covering of long hair and an alert, friendly face. Usual coat coloration is black and white, but other colours are also commonly seen.
• **HISTORY** The ancestry of this newcomer is in no doubt at all: it is the result of crossings between the Lhasa Apso and the Maltese. Originating in California, the Kyi Leo is specifically designed for life as a companion dog and does not regard the lack of a garden or yard as a particular hardship.
• **REMARK** The Kyi Leo is an "easy-care" dog. Its long coat does require frequent brushing to remain in good condition but no clipping is necessary.

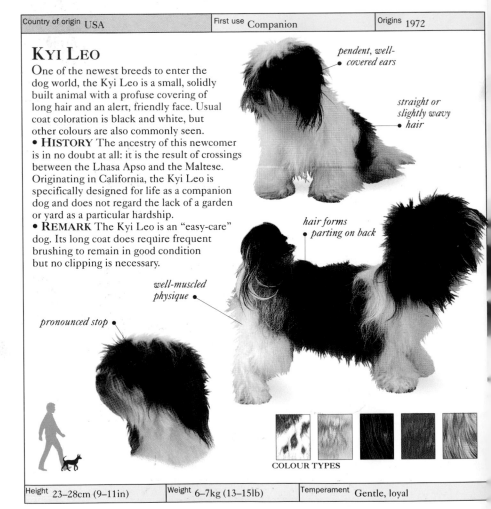

pendent, well-covered ears

straight or slightly wavy hair

hair forms parting on back

well-muscled physique

pronounced stop

COLOUR TYPES

Height 23–28cm (9–11in)	Weight 6–7kg (13–15lb)	Temperament Gentle, loyal

Country of origin USA	First use Companion	Origins 1900s

TOY AMERICAN ESKIMO

erect, triangular ears

plumed tail, set high and carried over the back

The face, coat, and lush tail of this dog identify it as a spitz-type breed. The pointed muzzle and erect ears are fox-like, its coat is long and thick, and its tail is well-plumed and carried in a curl over the back. Although a small dog, it is nevertheless sturdy, well-muscled, and powerful with a broad back. Solid white is the preferred coat colour, although it can sometimes be found with cream- or biscuit-coloured markings.

- **HISTORY** Descended from the German Spitz, American breeders favoured the white form and concentrated their efforts into developing this single colour type.
- **REMARK** Apart from size, all three American Eskimo dogs are judged against the same standard.

short, sturdy legs

Height 28–31cm (11–12in)	Weight 3–5kg (6–10lb)	Temperament Affectionate, obedient

Country of origin Great Britain	First use Baiting bulls	Origins 1800s

BULLDOG

very short, broad nose

undershot lower jaw

With a musculature almost out of proportion to its size, the Bulldog is a diminutive, but powerful, mastiff-type dog. Its head is enormous, the circumference of which may equal its height. Its eyes are set low. White predominates in the coat, although there are plenty of pied, brindle, and fawn Bulldogs.

- **HISTORY** Until the banning of bull baiting in England in 1835, this breed was very popular. Since then it has been made considerably gentler by selective breeding.
- **REMARK** Birth by Caesarean section is not uncommon, as the large head size of the pups may block the birth canal.
- **OTHER NAMES** English Bulldog.

powerful, compact body

extremely wide chest

COLOUR TYPES

Height 31–36cm (12–14in)	Weight 23–25kg (50–55lb)	Temperament Affectionate, docile

Country of origin Great Britain	First use Companion	Origins 1920s

CAVALIER KING CHARLES

A modern recreation of the old type of King
Charles Spaniel (below), the Cavalier can be
distinguished by its longer nose and heavier
build. Both breeds have identical coloration.
The chestnut and white of each breed is
described as the Blenheim, after the estate
of the Duke of Marlborough, where spaniels
of this colour were first developed.
• **HISTORY** Toy spaniels were a common
sight around the palaces of Europe during
the 17th century and were often portrayed
in paintings of the period. Cavaliers were
first registered by the British Kennel
Club as a separate breed in 1945.
• **REMARK** The prefix "Cavalier"
was chosen to distinguish it from
the King Charles Spaniel.

*long, well-
feathered ears*

*relatively flat,
undomed skull*

*long, silky coat
with no curls*

COLOUR TYPES

Height 31–33cm (12–13in)	Weight 5–8kg (10–18lb)	Temperament Friendly, obedient

Country of origin Great Britain	First use Companion	Origins 1600s

KING CHARLES SPANIEL

Squarely built with a distinctive domed skull,
this breed's affectionate nature has made it a
popular pet for centuries. The large, dark
eyes are particularly appealing.
• **HISTORY** This breed was greatly
favoured by King Charles II (1630–85).
He regularly exercised his dogs in St.
James's Park, London.
• **REMARK** The breed today is
larger than its ancestors.
• **OTHER NAMES**
English Toy Spaniel.

domed skull

COLOUR TYPES

short back

*short nose,
with wide,
turned-up
muzzle*

*deep,
broad chest*

Height 25–27cm (10–11in)	Weight 4–6kg (8–14lb)	Temperament Obedient, affectionate

Country of origin Mexico	First use Companion	Origins 1800s

CHIHUAHUA

There are two varieties of this tiny, plucky
dog, which can be separated on the basis of
coat length. The smooth-coated form has a
glossy, short coat, while the long-haired form
has a significantly longer, slightly wavy coat.
The long-haired form is the result of crossings
of Smooth-coated Chihuahuas with Yorkshire
Terriers (see p.219) and Papillons (see p.47).
Selective breeding has since taken place to
ensure that in all other respects the two forms
are indistinguishable. Common colours are
fawn, chestnut, steel-blue, and silver, often
seen in combinations.

• HISTORY The name "Chihuahua" derives
from the Mexican state of that name where this
dog may possibly have originated. It was first
seen in the USA towards the end of the 19th
century, before being taken to Europe. Most
of today's bloodlines are descended from the
original 50 dogs taken to the USA.

• REMARK The Chihuahua can
be sensitive to cold. It also shivers
when excited or nervous.

COLOUR TYPES

relatively
muscular
hindquarters •

short, •
soft, and
glossy
coat

SHORT-HAIRED
CHIHUAHUA

• ruff on neck

muscular, well-
• feathered legs

• short,
pointed
muzzle

LONG-HAIRED
CHIHUAHUA

coat may be
slightly wavy
but never
• curled

long tail
resembles
a plume •

• dainty feet

Height 15–23cm (6–9in)	Weight 1–3kg (2–6lb)	Temperament Bold, playful

Country of origin Mexico	First use Companion	Origins 1500s

MEXICAN HAIRLESS

Three forms of this breed are now recognized: the Standard (shown here), the Miniature, and the smaller Toy version. There is also a so-called "Powder-puff" version of each size, which does have a coat of hair but cannot be exhibited. The Mexican Hairless has a noble stance, not unlike that of a sight hound, and the build of a terrier.

• **HISTORY** Utilized as bed-warmers, pets, and, less comfortingly, as ritual sacrifices, this dog was widely kept in ancient Aztec settlements.

• **REMARK** A breeding programme initiated by the Mexican Kennel Club in the 1950s saved this dog from certain extinction. They are, however, still quite scarce, even today.

• **OTHER NAMES** Tepeizeuintli, Xoloitzcuintli.

traces of hair apparent on top of head

pointed muzzle

ears positioned laterally and kept erect when dog is alert

tip of tail shows traces of hair

straight, parallel forelegs

long, slightly arched neck

firm, broad, well-muscled back

exposed skin is susceptible to sunburn

COLOUR TYPES

Height 28–31cm (11–12in)	Weight 4–8kg (9–18lb)	Temperament Lively, alert

Country of origin Peru	First use Warming beds	Origins 1200s

INCA HAIRLESS DOG

This group of dogs is found in three distinct categories, based on size. It is not clear if all the New World hairless breeds are related, but these particular dogs occur predominantly in solid colours only.
• **HISTORY** Although rare in their homeland today, they were once the favoured companions of the Incas.
• **REMARK** As with the Mexican Hairless (see p.42) "Powder-puff" versions of these dogs also occur.
• **OTHER NAMES** Peruvian Hairless Dog.

some hair on head, extending over the ears

ears set low on head

long thigh muscles

small, dark eyes

COLOUR TYPES

Height 25–71cm (10–28in)	Weight 4–25kg (9–55lb)	Temperament Affectionate, loyal

Country of origin Cuba	First use Companion	Origins 1700s

HAVANESE

This dog is of bichon stock, and is related to such breeds as the Bichon Frise (see p.58). It has a profuse double coat and is usually cream, gold, silver, blue or black.
• **HISTORY** It is believed to have been brought to Cuba by sailors from the Canaries.
• **REMARK** This breed is becoming popular in the USA.
• **OTHER NAMES** Bichon Havanais.

dense crest of long hair on head

tail carried forwards in a curl

small, rounded feet covered in hair

broad, well-muscled thighs

COLOUR TYPES

Height 20–28cm (8–11in)	Weight 3–6kg (7–12lb)	Temperament Responsive, friendly

Country of origin Germany	First use Companion	Origins 1800s

GIANT GERMAN SPITZ

The face of this breed is a little fox-like. The outercoat is long and harsh, while the undercoat is dense and soft. The Giant German Spitz, as its name suggests, is the second largest of this German group of spitz dogs, and is bred in solid colours only.

- **HISTORY** The ancestors of these dogs were probably brought to Holland and Germany by the Vikings.
- **REMARK** Certain colours became associated with particular regions, such as the black with Wurttemberg.
- **OTHER NAMES** Deutscher Gross Spitz.

tail curls up and lies over back

erect, triangular-shaped ears

rounded, cat-like feet

COLOUR TYPES

Height 41cm (16in)	Weight 18kg (40lb)	Temperament Lively, playful

Country of origin Germany	First use Working on farms	Origins 1800s

GERMAN SPITZ: MITTEL

The Mittel, or standard, form of the German Spitz is the third largest of the five varieties. Like the Giant (above), it is usually bred in solid colours, but in Britain all varieties and markings are acceptable.

- **HISTORY** The watchful demeanour of these dogs initially led to their being highly valued on farms, but they also make rewarding companions.
- **REMARK** Like the other German Spitz, the Mittel has a harsh, long outercoat and a soft, woolly undercoat.
- **OTHER NAMES** Deutscher Mittel Spitz.

luxuriant tail

oval-shaped eyes

compact, firm condition

COLOUR TYPES

Height 29–36cm (11½–14in)	Weight 11kg (25lb)	Temperament Lively, playful

| Country of origin Germany | First use Lap dog | Origins 1800s |

GERMAN SPITZ: KLEIN

The German Spitz breeds are compact and squarely built, and can be distinguished essentially on the basis of size. The Spitz is protected from harsh weather by its thick coat, which varies greatly in colour and has a dense undercoat.
- **HISTORY** The German Spitz is descended from much larger, sledge-pulling spitz breeds.
- **REMARK** Since 1985, this breed has undergone a revival outside Germany.
- **OTHER NAMES** Deutsche Spitz.

tail curls over back

small, triangular-shaped ears

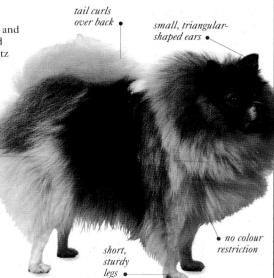

no colour restriction

short, sturdy legs

COLOUR TYPES

| Height 23–28cm (9–11in) | Weight 8–10kg (18–22lb) | Temperament Lively, playful |

| Country of origin Germany | First use General companion | Origins 1800s |

POMERANIAN

The smallest member of the German Spitz group, the Pomeranian is characterized by an upright tail that tilts forward over its body. This breed is a devoted and affectionate companion. The coat takes three years to reach full maturity, the whole colours include white, red orange, grey, and black.
- **HISTORY** This breed is thought to have developed in northern Germany from larger spitz dogs.
- **REMARK** Despite its diminutive size it makes a good watchdog.

erect, fox-like ears

harsh, long hair on tail

COLOUR TYPES

| Height 28cm (11in) | Weight 2–3kg (4–5½lb) | Temperament Friendly, active |

| Country of origin Netherlands | First use Barge companion | Origins 1500s |

KEESHOND

This lively breed is distinguished by its wolf-grey coat. Its coloration tends to be lighter on the head, creating the impression of dark "spectacles" around the eyes.

- **HISTORY** It is named after the Dutchman de Gyselaer, whose nickname was Kees.
- **REMARK** A fine watchdog, the Keeshond provides good security as well as company.
- **OTHER NAMES** Wolf Spitz, Chien Loup.

*tightly curled tail;
• double curl preferred*

*• no feathering
below hocks*

• dense ruff

| Height 43–48cm (17–19in) | Weight 25–30kg (55–66lb) | Temperament Independent, affectionate |

| Country of origin Belgium | First use Companion | Origins 1600s |

CONTINENTAL TOY SPANIEL: PHALENE

Closely related to the Papillon (see p.47), the Phalene can be readily distinguished from it by its ears, which hang down on the sides of its head.

- **HISTORY** The breed was popular in Italy during the Renaissance, and was well known in European royal circles.
- **REMARK** In the USA, the Phalene is not distinguished from the Papillon, which is accepted in both ear forms.
- **OTHER NAMES** Épagneul Nain, Continental Phalene.

*white blaze
• on face*

*high-set
• bushy tail*

hare-like feet •

COLOUR TYPES

| Height 20–28cm (8–11in) | Weight 4.1–4.5kg (9–10lb) | Temperament Friendly, alert |

Country of origin France	First use Companion	Origins 1600s

CONTINENTAL TOY SPANIEL: PAPILLON

This dainty little dog is closely related to the Phalene (see p.46), but it can easily be distinguished by its erect ears. Its name, *Papillon*, the French for "butterfly", refers to the shape of its ears.

• **HISTORY** This breed often featured in paintings by the Flemish artist Van Dyke.
• **REMARK** Daily grooming is essential.
• **OTHER NAMES** Épagneul Nain.

symmetrical head markings and blaze

slightly rounded skull

very large, well-fringed ears

fine, hare-like feet with long hair between toes

Height 20–28cm (8–11in)	Weight 4–4.5kg (9–10lb)	Temperament Friendly, alert

Country of origin France	First use Companion	Origins 1400s

TOY POODLE

Identical in all respects to its larger relatives except in height, this is the smallest of the three varieties of poodle. Pictured here is the lion trim, preferred for showing.

• **HISTORY** Miniaturization of the Standard Poodle gave rise to this dog. They were portrayed by the German artist Dürer in 1500.
• **REMARK** The coat of this and other poodles is not moulted, so it needs clipping approximately every six to eight weeks.
• **OTHER NAMES** Caniche.

tail carried at an angle to body

long, fine head

deep, relatively wide chest

dense, very profuse coat

well-sprung ribs

small, oval-shaped feet

COLOUR TYPES

Height 25–28cm (10–11in)	Weight 7kg (15lb)	Temperament Loyal, sociable

Country of origin France	First use Water-dog	Origins 1600s

MINIATURE POODLE

Well-proportioned and squarely built, the Miniature Poodle lies between the larger Standard (see p.254) and the tiny Toy (see p.47) in size. This intelligent breed has a sporty disposition, and is easy to train.
• **HISTORY** Poodles probably derive from the Pudel, an old German water-dog.
• **REMARK** From the late 1940s to the 1960s, the Miniature Poodle was the most popular dog breed in the world.
• **OTHER NAMES** Barbone, Caniche.

long, wide ears

strong neck

thick, harsh-textured coat

straight forelegs

long, straight muzzle

muscular hindlegs

small, oval-shaped feet

COLOUR TYPES

Height 28–38cm (11–15in)	Weight 12–14kg (26–30lb)	Temperament Intelligent, lively

Country of origin France	First use Companion	Origins 1500s

LÖWCHEN

With its long, silky coat trimmed in the traditional "lion clip", this dog is easily distinguished from other members of the bichon group. The tail is clipped along part of its length, leaving just a plume of hair, completing this attractive, lively breed's distinctive parody of the "king of the beasts".

- **HISTORY** This breed found favour with the European aristocracy at an early stage in its development. It featured in a painting by Goya of the Duchess of Alba in the late 1700s. However, its popularity declined to the extent that by 1960 it was considered to be the world's rarest dog breed.
- **REMARK** This intelligent, good-natured breed has recently undergone a welcome growth in popularity, particularly in the USA.
- **OTHER NAMES** Little Lion Dog.

short head with dark nose

long, silky "mane"

large, dark, round eyes

tail curls forwards over back

well-muscled hindquarters

long, pendent, well-fringed ears

COLOUR TYPES

Height 25–33cm (10–13in)	Weight 4–8kg (8–18lb)	Temperament Active, affectionate

Country of origin Italy	First use Lady's companion	Origins 500BC

ITALIAN GREYHOUND

A miniature form of the Greyhound, this breed is far less fragile than it looks. It has a gait similar to the larger dog's, and the same rapid acceleration, facilitated by long, muscular hindquarters. The long, graceful neck heightens its refined air.
• **HISTORY** This breed has survived since the time of the pharaohs. More recently, however, it has suffered from the introduction of English Toy Terrier blood (see p.210).
• **REMARK** Similar dogs have been found, mummified, in Egyptian tombs.
• **OTHER NAMES** Piccolo Levrieri Italiani.

ears well back on head

flat and narrow skull

ITALIAN GREYHOUND PUPPIES

elegant arched back slopes down over hindquarters

deep, narrow chest

thin, glossy coat with satin-like texture

straight, fine-boned forelegs

longish tail carried low

COLOUR TYPES

Height 33–38cm (13–15in)	Weight 3.6kg (8lb)	Temperament Quiet, affectionate

Country of origin Italy	First use General companion	Origins 1200s

BOLOGNESE

Descended from bichon stock, and so having the characteristic white, cottony coat associated with this group, the Bolognese may in fact have blond markings, although these are not considered desirable. This is a square-built and solid dog for its size.

• **HISTORY** The breed's ancestry dates back to the bichons that first appeared in southern Italy in the 13th century. It became a popular court dog but is now relatively scarce.

• **REMARK** The Bolognese has always been a companion dog and bonds very closely with people.

• **OTHER NAMES** Bichon Bolognese.

flat cheeks

dark skin under fur

round, black, shiny nose

soft hair forms tufts, with no undercoat •

small, • rounded feet

Height 25–31cm (10–12in)	Weight 3–4kg (5½–9lb)	Temperament Friendly, loyal

Country of origin Italy	First use General companion	Origins 1600s

VOLPINO ITALIANO

This small Italian breed is unmistakably a spitz type, its face being not unlike that of a fox, with the muzzle short, straight, and rather pointed. The Volpino is usually pure white in coloration, the sable form now being rare. A fawn variety existed at one time, but this has now been lost.

• **HISTORY** The early ancestors of the Volpino Italiano were originally brought from northern Europe in the 1600s, but the breed itself was developed entirely within Italy. Today, it is quite scarce in its homeland.

• **REMARK** The name "Volpino" originates from the Italian word, *volpe*, which translates as "fox".

• **OTHER NAMES** Cane de Quirinale.

large, rounded, • dark eyes

small, triangular-shaped ears •

tail curls back • over body

profuse, thick coat

dainty • hindfeet

• cobby body shape

COLOUR TYPES

Height 28cm (11in)	Weight 5kg (10lb)	Temperament Affectionate

Country of origin China	First use Companion	Origins 100s

PEKINGESE

The Pekingese is a short-legged breed of dog with a characteristic rolling gait. It has a relatively compact, flattened face fringed with longer hair, which gives the impression of the dog having a mane. This breed makes a bold and alert watchdog for the home.

• **HISTORY** It was first seen in the West after the British overran Beijing in 1860. Prior to this, the Pekingese had been the jealously guarded, exclusive possession of the Chinese emperor.

• **REMARK** Pekingese used to be known as "sleeve dogs" because they could be carried in the long, flowing sleeves of Chinese courtiers.

• **OTHER NAMES** Peking Palasthund.

large, round, dark eyes

very evident stop to nose

well-feathered tail is set high and curled over to one side

long, silky coat

broad nose with large nostrils

large head with broad skull

skull is flat between ears

heart-shaped ears set level with skull

COLOUR TYPES

Height 15–23cm (6–9in)	Weight 3–6kg (7–12lb)	Temperament Independent, lively

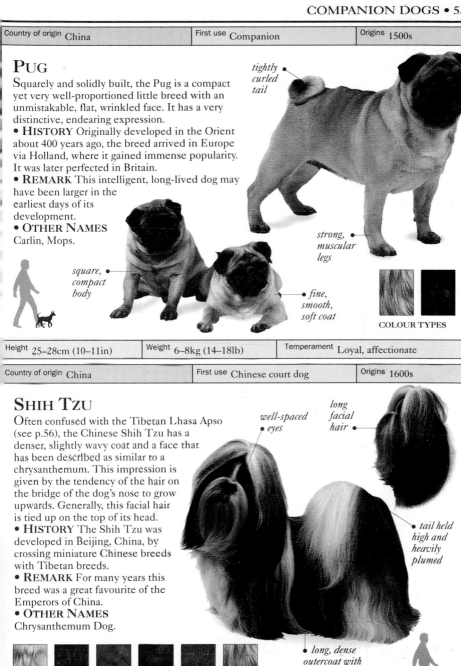

| Country of origin China | First use Companion | Origins 1500s |

PUG

Squarely and solidly built, the Pug is a compact yet very well-proportioned little breed with an unmistakable, flat, wrinkled face. It has a very distinctive, endearing expression.
• **HISTORY** Originally developed in the Orient about 400 years ago, the breed arrived in Europe via Holland, where it gained immense popularity. It was later perfected in Britain.
• **REMARK** This intelligent, long-lived dog may have been larger in the earliest days of its development.
• **OTHER NAMES** Carlin, Mops.

tightly curled tail

strong, muscular legs

square, compact body

fine, smooth, soft coat

COLOUR TYPES

| Height 25–28cm (10–11in) | Weight 6–8kg (14–18lb) | Temperament Loyal, affectionate |

| Country of origin China | First use Chinese court dog | Origins 1600s |

SHIH TZU

Often confused with the Tibetan Lhasa Apso (see p.56), the Chinese Shih Tzu has a denser, slightly wavy coat and a face that has been described as similar to a chrysanthemum. This impression is given by the tendency of the hair on the bridge of the dog's nose to grow upwards. Generally, this facial hair is tied up on the top of its head.
• **HISTORY** The Shih Tzu was developed in Beijing, China, by crossing miniature Chinese breeds with Tibetan breeds.
• **REMARK** For many years this breed was a great favourite of the Emperors of China.
• **OTHER NAMES** Chrysanthemum Dog.

well-spaced eyes

long facial hair

tail held high and heavily plumed

long, dense outercoat with good undercoat

COLOUR TYPES

| Height 27cm (10½in) | Weight 5–7kg (10–16lb) | Temperament Gentle, loyal |

Country of origin China	First use Companion	Origins 100BC

CHINESE CRESTED DOG

This nimble little dog comes in two varieties. One form, the Hairless, only has hair as a crest on its head and toes, and a plume on its tail. The Powder Puff variety is covered with long, soft hair. Both are found in a mixture of colours.

• **HISTORY** Known for centuries in China, this dog first came to prominence in the Han dynasty, but was not exhibited in the West until the Westminster Show in New York in 1885. It was not until 1975 that a specialist breed club was established in the USA.

• **REMARK** The texture of the skin of the Hairless should be smooth and fine-grained. This dog is vulnerable to sunburn.

POWDER PUFF

ears are normally erect

long, slightly rounded skull

deep, broad chest

Powder Puff has undercoat and a soft veil of long hair

skin may be plain or spotted, and may lighten in summer

long, tapering, fairly straight tail

no hair above first joint of leg

ears sometimes droop under weight of hair

HAIRLESS

hairless body

hare-like feet

Height 23–33cm (9–13in)	Weight 2–5.5kg (5–12lb)	Temperament Affectionate, lively

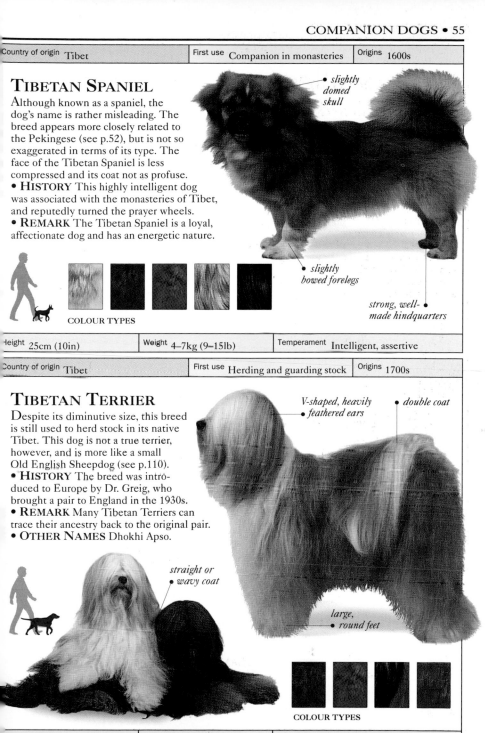

| Country of origin Tibet | First use Companion in monasteries | Origins 1600s |

TIBETAN SPANIEL

Although known as a spaniel, the dog's name is rather misleading. The breed appears more closely related to the Pekingese (see p.52), but is not so exaggerated in terms of its type. The face of the Tibetan Spaniel is less compressed and its coat not as profuse.
• **HISTORY** This highly intelligent dog was associated with the monasteries of Tibet, and reputedly turned the prayer wheels.
• **REMARK** The Tibetan Spaniel is a loyal, affectionate dog and has an energetic nature.

slightly domed skull

slightly bowed forelegs

strong, well-made hindquarters

COLOUR TYPES

| Height 25cm (10in) | Weight 4–7kg (9–15lb) | Temperament Intelligent, assertive |

| Country of origin Tibet | First use Herding and guarding stock | Origins 1700s |

TIBETAN TERRIER

Despite its diminutive size, this breed is still used to herd stock in its native Tibet. This dog is not a true terrier, however, and is more like a small Old English Sheepdog (see p.110).
• **HISTORY** The breed was introduced to Europe by Dr. Greig, who brought a pair to England in the 1930s.
• **REMARK** Many Tibetan Terriers can trace their ancestry back to the original pair.
• **OTHER NAMES** Dhokhi Apso.

V-shaped, heavily feathered ears

double coat

straight or wavy coat

large, round feet

COLOUR TYPES

| Height 36–41cm (14–16in) | Weight 8–14kg (18–30lb) | Temperament Friendly, alert |

Country of origin Tibet	First use Companion in monasteries	Origins 600s

LHASA APSO

Although small in stature, the Lhasa Apso is a hardy dog, has a fine sense of hearing, and makes an excellent watchdog. While the name "Lhasa" probably refers to the capital of Tibet, "apso" may mean "goat-like" – a reference to this breed's long, coarse coat. The luxuriant coat is its most distinctive feature. Hair falls well over its eyes, and it has a prominent beard and moustache.

• **HISTORY** This is the most recent of the Tibetan breeds to have reached Europe. The giving of a Lhasa Apso was a traditional gift of the Dalai Lama.

• **REMARK** The Lhasa Apso's long, cascading coat needs plenty of grooming.

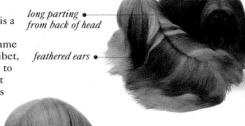

long parting from back of head

feathered ears

straight forelegs

COLOUR TYPES

Height 25–28cm (10–11in)	Weight 6–7kg (13–15lb)	Temperament Gentle, loyal

Country of origin Japan	First use Companion to aristocracy	Origins 700s

JAPANESE CHIN

There is a distinct similarity between this breed and the Pekingese (see p.52), but the Japanese Chin is both taller and of a lighter build. The coat of a puppy is relatively short compared with that of an adult dog.

• **HISTORY** Queen Victoria, a keen dog lover, had two Japanese Chins.

• **REMARK** Early examples of the breed were apparently quite delicate and tended to be even smaller than those seen today.

• **OTHER NAMES** Japanese Spaniel, Chin.

long hair on ears

large, dark eyes

slender feet

COLOUR TYPES

Height 23cm (9in)	Weight 2–3kg (4–7lb)	Temperament Intelligent, alert

| Country of origin Japan | First use Companion | Origins 1800s |

JAPANESE SPITZ

This delightful spitz breed has a striking, long coat, which must always be pure white in colour. This feature can serve to distinguish it from the miniature form of the American Eskimo (see p.39), which is otherwise extremely similar.

• **HISTORY** The Japanese Spitz is thought to bear no direct relationship to the American Eskimo; rather, it is believed to have been developed from the native Siberian Samoyed (see p.287).

• **REMARK** The Japanese Spitz is rapidly increasing in popularity in Europe.

high-set tail curls over back •

• *mane of longer hair extends down to brisket*

• *profuse, stand-off coat*

cat-like feet •

| Height 30–36cm (12–14in) | Weight 5–6kg (11–13lb) | Temperament Lively, intelligent |

| Country of origin Malta | First use Catching rats | Origins 500BC |

MALTESE

Of bichon stock, this tiny, attractive dog has a long, silky, pure-white coat which contrasts starkly with its dark, oval-shaped eyes and black eye rims. The coat may have slight lemon-coloured markings, notably in the vicinity of the head.

• **HISTORY** Possibly the oldest of Europe's toy breeds, the ancestors of the Maltese were thought to have been introduced to Malta by the Phoenicians. This lively, intelligent breed has since attracted countless generations of enthusiastic owners.

• **REMARK** Belying its "chocolate-box" appearance, this dog, once called a Maltese Terrier, was a renowned rat-catcher.

• **OTHER NAMES** Bichon Maltiase.

pure black nose •

stop is centred between tip of nose • *and occiput*

dark brown • *eyes*

long, straight coat should not impede the dog's action •

| Height 25cm (10in) | Weight 2–3kg (4–6lb) | Temperament Friendly, alert |

Country of origin Tenerife	First use Companion to royalty	Origins 1400s

BICHON FRISE

This bichon is distinguished by its double coat, which gives it a fluffy appearance. The coat is fine and silky, consisting of soft, corkscrew curls. These are trimmed back over the eyes to emphasize the rounded appearance of the face.

• **HISTORY** Originally, the Bichon Frise was popular in the royal courts of Europe. By the 1800s, however, the breed had lost favour and was more likely to be seen in circuses or accompanying organ grinders.

• **REMARK** Its long association with people makes the Bichon Frise a responsive pet.

• **OTHER NAMES** Tenerife Dog.

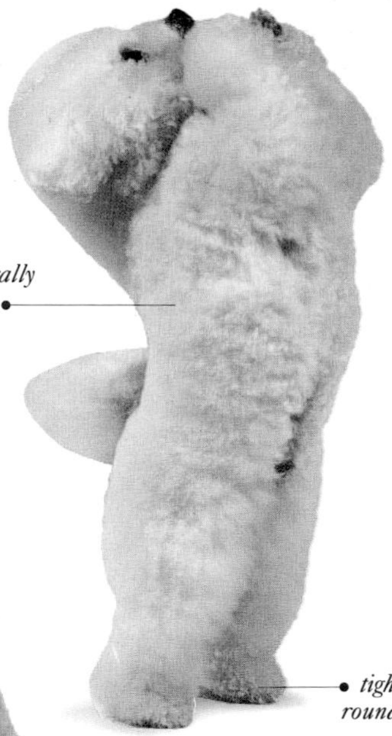

naturally agile

narrow, delicate ears

tight, round feet

tail curls over back

silky, cork-screw curls

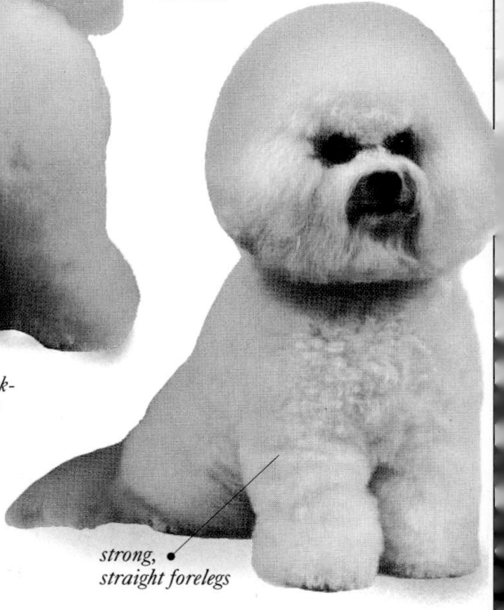

strong, straight forelegs

Height 23–31cm (9–12in)	Weight 3–6kg (7–12lb)	Temperament Friendly, active

Country of origin Zaire	First use Hunting dog	Origins 1500s

BASENJI

The most distinctive feature of the alert, finely
built Basenji becomes apparent only when it is
disturbed: instead of barking like other dogs, it
has unique yodelling and chortling calls.

• **HISTORY** The Basenji was developed as a
hunting dog in the Congo and it may be related
to similar dogs portrayed on ancient Egyptian
artefacts. The breed caused a sensation when it
was first shown at Crufts, in England, in 1937.
The owner called them "basenji", which is
an African word for "bush thing".

• **REMARK** Green vegetables are favoured by these dogs and should form part
of their regular diet. Bitches come on heat
only once a year instead of twice.

• **OTHER NAMES** Congo Dog.

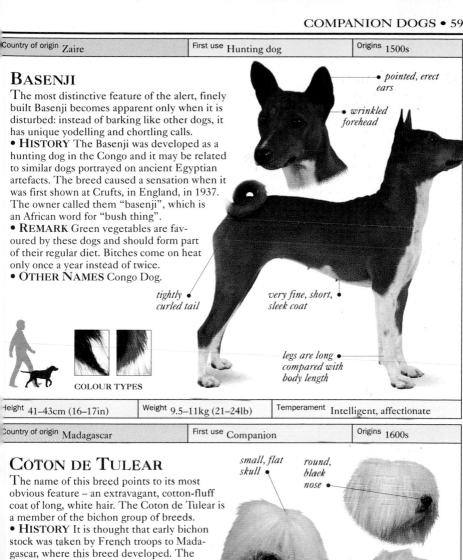

*pointed, erect
ears*

*wrinkled
forehead*

*tightly
curled tail*

*very fine, short,
sleek coat*

*legs are long
compared with
body length*

COLOUR TYPES

Height 41–43cm (16–17in)	Weight 9.5–11kg (21–24lb)	Temperament Intelligent, affectionate

Country of origin Madagascar	First use Companion	Origins 1600s

COTON DE TULEAR

The name of this breed points to its most
obvious feature – an extravagant, cotton-fluff
coat of long, white hair. The Coton de Tulear is
a member of the bichon group of breeds.

• **HISTORY** It is thought that early bichon
stock was taken by French troops to Madagascar, where this breed developed. The
similar, but now extinct, Chien Coton was
popular on the island of Réunion located
off the east coast of Madagascar.

• **REMARK** The breed is virtually unknown
outside its homeland.

*small, flat
skull*

*round,
black
nose*

*cotton-like
coat texture*

*rounded feet
with black
nails*

COLOUR TYPES

Height 25–30cm (10–12in)	Weight 5.5–7kg (12–15lb)	Temperament Lively, loyal

GUNDOGS

ORIGINALLY a sporting companion, the lively, loyal nature of the gundog has won it a place in the home as a family pet. Setters, spaniels, pointers, and retrievers are all classified as gundogs, and are characterized by their very responsive and friendly dispositions. However, they do require a great deal of exercise. Their longish, water-resistant coats protect them in al[l] weather, a feature bred into them i[n] their sporting days. A number o[f] gundog breeds have a localized dis[-] tribution, while others, such as the Spinone (see p.100), are now wel[l] known in show rings around the world Field trials are held regularly to tes[t] and maintain their working abilities.

Country of origin USA	First use Hunting small game	Origins 1800s

AMERICAN COCKER SPANIEL

Smaller than its English counterpart (see p.63), and with a much longer coat, the American Cocker Spaniel was developed in the USA in the last century. A black American Cocker must be jet black, with no trace of brown or liver shadings. To be classified as black and tan, tan markings must comprise no less than 10 per cent of the coat. The colour "tan" can vary from shades of cream to dark red.
• **HISTORY** This dog was bred from English Cocker Spaniels taken to the USA. It was first recognized as a separate breed in 1946.
• **REMARK** This keen and industrious breed specialized in retrieving quails.
• **OTHER NAMES** Cocker Spaniel.

clearly defined stop

lobular ears

rounded head shape

muscular, well-boned hindquarters

rounded, firm feet with thick pads

profuse covering of wavy or flat silky hair

COLOUR TYPES

Height 36–38cm (14–15in)	Weight 11–13kg (24–28lb)	Temperament Active, friendly

Country of origin USA	First use Retrieving water-fowl	Origins 1800s

CHESAPEAKE BAY RETRIEVER

The broad skull, wedge-shaped forehead, and powerful jaws of this breed make it ideal as a retriever, and its very dense coat serves to protect it from the cold waters of the Chesapeake Bay region of the USA, where it was first developed. The oily texture of the hair gives this retriever a rather distinctive smell.

• **HISTORY** The breed evolved from two pups rescued from a ship that ran aground off the coast of Maryland, USA, in 1807. The two dogs were trained to retrieve duck, a skill that was refined through crossings with Flat and Curly-coated Retrievers and Otter Hounds.

• **REMARK** The webbed toes of this breed assist in swimming.

broad, rounded head

distinctive yellow or amber eyes

thin, not pendulous, lips

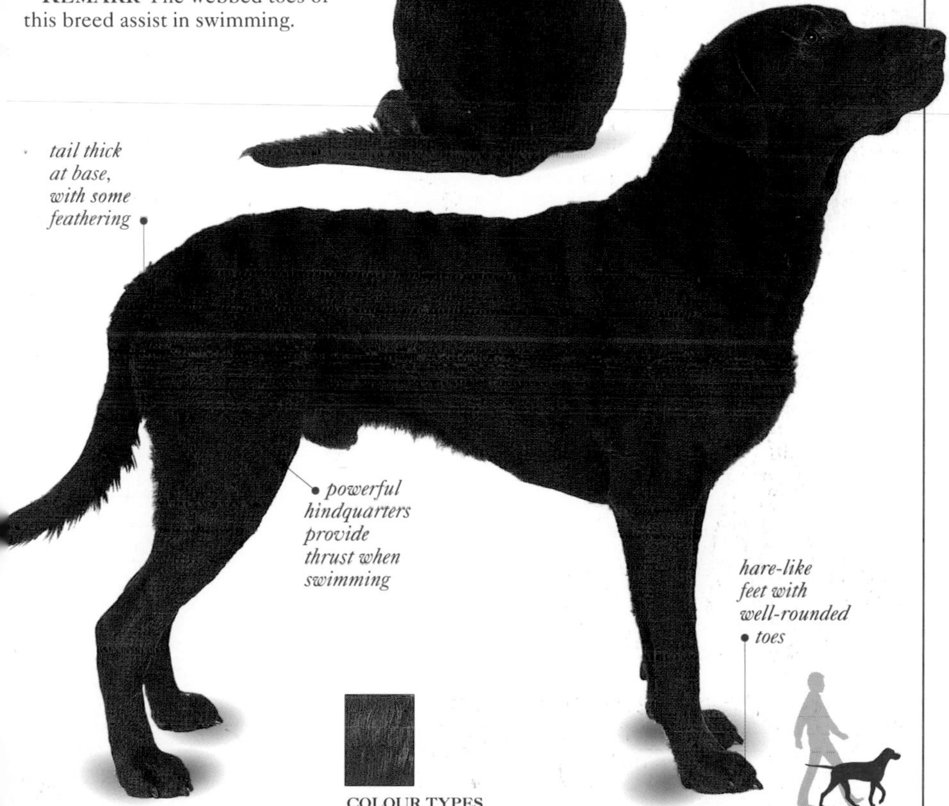

tail thick at base, with some feathering

powerful hindquarters provide thrust when swimming

hare-like feet with well-rounded toes

COLOUR TYPES

Height 53–66cm (21–26in)	Weight 25–34kg (55–75lb)	Temperament Responsive, industrious

Country of origin Great Britain	First use Tracking and retrieving game	Origins 1800s

CLUMBER SPANIEL

This large, bulky spaniel is not as speedy in the field as some of its more streamlined relatives, but it is vigorous and works well, especially in areas of heavy cover. The Clumber has a large, wide head, a pronounced stop, and deep-set eyes. Its attractive, pure-white, silky coat is heavily feathered on the neck and chest. Lemon- or orange-coloured markings are permissible.

• **HISTORY** The Duke of Newcastle was instrumental in developing this breed in Britain at the family home in Clumber Park. He may have obtained the ancestral stock from France. Later, Prince Albert, as well as his son, who became King Edward VII, both favoured this spaniel, as did King George V.

• **REMARK** Despite royal patronage, this spaniel has never been generally popular.

• massive, square skull with heavy brow and deep stop

• lemon markings on ears preferred

• long ears, shaped like vine leaves

• plain white body preferred

well-feathered tail •

thick, powerful neck

short, well-boned legs

exceedingly • powerful hindquarters

Height 48–51cm (19–20in)	Weight 29–36kg (65–80lb)	Temperament Dedicated, responsive

Country of origin Great Britain	First use Retrieving game	Origins 1800s

COCKER SPANIEL

This breed of gundog has a broad nose for scenting, a generous, square muzzle, a pronounced stop, and a precise yet delicate bite, ideal for retrieving game. Its long coat is silky in texture but not curly. In solid-coloured dogs, white markings are permissible only on the chest.

• **HISTORY** The Cocker Spaniel was originally developed in Wales and southwestern parts of England to flush woodcock, a popular game-bird.

• **REMARK** Its long ears hang close to the ground and often harbour ticks and burrs, which can lead to disease and injury.

• **OTHER NAMES** English Cocker Spaniel.

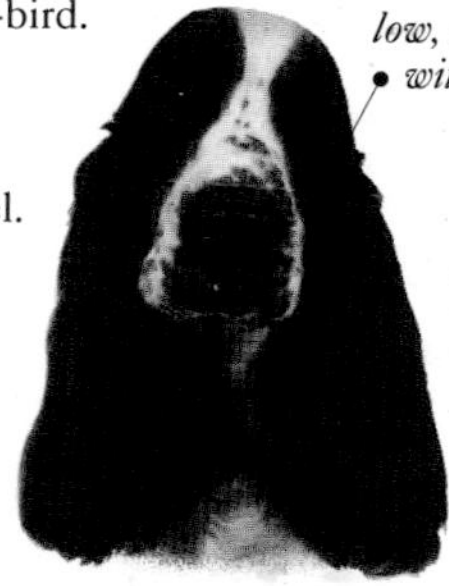

ears set low, level with eyes

long, silky hair on ears

strong, compact body

flat, silky coat with feathering

tail set low and may be moderately docked

medium-length, muscular neck merging into sloping shoulders

stifles well-bent

straight, well-boned legs

thickly padded feet

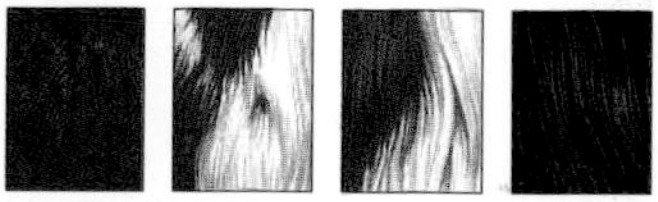

COLOUR TYPES

eight 38–41cm (15–16in)	Weight 13–15kg (28–32lb)	Temperament Responsive, affectionate

Country of origin Great Britain	First use Retrieving water-fowl	Origins 1800s

CURLY-COATED RETRIEVER

This robust, agile breed of retriever has a generally neat appearance. Its body is covered with a tightly curled, black- or liver-coloured coat, which does not need trimming. By contrast, its facial hair is distinctively smooth.

- **HISTORY** The precise ancestry of the Curly-coated Retriever is unclear, but Water Spaniels are probably responsible for its distinctive coat. Early Labradors may also have contributed to its development, as may poodles.
- **REMARK** The Curly-coated Retriever is one of the oldest breeds of retriever and is still a popular choice in Australia and New Zealand for quail and water-fowl hunting. They enter water without hesitation, and their water-resistant coat dries quickly.

long head •

small ears
lying close
• to head

dense, tightly
• curled coat

curls present
on ears •

moderately
long legs

deep •
shoulders and
muscular body

tail •
tapers
towards
point

straight forelegs •

strong hind-
quarters and
low hocks •

round, •
compact feet

COLOUR TYPES

Height 64–69cm (25–27in)	Weight 32–36kg (70–80lb)	Temperament Responsive, friendly

Country of origin Great Britain	First use Retrieving birds	Origins 1800s

ENGLISH SETTER

The mottled coloration of the English Setter serves to distinguish it from other breeds of setter. Essentially it is a working dog which can be developed into an extremely responsive gundog, and it requires a lot of exercise to remain healthy. A popular dog in the show ring, the breed's friendly nature guarantees it strong support. Careful grooming is important if this breed is to be seen at its best.

• **HISTORY** The old Setting Spaniel is the probable ancestor of this breed. It was developed initially by a Mr. Edward Laverack, who began a breeding programme in 1825, and for a period these dogs were known simply as Laverack Setters.

• **REMARK** The term "setter" originates from the way such dogs "set" (sit) after they have located game.

dark hazel eyes

velvety tips to ears

close, compact feet

tail forms a line with the back

deep chest

medium-length body

feathering is longest towards middle of tail

COLOUR TYPES

Height 61–69cm (24–27in)	Weight 25–30kg (56–66lb)	Temperament Responsive, friendly

Country of origin Great Britain	First use Retrieving birds	Origins 1600s

GORDON SETTER

The black-and-tan coloration of the Gordon is distinctive among setters. It is an adept sporting dog, being skilled at locating game, and is also an impressive sight in the show ring. Puppies are slow to mature, however, and appear rather uncoordinated.
• **HISTORY** The Gordon Setter was developed by the 4th Duke of Richmond and Gordon, at his ancestral seat in Banffshire, Scotland, from various breeds including bloodhounds and collies.
• **REMARK** It is the only setter developed in Scotland.

clearly defined stop

silky, glossy coat

• *long muzzle*

• *forelegs are well feathered*

Height 62–66cm (24½–26in)	Weight 25–30kg (56–65lb)	Temperament Obedient, loyal

Country of origin Great Britain	First use Flushing out game	Origins 1800s

ENGLISH SPRINGER SPANIEL

As well as being the ancestor of most other contemporary spaniels, the English Springer is also one of the tallest. A division between working and show strains has arisen, the former being shorter and stockier.
• **HISTORY** This gundog was originally used to "spring" (flush) game from the ground.
• **REMARK** The Springer makes a good family pet if it receives sufficient exercise.

strong jaws

lobe-shaped ears

weather-resistant coat

COLOUR TYPES

Height 48–51cm (19–20in)	Weight 22–24kg (49–53lb)	Temperament Willing, active

| Country of origin Great Britain | First use Retrieving birds | Origins 1800s |

FIELD SPANIEL

The Field Spaniel has a long body in relation to its height, and a silky, flat coat. The breed was originally divided into two categories, the lighter of which became the Cocker Spaniel (see p.63).
• HISTORY After the Field Spaniel was separated from the Cocker in 1892, crossings with Sussex Spaniels (see p.72) led to a temporary deterioration in type and soundness, which threatened the breed's existence.
• REMARK Although popular as a gundog, the breed has not done well in the show ring.

wide, almond-
• *shaped eyes*

long, well-feathered
• *ears*

• *very long ribcage*

COLOUR TYPES

| Height 46cm (18in) | Weight 16–23kg (35–50lb) | Temperament Responsive, friendly |

| Country of origin Great Britain | First use Retrieving fowl | Origins 1800s |

FLAT-COATED RETRIEVER

As its name suggests, the coat of this retriever lies close to the body. It is dense and fine-textured, with feathering on the legs and tail.
• HISTORY Although a British dog, it derives from two American breeds – the Labrador (see p.69) and the Newfoundland (see pp.240–41).
• REMARK The breed declined after the First World War, having been kept largely as a working dog.

flat skull and long head •

• *short, well-feathered tail*

round, strong feet with arched toes
• *and thick soles*

straight, well-boned
• *forelegs*

| Height 56–58cm (22–23in) | Weight 27–32kg (60–70lb) | Temperament Attentive, friendly |

Country of origin Great Britain	First use Retrieving birds	Origins 1800s

GOLDEN RETRIEVER

The coloration of this retriever has helped to make it one of the most popular of all breeds. The coat can vary from shades of cream to gold, but must not be red. The Golden Retriever is a responsive dog to train, and provided it receives plenty of exercise it makes an excellent family companion.

• **HISTORY** Although it has been suggested that this retriever evolved from Russian circus dogs, it is more likely it was bred from crossings that started with a yellow Flat-coated Retriever (see p.67) and a Tweed Water Spaniel, with Irish Setter, Labrador, and Bloodhound introduced later.

• **REMARK** Until 1920 it was known as the Golden Flat-coat.

• **OTHER NAMES** Yellow Retriever or Russian Retriever.

broad skull and powerful muzzle

well-spaced, brown eyes

ears level with eyes

black nose preferred

well-defined stop

wavy or flat coat

tail level with back, and carried horizontally

straight, well-boned forelegs

good feathering on tail

round, rather cat-like feet

Height 51–61cm (20–24in)	Weight 27–36kg (60–80lb)	Temperament Responsive, alert

Country of origin Canada	First use Helping fishermen	Origins 1800s

LABRADOR RETRIEVER

The tail is the most distinctive feature of this intelligent, short-coated retriever. It has a thick base, tapering along its length, with no signs of feathering. A short-coupled, solid dog, it has a broad skull, wide nose, and powerful neck.

• **HISTORY** The Labrador Retriever came from Newfoundland, where it used to help haul the fishermen's nets ashore. Today, apart from being a gundog, Labradors often act as guide dogs, have been trained to detect drugs and explosives, and are popular as companions.

• **REMARK** Unless regularly exercised, Labradors tend towards obesity.

wide skull and slightly pronounced brow

smooth, black, chocolate, or yellow double coat

long shoulders

otter-like, medium-length tail

well-developed hindquarters

wide, powerful, chest with barrel-shaped ribcage

well-arched toes and thick pads

COLOUR TYPES

Height 54–57cm (21½–22½in)	Weight 25–34kg (55–75lb)	Temperament Responsive, friendly

Country of origin Great Britain	First use Tracking hares	Origins 1600s

POINTER

This breed has an agile and athletic build. The muzzle has a distinctively concave profile and is often raised high as the dog tests the air. The Pointer is prized for its exceptional sense of smell and displays considerable pace on the field, covering enormous distances. This elegant dog retains strong working instincts and requires a great deal of exercise if it is to be kept as a pet.

• **HISTORY** The Pointer has been a hunting dog since the 17th century. Originally it was trained to detect hares, which were then run down, or "coursed", by greyhounds.

• **REMARK** In the presence of game, this dog freezes in a characteristic "pointing" stance to indicate the quarry's direction.

• **OTHER NAMES** English Pointer.

pronounced occipital bone

well-defined stop on the muzzle

long, sloping shoulders

wide chest

straight forelegs

hard, short coat with good gloss

Height 61–69cm (24–27in)	Weight 20–30kg (44–66lb)	Temperament Responsive, lively

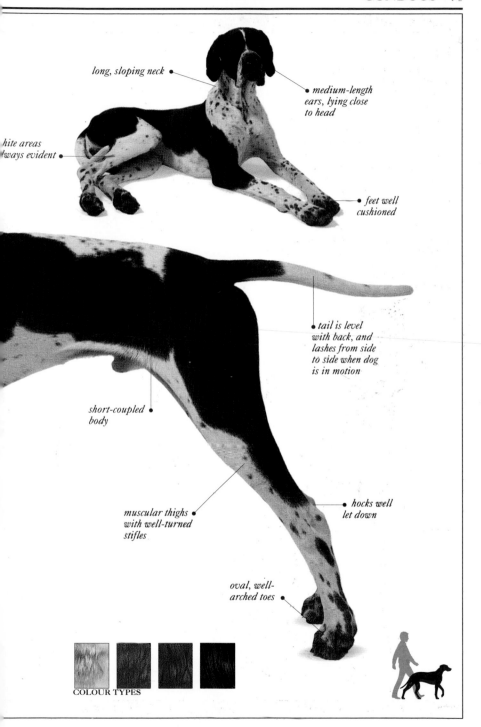

long, sloping neck

medium-length
ears, lying close
to head

hite areas
ways evident

feet well
cushioned

tail is level
with back, and
lashes from side
to side when dog
is in motion

short-coupled
body

muscular thighs
with well-turned
stifles

hocks well
let down

oval, well-
arched toes

COLOUR TYPES

Country of origin Great Britain	First use Springing hidden game	Origins 1500s

WELSH SPRINGER SPANIEL

Although possibly sharing common origins with the English Springer (see p.66), the Welsh Springer Spaniel is generally smaller, has a finer head, and always has rich, dark-red markings on a white coat.

HISTORY A clue to the possible age of this breed comes from a 16th-century manuscript which refers to what could be an early ancestor of the Welsh Springer Spaniel.

• **REMARK** The description "springer" refers to the breed's ability to "spring" hidden game.

slightly domed skull

long, muscular neck

square, medium-length muzzle

silky, dense coat, never wavy or wiry

Height 46–48cm (18–19in)	Weight 16–20kg (35–45lb)	Temperament Attentive, friendly

Country of origin Great Britain	First use Scenting game	Origins 1700s

SUSSEX SPANIEL

The Sussex is a lower, longer, slower dog than other spaniels. Its abundant, flat coat is rich golden liver in colour, with the hairs becoming golden at their tips.

• **HISTORY** This is one of the oldest spaniel breeds, first recognized in 1855.

• **REMARK** Unusually for spaniels, the Sussex will "give tongue" (bay) when on the scent of game, in the fashion of hounds.

broad skull and wrinkled brows

short, strong legs

long body

Height 38–41cm (15–16in)	Weight 18–23kg (40–50lb)	Temperament Friendly, determined

Country of origin Canada	First use Retrieving water-fowl	Origins 1800s

NOVA SCOTIA DUCK TOLLING RETRIEVER

This muscular, medium- to heavy-boned retriever has a dense, water-repellent coat. The feathering is paler than the ground colour, which can be various shades of red, often with white markings.

• HISTORY This Retriever was developed in Canada in the late 19th century to perform a unique role in hunting. It is used to toll (lure) curious ducks within range of the concealed hunters' guns by creating a disturbance at the water's edge.

• REMARK Foxes occasionally lure their prey towards them in this cunning fashion.

wedge-shaped head •

• brown nose.

• pale feathering

deep chest •

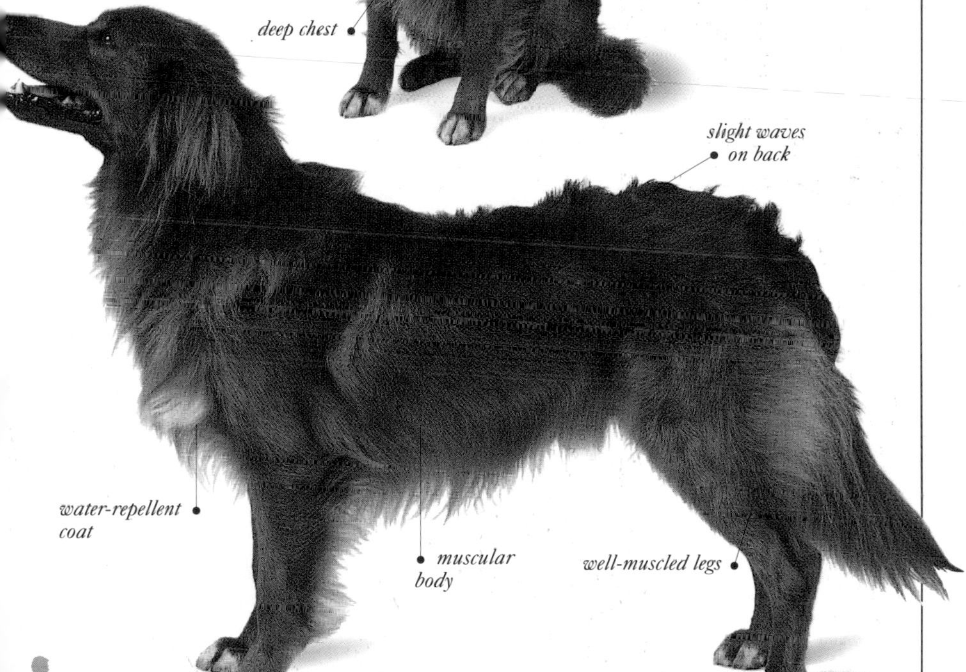

slight waves • on back

water-repellent coat •

• muscular body

well-muscled legs •

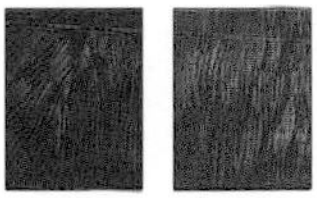

COLOUR TYPES

Height 43–53cm (17–21in)	Weight 17–23kg (37–51lb)	Temperament Responsive, active

| Country of origin Denmark | First use Scenting and pointing game | Origins 1700s |

OLD DANISH POINTER

By the standards of most pointers, this dog is not tall, but it is nevertheless a robust animal, well-balanced, with muscular thighs, a heavy head, and a long and powerful neck with dewlap. Its short coat is brown and white in colour, some ticking being permitted.

- **HISTORY** The origins of the Old Danish Pointer are uncertain, but it may have resulted from crossings between Spanish Pointers, brought to Denmark by gypsies, and local bloodhound breeds. The breed is little known outside its Danish homeland.
- **REMARK** Its excellent scenting abilities makes it ideal for tracking wounded animals.
- **OTHER NAMES** Gammel Dansk Honsehund.

long, pendent ears, rounded at tips

broad forehead

liver-coloured nose

hazel-coloured eyes

some ticking evident in coat

broad, straight back

tapering tail, thick at base

long neck with dewlap

broad, muscular chest

short, dense coat

well-developed, powerful thighs

| Height 51–58cm (20–23in) | Weight 18–24kg (40–53lb) | Temperament Active, responsive |

Country of origin Germany	First use Hunting quail	Origins 1900s

GERMAN SPANIEL

Although somewhat similar in appearance to the English Springer Spaniel (see p.66), the German Spaniel is slightly shorter in the leg. This versatile dog operates as a talented retriever, often working in marshland. It resembles hounds in that it is also highly respected as a tracker.

• **HISTORY** Various breeds contributed to its development, including the old German Stöber.

• **REMARK** Essentially a working dog, this breed is not normally kept as a pet in Germany.

• **OTHER NAMES** Deutscher Wachtelhund.

predominantly smooth coat on head

pendent ears covered with longer hair

broad, brown nose with large nostrils

body is long compared with its height

slight feathering on tail

feathering present on backs of forelegs

long ears hang back, behind eyes

elongated, but not pointed, muzzle

thick, medium-length, wavy coat

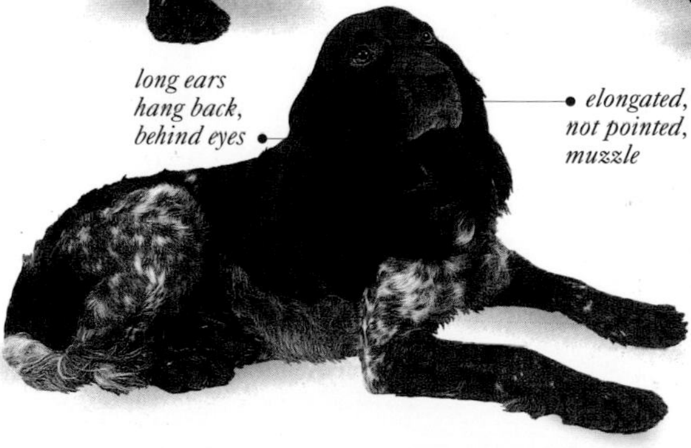

COLOUR TYPES

Height 40–51cm (16–20in)	Weight 20–30kg (44–66lb)	Temperament Gentle, obedient

Country of origin Germany	First use Tracking large game	Origins 1600s

WEIMARANER

A sleek, uniformly grey coat colour and fine, aristocratic features are the main hallmarks of this medium-sized hunting dog. It has a strong muzzle and only a moderate stop. The Weimaraner, originally known as the Weimar Pointer, comes from a long tradition of German hunting dogs, many of which have found favour in other countries all over the world. This indefatigable breed has long, muscular limbs, a good sense of smell, and an obedient and friendly nature – all the attributes of a good, all-round hunting dog. It is one of only seven breeds of hunt, point, and retrieve dogs. Long- and short-haired forms of the Weimaraner are found, although the long-haired form is not officially recognized in the USA. The coat colour is slightly lighter on the head and on the ears.

• **HISTORY** There is no confirmed history of the development of this dog. One theory suggests that the Weimaraner is the result of an albino mutation that appeared in some of the ancient German pointers. It may have descended from the German Braken, or from crossings between a regular pointer and an unnamed yellow pointer, overseen by Grand Duke Karl August of Weimar.

• **REMARK** The exact origins of this dog are unknown. However, it can be positively dated to the 1600s when it appeared in an early painting by the Flemish artist Van Dyck.

• **OTHER NAMES** Weimaraner Vorstehhund.

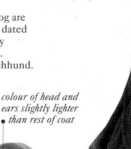

well-developed, muscular hindquarters

level back

tail is traditionally docked to approximately 15cm (6in)

colour of head and ears slightly lighter than rest of coat

coat length 3–6cm (1–2in)

coat has almost metallic sheen

LONG-HAIRED WEIMARANER

fringing evident

Height 56–69cm (22–27in)	Weight 32–39kg (70–86lb)	Temperament Responsive, alert

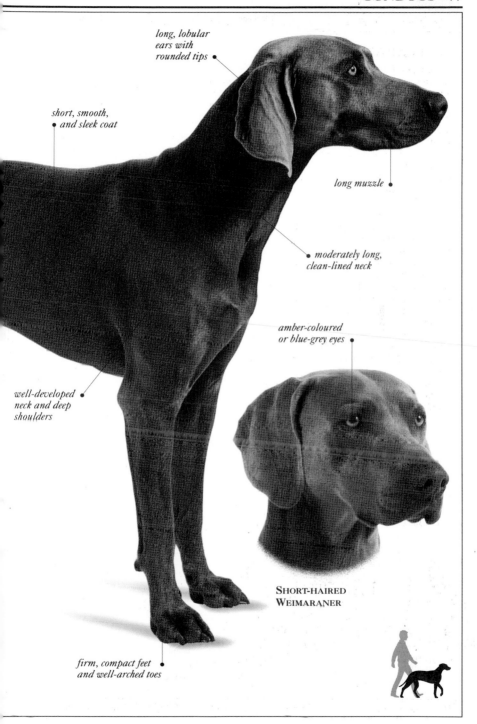

long, lobular
ears with
rounded tips

short, smooth,
and sleek coat

long muzzle

moderately long,
clean-lined neck

amber-coloured
or blue-grey eyes

well-developed
neck and deep
shoulders

firm, compact feet
and well-arched toes

**SHORT-HAIRED
WEIMARANER**

Country of origin Germany	First use Retrieving birds	Origins 1800s

GERMAN WIRE-HAIRED POINTER

The harsh, wiry coat and the longer hair above the eyes and on the jaws distinguish this sturdy breed from the other forms of German pointer. The distinctive texture of the coat helps to prevent twigs and other debris becoming entangled when the dog is working.

• **HISTORY** First recognized in Germany in 1870, the breed has developed into its present condition through the infusion of German Shepherd and griffon blood.

• **REMARK** Highly valued as a gundog, it is able to fulfil a variety of tasks.

• **OTHER NAMES** Deutscher Drahthaariger Vorstehhund.

medium-length head

pronounced beard

harsh, flat outercoat

tail often kept nearly horizontal

powerful muzzle

straight forelegs

deep chest

well-arched toes with sturdy nails

COLOUR TYPES

Height 56–66cm (22–26in)	Weight 20–34kg (45–75lb)	Temperament Active, responsive

Country of origin Germany	First use Pointing	Origins 1800s

SMALL MÜNSTERLÄNDER

This sturdy breed can be distinguished from its larger relative not only by its size, but also by its coloration, which is invariably liver and white. It is otherwise of similar type, being a powerful, muscular dog very well suited to working in the field for long periods.

• **HISTORY** The breed's origins can be traced back to Westphalia in Germany. It was developed from crossings involving French spaniels and dogs similar to the Dutch Partridge Dog (see p.82). It was used as a bird dog, and valued especially for its pointing skills. It reached its greatest prominence in the early 1900s.

• **REMARK** This good-natured dog is now becoming more popular outside Germany.

• **OTHER NAMES** Kleiner Münsterländer Vorstehhund, Heidewachtel, Spion.

predominantly liver-coloured head

sleek coat with signs of feathering

variable amount of ticking

skin is tight over body

well-feathered tail

straight forelegs

strong, rather setter-like body

considerable feathering at back of hindlegs

tight feet, with thick pads

Height 48–56cm (19–22in)	Weight 15kg (33lb)	Temperament Responsive, friendly

| Country of origin Germany | First use Tracking and retrieving game | Origins 1800s |

LARGE MÜNSTERLÄNDER

The Large Münsterländer can be instantly
distinguished from its smaller relative
(see p.79) by its distinctive
coloration, which is a
striking combination
of black and white,
rather than liver and
white. The larger breed
should also have ticking
or roaning in the white.

• **HISTORY** Originally, the
German Long-haired Pointer Club
accepted only liver-and-white dogs
for registration, and so black-and-white
pups were often simply given away. It
was from these that the Large Münsterländer evolved.

• **REMARK** The first breed club for this
dog was formed in 1919.

• **OTHER NAMES** Grosser
Münsterländer Vorstehhund.

*strong,
muscular neck*

*broad, slightly
rounded head*

*wide chest
with good depth*

straight forelegs

*strong,
black nails*

| Height 59–61cm (23–24in) | Weight 25–29kg (55–65lb) | Temperament Responsive, friendly |

dark brown,
medium-
sized eyes

broad, round-
tipped ears,
lying flat on
the sides

solid back,
sloping slightly
downwards

well-formed
black nose

tail is in line
with back, tapering
to the tip

taut abdomen

dense hair
between toes

Country of origin Netherlands	First use Hunting game	Origins 1600s

DUTCH PARTRIDGE DOG

The coat of this medium-sized, strongly built breed appears long, mainly because of fringes present on the ears. These extend down the neck, and on the legs and tail. When walking, the tail is extended horizontally, and is slightly curled at the tip, but it is held down when the dog is at rest.

fringes on ears

• **HISTORY** This breed originated in the Drentse district of the Netherlands; it probably stems from the same ancestral stock as today's spaniels and setters. It frequently hunts pheasants and rabbits, as well as partridges.

• **REMARK** The Dutch Partridge Dog tends to rotate its tail in a circle when it has located game.

• **OTHER NAMES** Drentse Partijshond.

strong, sturdy legs with thick pads on feet •

COLOUR TYPES

• coarse, straight coat

Height 56–64cm (22–25in)	Weight 23kg (50lb)	Temperament Responsive, loyal

Country of origin Netherlands	First use Hunting small game	Origins 1700s

KOOIKER DOG

ears set high • on head

This lightly-built, well-proportioned dog has well-feathered ears, a slightly wavy, moderate-length coat, and pronounced fringing to the ears, chest, and tail. In general appearance it is not unlike a small setter with a long, bushy tail.

• conspicuous black nose

• **HISTORY** This breed is well known in the Netherlands and is reputed to have foiled an assassination attempt on Prince William II of Orange (1626–1650) by barking and waking him just in time.

white blaze on face •

• **REMARK** The bushy tail of the Kooiker is used to lure wild ducks so that they can be banded and then released.

• **OTHER NAMES** Kooikerhondje.

• medium-length, wavy coat

well-feathered • forelegs

• well-feathered ears with black tips

Height 35–41cm (14–16in)	Weight 9–11kg (20–24lb)	Temperament Industrious, intelligent

Country of origin Netherlands	First use Catching moles	Origins 1600s

STABYHOUN

This spaniel-like breed has a slightly elongated but well-balanced body, a wide head, and a muzzle tapering towards the nose. Its coat is long, sleek, and well feathered, and is seen in dappled colours of black, brown, orange, and blue.

• **HISTORY** The breed originated in Friesland, in the Netherlands. Crossings between the Drentse Patrijshond, a larger Dutch gundog, and spaniels probably occurred.

• **REMARK** This popular gundog is able to locate, point, and retrieve game. It adapts well to family life.

broad skull

well-boned, straight forelegs

long, sleek coat, with feathering evident

COLOUR TYPES

Height 50–53cm (19½–21in)	Weight 15–20kg (33–44lb)	Temperament Responsive, gentle

Country of origin Netherlands	First use Hunting otters	Origins 1600s

WETTERHOUN

The Wetterhoun is a dog for all seasons. Its coat provides a covering of tight, water-resistant curls, except on the head and legs, and its solid and rugged build made it an ideal hunter of otters.

• **HISTORY** The Wetterhoun, Dutch for "water dog", probably descended from the now-extinct Old Water Dog.

• **REMARK** This strong-willed dog benefits from good training when young.

• **OTHER NAMES** Otterhoun, Dutch Spaniel.

spatula-shaped ears on a broad head

curly coat except for head and legs

powerful, thick-set neck

COLOUR TYPES

Height 53–58cm (21–23in)	Weight 15–20kg (33–44lb)	Temperament Independent, active

Country of origin Ireland	First use Retrieving water-fowl	Origins 1800s

IRISH WATER SPANIEL

Standing taller than any other breed of spaniel, and with a unique coloration showing a purplish hue described as puce liver, this breed has a powerful presence. The coat is comprised of tight ringlets and is naturally oily and water-repellent. The first 10cm (4in) of tail has curly hair, whereas the rest to the tip is either bare skin or is covered with straight hair.

• **HISTORY** The Irish Water Spaniel may have been developed from the Portuguese Water Dog or a poodle, crossed with native Irish spaniels. The breed's founder, Justin McCarthy, kept the breed's origins a closely guarded secret and refused to reveal details of its precise ancestry.

• **REMARK** This spaniel is a powerful swimmer and is large enough to retrieve game the size of geese from deep water.

large nose, the colour of dark liver

long, oval-shaped ears

head set well above body

long curls on head

powerful, arching neck

tight ringlets of hair cover body

V-shaped patch of smooth hair

short, straight, tapering tail

smooth hair on front of hindlegs below the hocks

straight, powerful forelegs

Height 51–58cm (20–23in)	Weight 20–29kg (45–65lb)	Temperament Responsive, playful

Country of origin Ireland	First use Retrieving game	Origins 1700s

IRISH RED AND WHITE SETTER

Well-proportioned and athletic, the Irish
Red and White Setter is a powerful,
good-natured dog. Similar to the Irish
Setter (see p.86), it is more heavily built
with a broader head and a more
prominent occipital peak. The finely-
textured, feathered coat has a pure white
ground colour with solid red patches. Some
mottling or flecking is common; roaning,
however, is frowned upon in show circles.
Setters are renowned for their highly
developed sense of smell and ability to
excel at any kind of hunting in any type
of terrain or weather conditions.
• **HISTORY** Originally called the Parti-
coloured Setter, this hardy breed derives from
the same root-stock as the graceful Irish Setter.
Although the Irish Red and White Setter is an
excellent working dog in the field, it came very
close to extinction before undergoing a revival
in recent years.
• **REMARK** The Irish Red and White Setter
makes an affectionate family pet, but requires
a great deal of exercise and rigorous training.

domed skull

solid red patches

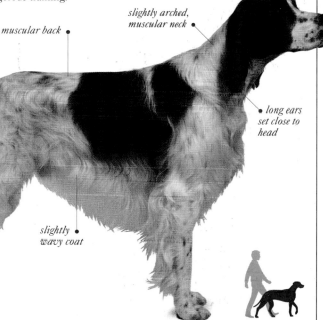

strong, well-feathered tail, carried level with, or below, back

muscular back

slightly arched, muscular neck

long ears set close to head

slightly wavy coat

Height 58–69cm (23–27in)	Weight 27–32kg (60–70lb)	Temperament Active, affectionate

| Country of origin Ireland | First use Retrieving game | Origins 1700s |

IRISH SETTER

In spite of its formal name, the Irish Setter is often better known simply as the Red Setter, due to its distinctive coloration. Built on racier lines than its red and white cousin, it is a lively, active dog, perpetually ready for fun. It is popular as a pet but must have plenty of exercise. To ensure obedience it requires more training than other similar breeds, but in the end the Irish Setter should become a superb working companion.

• **HISTORY** The breed evolved in Ireland, where Irish Water Spaniels, Gordon Setters, and Springer Spaniels are all believed to have played a part in its development.

• **REMARK** A small amount of white on the chest is quite common, and will not lead to disqualification from a show ring.

• **OTHER NAMES** Red Setter.

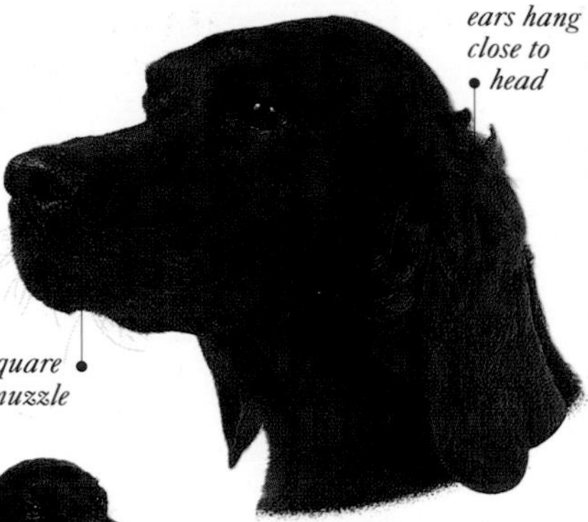

ears hang close to head

square muzzle

rich, chestnut coat

long, muscular neck

feathered, low-set tail

straight, sinewy forelegs

deep, narrow chest

long, fine feathering on back of legs

| Height 64–69cm (25–27in) | Weight 27–32kg (60–70lb) | Temperament Active, affectionate |

Country of origin France	First use Hunting small game	Origins 1700s

BRAQUE ST. GERMAIN

This pointer has a predominantly white coat broken by orange areas of variable size. Although slightly leggier than the English Pointer (see pp.70–71), the elegant Braque St. Germain is a dog of fine proportions.

• HISTORY The breed's ancestry traces back to two English Pointers given to King Charles X of France. When one died, the other was mated with a Braque Francais. The offspring laid the foundations of this breed.

• REMARK This dog is not favoured for retrieving from water as its coat does not provide sufficient insulation when it is wet.

• OTHER NAMES St. Germain Pointer.

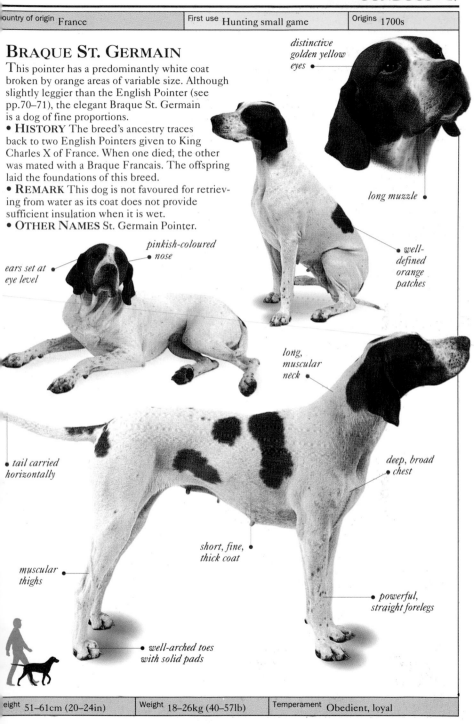

distinctive golden yellow eyes

long muzzle

well-defined orange patches

pinkish-coloured nose

ears set at eye level

long, muscular neck

tail carried horizontally

deep, broad chest

muscular thighs

short, fine, thick coat

powerful, straight forelegs

well-arched toes with solid pads

Height 51–61cm (20–24in)	Weight 18–26kg (40–57lb)	Temperament Obedient, loyal

Country of origin France	First use Scenting and pointing game	Origins 1600s

LARGE FRENCH POINTER

One of France's oldest breeds, the Large French
Pointer is an imposing dog, with a strong, well-
muscled physique. The breed, which originated in the
Pyrenean region of France, is a slightly taller dog than
the better-known English Pointer (see pp.70–71), but
in general physique they are very similar. A smaller
version of the breed, from Gascony, has a more
refined appearance.

• HISTORY It is popularly believed that
the Large French Pointer is descended
from the old, extinct Southern Hound, and
that it is also closely related to the Italian
and Spanish Pointers (see pp.101 and 102).
There is certainly a hound-like aura attaching
to this breed, which lends credence to this belief.

• REMARK During the latter part of the 19th century
the breed declined in popularity, and was in danger of
dying out. However, recent efforts among enthusiasts
have resulted in a considerable boost in the numbers
of these pointers. Although not common, its future
does now seem assured, as a new generation of hunters
learns to appreciate its working skills.

• OTHER NAMES Braque Francais de Grande Taille.

*head often held upwards to
detect scent when working
• in open surroundings*

*convex head
has broad,
rectangular
muzzle •*

*ticking
present on
this specimen •*

*broad, •
deep chest*

*fine hair
covering on
ears and
head •*

*straight, well-
boned forelegs •*

*• ears show
signs of
pleats*

Height 56–68cm (22–27in)	Weight 20–32kg (45–71lb)	Temperament Well-balanced, steady

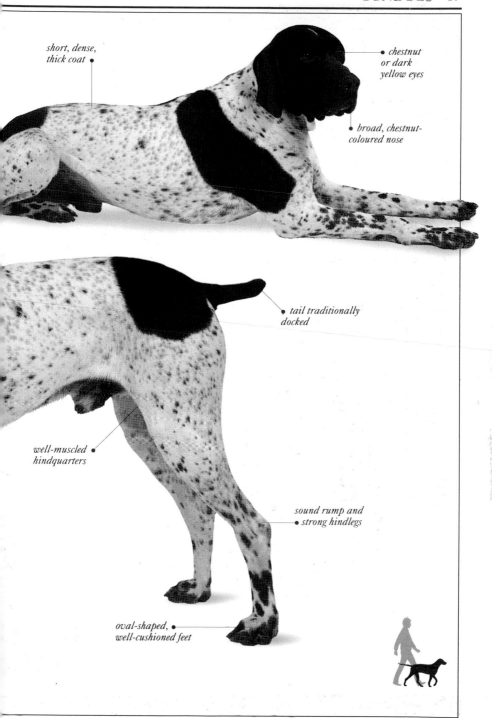

short, dense,
thick coat •

• chestnut
or dark
yellow eyes

• broad, chestnut-
coloured nose

• tail traditionally
docked

well-muscled •
hindquarters

sound rump and
• strong hindlegs

oval-shaped, •
well-cushioned feet

| Country of origin France | First use Pointing and retrieving game | Origins 1800s |

AUVERGNE POINTER

The Auvergne Pointer is a large and relatively heavy gundog, with distinctive coloration and markings. It is an important breed characteristic that the ears and the area around the eyes are black. Elsewhere on the body, blue roaning, resulting from overlapping black and white hairs, is desirable. This patterning is known as "charbonnée", or "charcoaled", although some Auvergnes show clearly defined black markings on a white background.

• **HISTORY** It is thought that Gascony Hounds (see pp.170–71) contributed to the breed's ancestry, although any residual traces of tan markings now merit disqualification in the show ring.

• **REMARK** This pointer is still kept essentially for sporting purposes.

• **OTHER NAMES** Braque d'Auvergne.

black markings on ears and around eyes are essential

rounded, domed skull with well-defined stop

wide, moist nostrils

long, straight forelegs

good sheen to coat

large, deep chest

very powerful hindquarters

large feet supported on well-cushioned pads

| Height 56–61cm (22–24in) | Weight 22–28kg (49–62lb) | Temperament Responsive, lively |

Country of origin France	First use Hunting game	Origins 1500s

BRAQUE DU BOURBONNAIS

The coat of the Braque du Bourbonnais is basically white with very evident roaning and as few clear patches of coloration as possible. This moderately large pointer is born with either no tail or a very rudimentary stump.

• **HISTORY** As its name implies, the Braque du Bourbonnais originated in the French province of Bourbon, and a dog very similar to today's breed can be found in paintings dating back to the 16th century. The breed flourished in France during the 1800s but then declined from about the First World War. Enthusiasts have, however, now pooled their breeding stock to ensure its continued success as a fine French pointing dog.

• **REMARK** This versatile breed is equally at home in scrubland or marshes, and is happy hunting all manner of game.

• **OTHER NAMES** Bourbonnais Pointer.

slightly curled, pendent ears

dark amber eyes

strong, broad muzzle

short, muscular neck and slight dewlap

liver-coloured nose with well-developed nostrils

rudimentary tail

pear-shaped head

deep, powerful chest

very straight forelegs

COLOUR TYPES

Height 56cm (22in)	Weight 18–26kg (40–57lb)	Temperament Intelligent, affectionate

Country of origin France	First use Flushing and retrieving game	Origins 1600s

ÉPAGNEUL FRANCAIS

Being relatively tall and powerfully built, the
Épagneul Francais, one of the oldest breeds of
French spaniel, shows a distinct relationship
to the setters. Its head is square, with a short
neck which joins a muscular body of fine
proportions. The coat is short and flat
with some feathering.

• HISTORY The ancestry of this breed is
not known. Competition from other gundogs once brought it close to extinction,
but it is now firmly re-established.

• REMARK The breed is not well-
known outside its native France.

• OTHER NAMES French
Spaniel.

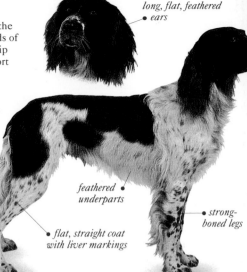

long, flat, feathered ears

feathered underparts

strong-boned legs

long, feathered tail

flat, straight coat with liver markings

Height 53–61cm (21–24in)	Weight 20–25kg (44–55lb)	Temperament Intelligent, responsive

Country of origin France	First use Retrieving water-fowl	Origins 1700s

ÉPAGNEUL PICARD

This is another of the older French
breeds of spaniel which displays an obvious relationship to the setters. The
Picard can be distinguished
by its characteristic tri-coloured
appearance, with tan, liver, and
white areas apparent in its coat.

• HISTORY Closely related to
the Épagneul Francais (above), the
Picard's ancestry is equally uncertain.

• REMARK This spaniel is highly
prized as a water-fowl retriever, working
in the marshlands of Picardy, France.

• OTHER NAMES Picardy Spaniel.

broad, round skull

finer, longer hair on ears

flat, straight coat

ticking clearly evident in coat

large feet for body size

feathering apparent at back of legs

Height 56–61cm (22–24in)	Weight 20kg (44lb)	Temperament Intelligent, friendly

Country of origin France	First use Retrieving game	Origins 1700s

BRITTANY

Frequently described as a spaniel, in behaviour the rather square-built Brittany appears to have more in common with the setters, certainly in terms of height. It is not a particularly gainly dog, the legs appearing rather out of proportion to the body. The tail is naturally short in length, but it is customarily docked to a maximum length of 10cm (4in).
• HISTORY An old breed, it underwent a revival in its native France in the early 1900s. It has since become popular in the USA.
• REMARK A good all-rounder in the field, the Brittany can hunt, point, and retrieve.
• OTHER NAMES Épagneul Breton.

wide-open nostrils enable scent to be detected more easily

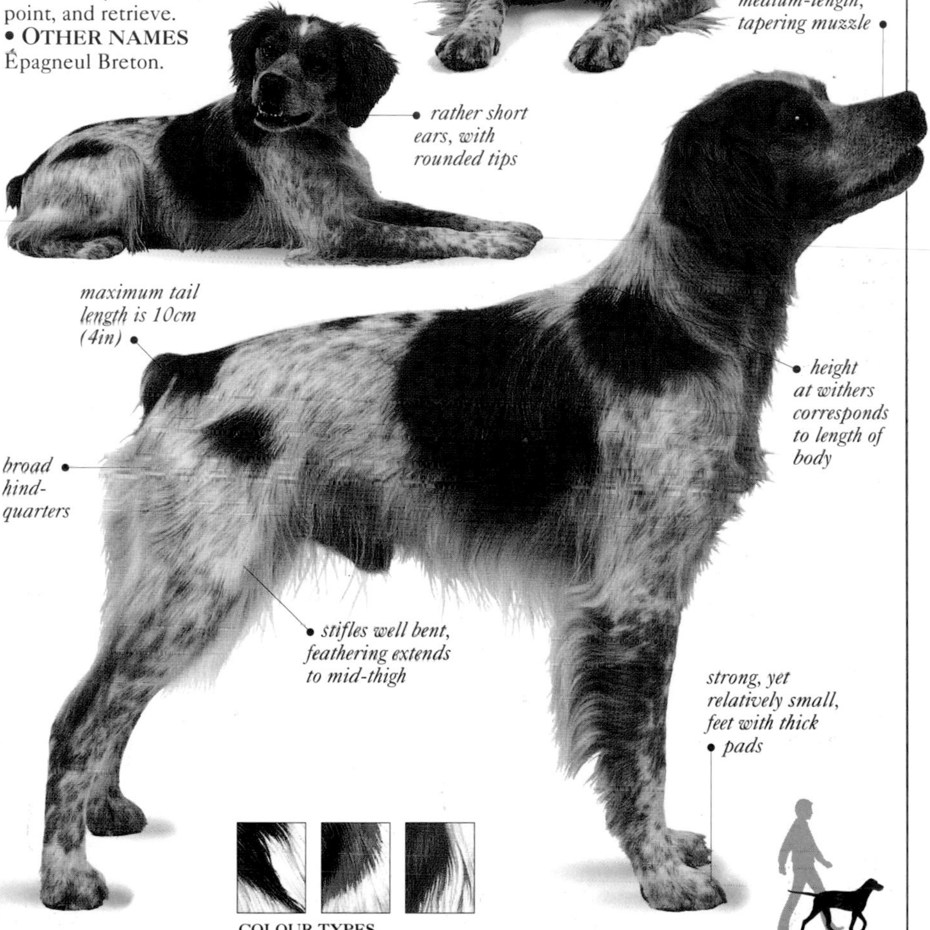

medium-length, tapering muzzle

rather short ears, with rounded tips

maximum tail length is 10cm (4in)

height at withers corresponds to length of body

broad hind-quarters

stifles well bent, feathering extends to mid-thigh

strong, yet relatively small, feet with thick pads

COLOUR TYPES

Height 46–52cm (18–20½in)	Weight 13–15kg (28–33lb)	Temperament Loyal, obedient

Country of origin France	First use Flushing and retrieving game	Origins 1600s

ÉPAGNEUL PONT-AUDEMER

The presence of a curly top-knot gives this spaniel a distinctive appearance. The rest of the liver, or liver-and-white, coat is long and curly, covering a medium-sized, well-built dog.

• **HISTORY** Crosses involving the Irish Water Spaniel, or similar ancestral stock, gave rise to this breed. Old French spaniels also probably contributed to the bloodline. The breed was developed in the area of Pont-Audemer in Normandy. After the Second World War, the breed declined drastically, and Irish Water Spaniels were used to increase numbers.

• **REMARK** The Épagneul Pont-Audemer remains scarce today, but a society has been established to safeguard its future.

• **OTHER NAMES** Pont-Audemer Spaniel.

short hair on face

long, pendent well-feathered ears

weather-resistant, wavy coat

ticking may be apparent in white areas of coat

tail traditionally docked to a third of full length

well-proportioned body

COLOUR TYPES

Height 51–58cm (20–23in)	Weight 18–24kg (40–53lb)	Temperament Responsive, docile

Country of origin France	First use Retrieving water-fowl	Origins 1600s

BARBET

The coat of the Barbet is thick and woolly, protecting the dog even from freezing water conditions. It is shiny and may be curly or wavy, with a rather becoming tasselled appearance. The Barbet has played a central role in the development of many of today's water dogs.

• **HISTORY** Although the precise ancestry of the Barbet is unknown, it is an ancient breed, and is thought to be the forerunner of such breeds as poodles, Irish Water Spaniels, and Otterhounds. It is also thought to resemble the now-extinct English Water Dog.

• **REMARK** As well as retrieving water-fowl, the Barbet would also return the fallen arrows of hunters who had missed their target.

• **OTHER NAMES** Griffon d'Arret à Poil Laineux.

long, pendent ears lying close to the head

large, prominent nostrils

good covering of long, water-resistant hair

solid, muscular body

undocked tail with slight upwards curve

powerful, well-boned legs

large, rounded feet with webbing between toes

COLOUR TYPES

Height 46–56cm (18–22in)	Weight 15–25kg (33–55lb)	Temperament Intelligent, obedient

Country of origin France	First use Hunting snipe	Origins 1800s

ÉPAGNEUL BLEU DE PICARDIE

The distinctive blue roan coloration of this breed helps to distinguish it from the Épagneul Picard (see p.92), another form of the same dog but with flecks and patches of liver and tan in its coat. In terms of its size, general proportions, and head shape, the breed conforms more to today's definition of a setter than a spaniel, and it looks a little like the engravings of early Gordon Setters (see p.66).

• **HISTORY** This form of the Picard was developed in the French province of Picardy, and is descended from crossings of the blue belton (blue mixed with white) English Setter with the Picard itself. The result is a taller, lighter-boned dog with a better nose than the old type of French spaniel.

• **REMARK** The Épagneul Bleu de Picardie is an exceedingly hardworking gundog and develops a very close bond with its master.

• **OTHER NAMES** Blue Picardy Spaniel.

hair longer and finer on ears

flat, relatively long, straight coat

dark brown, expressive eyes

good covering of hair on feet

ram-shaped muzzle with prominent nose

hair longer on tail than on body

deep chest

strong, well-boned legs

large feet

Height 56–61cm (22–24in)	Weight 20kg (44lb)	Temperament Intelligent, friendly

Country of origin France	First use Hunting and retrieving game	Origins 1800s

WIRE-HAIRED POINTING GRIFFON

The hard, coarse coat of this dog gives it rather an unkempt appearance. In reality it requires little grooming, aside from periodic brushing. Facially, this breed is characterized by bushy eyebrows and a heavy beard of long, thick hair.
• **HISTORY** The breed was developed by Dutchman Eduard Karel Korthals, possibly by crossing griffons with French Pointers.
• **REMARK** As well as pointing and retrieving, the versatile Wire-haired Pointing Griffon will also hunt rodents and pursue foxes.
• **OTHER NAMES** Korthals Griffon.

long, large head

powerful, straight forelegs

short legs compared with body

muscular hindquarters

COLOUR TYPES

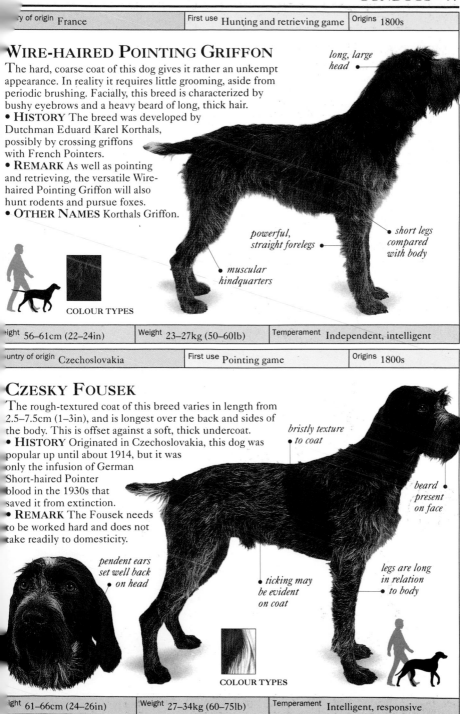

Height 56–61cm (22–24in)	Weight 23–27kg (50–60lb)	Temperament Independent, intelligent

Country of origin Czechoslovakia	First use Pointing game	Origins 1800s

CZESKY FOUSEK

The rough-textured coat of this breed varies in length from 2.5–7.5cm (1–3in), and is longest over the back and sides of the body. This is offset against a soft, thick undercoat.
• **HISTORY** Originated in Czechoslovakia, this dog was popular up until about 1914, but it was only the infusion of German Short-haired Pointer blood in the 1930s that saved it from extinction.
• **REMARK** The Fousek needs to be worked hard and does not take readily to domesticity.

bristly texture to coat

beard present on face

pendent ears set well back on head

ticking may be evident on coat

legs are long in relation to body

COLOUR TYPES

Height 61–66cm (24–26in)	Weight 27–34kg (60–75lb)	Temperament Intelligent, responsive

| Country of origin Hungary | First use Hunting and retrieving game | Origins 1000s |

HUNGARIAN VIZSLA

This medium-sized, athletic gundog gives an immediate impression of being lean, lively, and muscular. Its coat is particularly striking, being smooth, shiny, sleek, and golden russet in colour. White patches are undesirable.

• **HISTORY** It is thought that the ancestors of the Vizsla accompanied the Magyars in their invasion of Hungary. Its bloodline probably includes the ancient Transylvanian Hound and the Turkish Yellow Dog, with more recent additions of pointer blood.

• **REMARK** The Vizsla is adept at hunting, pointing, and retrieving in any terrain, including marshes.

• **OTHER NAMES** Magyar Vizsla.

long, thin ears, set low, and with rounded tips

long, tapering muzzle

short, tightly fitting coat

lean, elegant head

robust, medium-boned frame

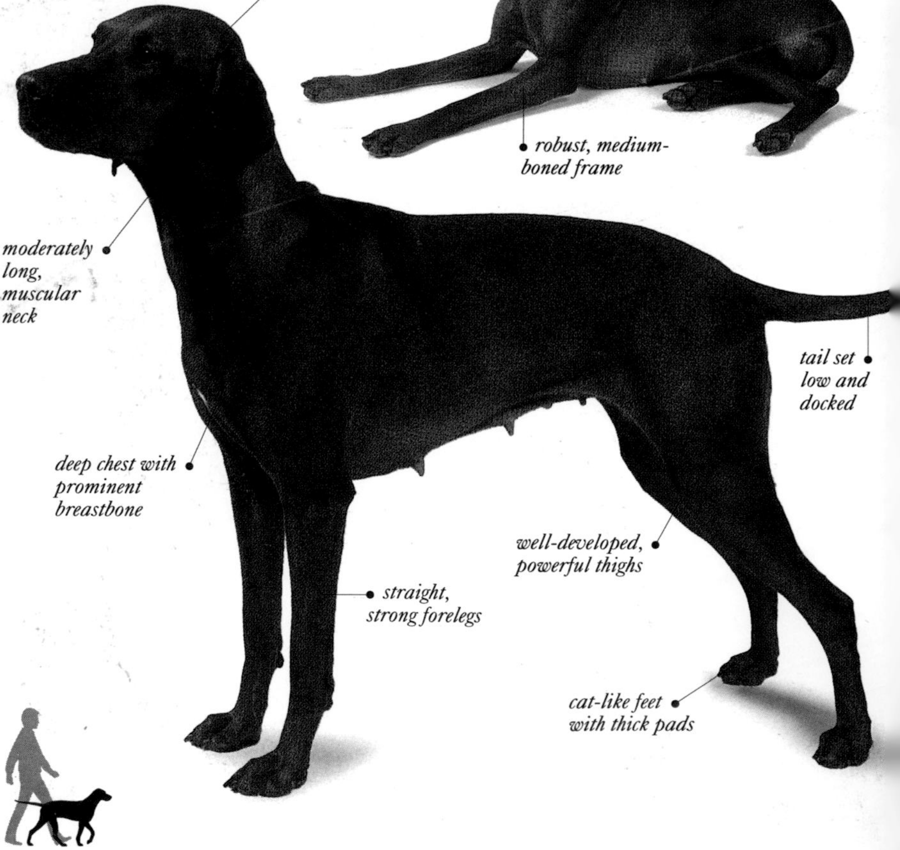

moderately long, muscular neck

tail set low and docked

deep chest with prominent breastbone

well-developed, powerful thighs

straight, strong forelegs

cat-like feet with thick pads

| Height 57–64cm (22½–25in) | Weight 22–30kg (48½–66lb) | Temperament Gentle, responsive |

Country of origin Hungary	First use Gundog	Origins 1930s

WIRE-HAIRED VIZSLA

The wire-haired form of the vizsla is much rarer than its smooth-coated counterpart. It is a relative newcomer to the gundog scene and has yet to receive widespread recognition as a separate breed. In its Hungarian homeland, it is favoured for working in water because it is less vulnerable to the cold.

• **HISTORY** Cross-breedings between the German Wire-haired Pointer and vizslas, which took place during the 1930s, gave rise to this breed.

• **REMARK** The Hungarian word *vizsla* translates as "responsive", "alert".

• **OTHER NAMES**
Drótszörü Magyar Vizsla.

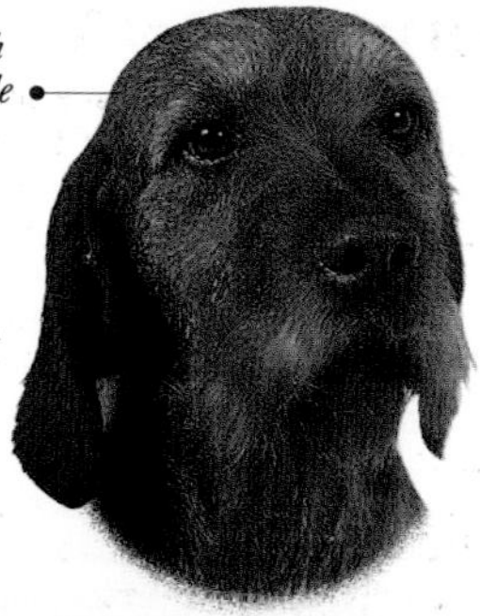

noble head with tapering muzzle

beard and eyebrows evident

nails slightly darker than coat

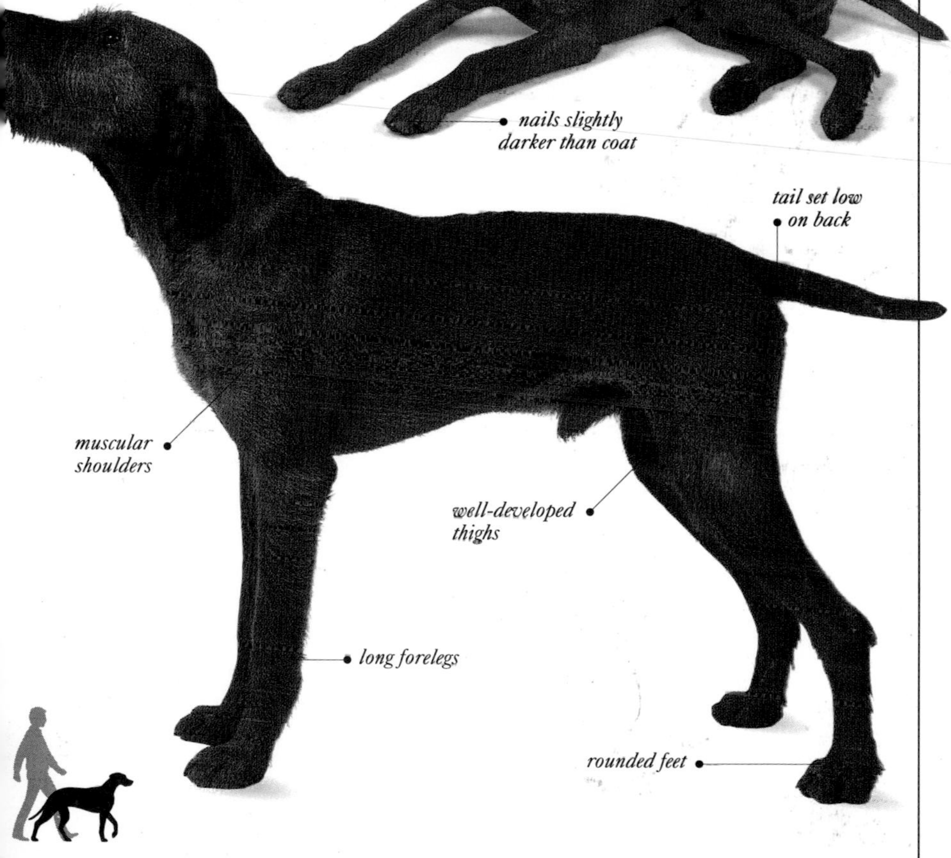

tail set low on back

muscular shoulders

well-developed thighs

long forelegs

rounded feet

Height 56–61cm (22–24in)	Weight 22–30kg (48–66lb)	Temperament Responsive, intelligent

Country of origin Italy	First use Retrieving game	Origins 1200s

SPINONE

Solid and squarely built, the Spinone is one of
the most talented of all the hunting dogs. Long
appreciated in its homeland, it is becoming more
popular elsewhere in Europe and in the USA.
Its tracking abilities are particularly keen, and
few dogs have a "softer" mouth for retrieving
game unspoiled.

• **HISTORY** The ancestry of this dog dates
back many centuries, and probably
originated from griffon stock.

• **REMARK** A 15th-century fresco at
the Ducal Palace in Mantua, Italy,
depicts an early representation of
the breed.

• **OTHER NAMES** Spinone
Italiano, Italian Spinone.

friendly
expression

large eyes,
varying from
yellow to ochre

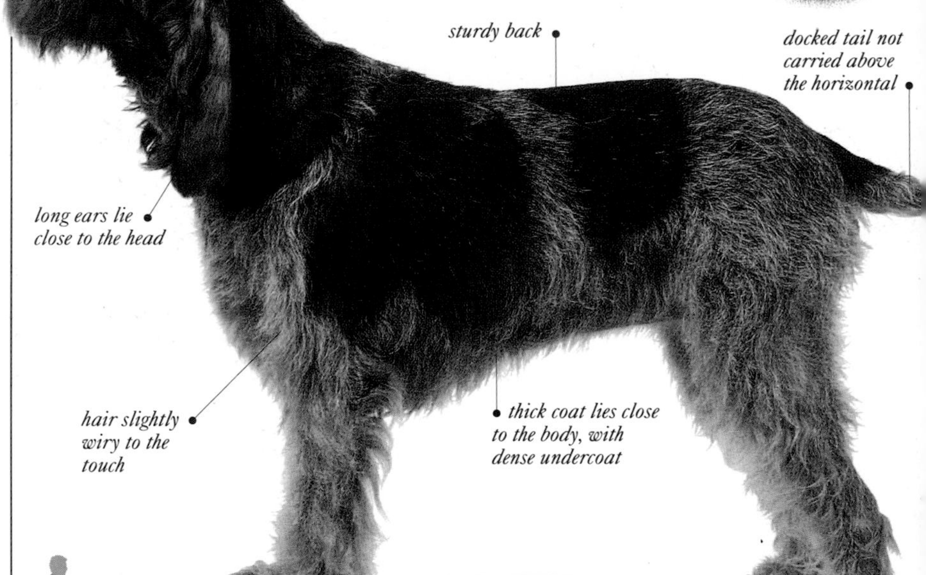

sturdy back

docked tail not
carried above
the horizontal

long ears lie
close to the head

hair slightly
wiry to the
touch

thick coat lies close
to the body, with
dense undercoat

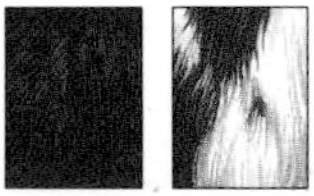

COLOUR TYPES

Height 61–66cm (24–26in)	Weight 32–37kg (71–82lb)	Temperament Responsive, loyal

Country of origin Italy	First use Gundog	Origins 1700s

BRACCO ITALIANO

This agile, square-framed dog is one of the oldest surviving gundog breeds, and shows very clear signs of its origins from ancient hound stock. The muzzle is unusual, being square almost to the point of convex when viewed in profile. Its coat, which is short and dense, has a finer quality on the head, neck, and lower body. The body of the Bracco Italiano resembles other pointer breeds in overall appearance.

• **HISTORY** This was a popular dog during the Renaissance period, and was often given as a gift from Italy to countries such as France and Spain. However, the Bracco Italiano declined in popularity by the 1800s, although it has recently undergone a revival in its homeland.

• **REMARK** It has changed little over the centuries and tends to be a little stubborn.

• **OTHER NAMES** Italian Pointer.

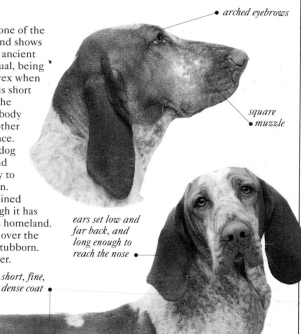

arched eyebrows

square muzzle

ears set low and far back, and long enough to reach the nose

muscular hindquarters

short, fine, dense coat

deep body

broad, deep chest

straight, firm forelegs

COLOUR TYPES

Height 56–67cm (22–26½in)	Weight 25–40kg (55–88lb)	Temperament Responsive, loyal

| Country of origin Spain | First use Hunting deer | Origins 1600s |

PERDIGUERO DE BURGOS

This breed of pointer has a massive head in relation to a rather slender, well-muscled body. Its coat is short and of a fine texture, being exclusively liver and white in coloration, often with prominent ticking.

• HISTORY The ancestry of this dog is not certain, but it undoubtedly belongs to an old breed, possibly one related to the ancient Sabueso Hound.

• REMARK The earlier form of this dog hunted deer; the quarry of today's breed is more likely to be partridge.

• OTHER NAMES Spanish Pointer.

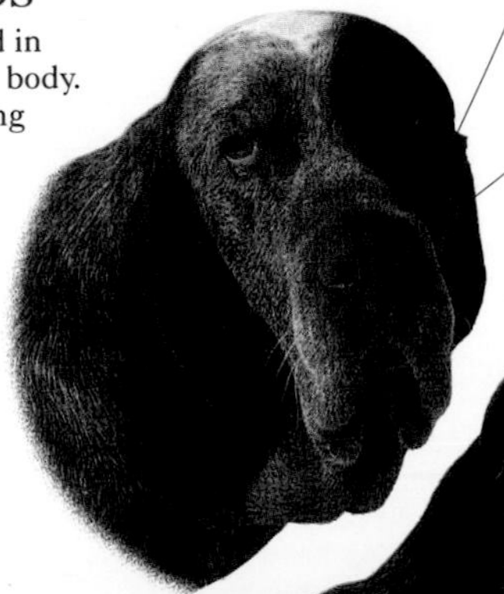

pendulous ears

square-shaped muzzle

large head

deep-chested appearance

powerful hindquarters

long, straight forelegs

ticking evident in coat

tail traditionally docked to one third of its full length

| Height 66–76cm (26–30in) | Weight 25–30kg (55–66lb) | Temperament Alert, responsive |

Country of origin Portugal	First use Retrieving from the sea	Origins 1500s

PORTUGUESE WATER DOG

There are two coat types associated with this breed, neither of which has an undercoat. In the first form, the hair is longish and wavy, with loose curls. In the second, the coat is shorter and thicker, and with more compact curls.

• **HISTORY** This breed is centuries old and was a valued fisherman's dog in the Algarve region of Portugal, capable of retrieving objects lost overboard and carrying messages between boats.

• **REMARK** Numbers of this breed fell to just 50 in 1960, although it is now widespread in Europe.

• **OTHER NAMES** Cão de Agua.

long, wavy hair

characteristic plume on tail

short, straight, muscular neck

profuse coat

deep chest

angulated hindquarters

powerful forelegs

COLOUR TYPES

Height 41–56cm (16–22in)	Weight 16–25kg (35–55lb)	Temperament Obedient, friendly

Country of origin Portugal	First use Hunting and retrieving game	Origins 1200s

PERDIGUERO PORTUGUESO

This is a medium-sized breed of pointer, which is still kept for working purposes in its homeland. The long-haired form is now relatively scarce, with the smooth-coated type predominating. It has a broad head and a distinctive stop to the nose.

- **HISTORY** So effective are the hunting abilities of this ancient breed that game suffered a dramatic decline. An ownership ban, from which only royalty was exempt, was imposed in the late 16th century.
- **REMARK** The name "Perdiguero" comes from the Portuguese word for partridge, the breed's chief quarry.
- **OTHER NAMES** Portuguese Pointer.

large, preferably dark eyes

ears have rounded tips

broad, black nostrils

triangular-shaped ears

smooth, short coat

tail traditionally docked

round, straight, powerful neck

short, broad body

well-arched toes

COLOUR TYPES

Height 52–56cm (20½–22in)	Weight 16–27kg (35–60lb)	Temperament Active, obedient

HERDING DOGS

ORIGINALLY, HERDING DOGS tended to be large and powerful, capable of protecting livestock from predators such as wolves and bears. As such threats declined, smaller, more agile breeds were adopted to take a more active role in controlling the movements of the herds. With various exceptions such as the German Shepherd Dog (see p.119), European herding breeds are less likely to be seen in the show ring, or in the home as family pets, but are still used for herding purposes. However, this is changing. Some breeds, such as the Tervuren (see p.128), are losing their popularity as herders, but finding new roles as companions and show dogs.

Country of origin USA	First use Herding sheep	Origins 1800s

AUSTRALIAN SHEPHERD

This attractive, long-haired breed has a bobtail and a striking, and remarkably varied, coat coloration: every dog has a unique pattern of markings. Eye coloration, too, is highly variable.
• **HISTORY** Despite its name, this breed was developed mainly in the USA. It is descended from collie stock, possibly crossed with other herding breeds. Its original ancestry can be traced back to the Basque region of France and Spain.
• **REMARK** This breed is highly prized wherever obedience is of vital importance, such as in search and rescue work.

triangular ears set high on head

thick ruff of fur on neck and chest

coat of moderate length and coarseness

deep chest with well-sprung ribs

COLOUR TYPES

Height 46–58.5cm (18–23in)	Weight 16–32kg (35–70lb)	Temperament Active, intelligent

| Country of origin Great Britain | First use Herding sheep | Origins 1500s |

BEARDED COLLIE

Not dissimilar to the Old English Sheepdog in appearance (see p.110), the Bearded Collie is much lighter and more slender in shape. It has a medium-length, tousled coat covering an agile and athletic, strong-limbed body.

• **HISTORY** The Bearded Collie is thought to have descended from Polish Lowland Sheepdogs brought to Scotland centuries ago by visiting sailors. Although an attentive and industrious worker, it seems to be adapting very well to its increasing popularity as a family pet and companion.

• **REMARK** Hardy and well protected, it is quite content to sleep outdoors.

• **OTHER NAMES** Beardie.

flat, broad skull

ears largely covered with hair

straight, level back

tail set low on back

strong, well-boned forelegs

legs covered with shaggy hair

medium-sized ears

COLOUR TYPES

oval-shaped feet with hair between toes

medium-length, harsh coat

| Height 51–56cm (20–22in) | Weight 18–27kg (40–60lb) | Temperament Friendly, active |

| Country of origin Great Britain | First use Herding sheep | Origins 1700s |

BORDER COLLIE

This graceful breed can be recognized by its distinctive black and white coloration, although a variety of colours are permissible. Its coat may be moderately long, or smooth.

- **HISTORY** A standard was not approved by the Kennel Club of Britain until 1976, but this dog had long been valued by farmers in the border region between Scotland and England as an excellent sheep herder.
- **REMARK** The Border Collie has an effortless gait, lifting its feet just a short distance off the ground.

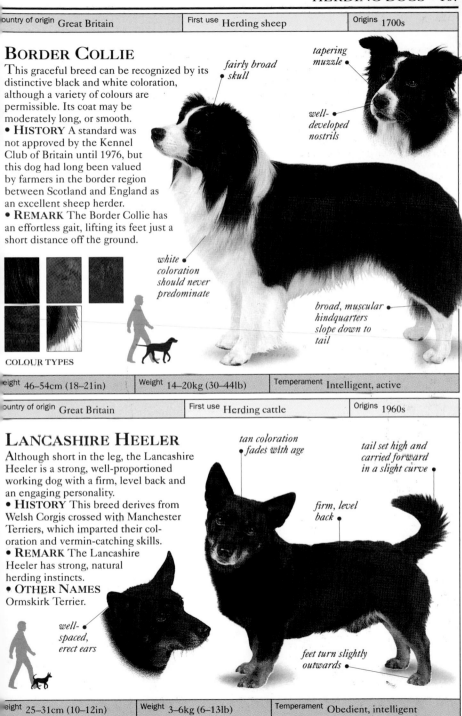

fairly broad skull

tapering muzzle

well-developed nostrils

white coloration should never predominate

broad, muscular hindquarters slope down to tail

COLOUR TYPES

| Height 46–54cm (18–21in) | Weight 14–20kg (30–44lb) | Temperament Intelligent, active |

| Country of origin Great Britain | First use Herding cattle | Origins 1960s |

LANCASHIRE HEELER

Although short in the leg, the Lancashire Heeler is a strong, well-proportioned working dog with a firm, level back and an engaging personality.

- **HISTORY** This breed derives from Welsh Corgis crossed with Manchester Terriers, which imparted their coloration and vermin-catching skills.
- **REMARK** The Lancashire Heeler has strong, natural herding instincts.
- **OTHER NAMES** Ormskirk Terrier.

tan coloration fades with age

tail set high and carried forward in a slight curve

firm, level back

well-spaced, erect ears

feet turn slightly outwards

| Height 25–31cm (10–12in) | Weight 3–6kg (6–13lb) | Temperament Obedient, intelligent |

Country of origin Great Britain	First use Herding sheep	Origins 1500s

ROUGH COLLIE

Truly spectacular in full coat, the Rough Collie is one of the most glamorous breeds in the world. It is unmistakable with its profuse mane and frill, and has a highly intelligent expression.

• **HISTORY** Essentially the same breed as the Smooth Collie (opposite), it derived from the same Scottish working collie stock. It enjoyed royal patronage when Queen Victoria kept the breed at Balmoral Castle, Scotland.

• **REMARK** The greatest of all film star dogs, Lassie, was a Rough Collie.

• **OTHER NAMES** Rough-haired Collie.

small, tipped ears

bushy tail

top of the skull is flat

long, tapering muzzle

long body

pronounced frill between forelegs

COLOUR TYPES

Height 51–61cm (20–24in)	Weight 18–30kg (40–65lb)	Temperament Loyal, responsive

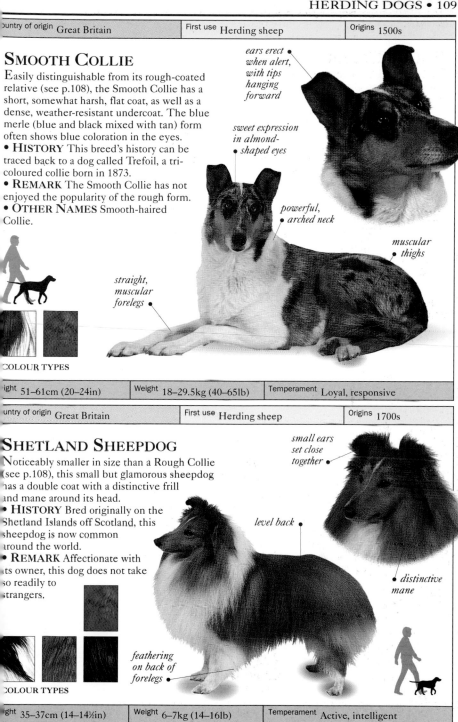

Country of origin Great Britain	First use Herding sheep	Origins 1500s

SMOOTH COLLIE

Easily distinguishable from its rough-coated relative (see p.108), the Smooth Collie has a short, somewhat harsh, flat coat, as well as a dense, weather-resistant undercoat. The blue merle (blue and black mixed with tan) form often shows blue coloration in the eyes.
• **HISTORY** This breed's history can be traced back to a dog called Trefoil, a tri-coloured collie born in 1873.
• **REMARK** The Smooth Collie has not enjoyed the popularity of the rough form.
• **OTHER NAMES** Smooth-haired Collie.

ears erect when alert, with tips hanging forward

sweet expression in almond-shaped eyes

powerful, arched neck

muscular thighs

straight, muscular forelegs

COLOUR TYPES

Height 51–61cm (20–24in)	Weight 18–29.5kg (40–65lb)	Temperament Loyal, responsive

Country of origin Great Britain	First use Herding sheep	Origins 1700s

SHETLAND SHEEPDOG

Noticeably smaller in size than a Rough Collie (see p.108), this small but glamorous sheepdog has a double coat with a distinctive frill and mane around its head.
• **HISTORY** Bred originally on the Shetland Islands off Scotland, this sheepdog is now common around the world.
• **REMARK** Affectionate with its owner, this dog does not take so readily to strangers.

small ears set close together

level back

distinctive mane

feathering on back of forelegs

COLOUR TYPES

Height 35–37cm (14–14½in)	Weight 6–7kg (14–16lb)	Temperament Active, intelligent

| Country of origin Great Britain | First use Herding sheep | Origins 1800s |

OLD ENGLISH SHEEPDOG

The immense, shaggy coat is the distinctive feature of this breed and requires a great deal of grooming. Thick-set and muscular, this strong, square-built dog has great symmetry and a distinctive rolling gait.

- **HISTORY** Developed from drover's dogs in the 1800s, it is probably related to shepherd's dogs found in mainland Europe, such as the Bergamasco (see p.135).
- **REMARK** This breed requires plenty of exercise if it is to remain healthy and happy.
- **OTHER NAMES** Bobtail.

hair extends over eyes

small ears on side of head, hidden by hair

coat is shaggy, not curly

thick-set, compact body

strong, straight forelegs

small, rounded feet

COLOUR TYPES

| Height 56–61cm (22–24in) | Weight 30kg (66lb) | Temperament Active, protective |

untry of origin Great Britain	First use Droving cattle	Origins 1200BC

CARDIGAN WELSH CORGI

The Cardigan is distinguishable from the Pembroke Welsh Corgi (below) by its long, fox's brush tail. The Cardigan's ears are also larger and more widely spaced, and the feet tend to have a more rounded appearance.

• **HISTORY** The Corgi is traditionally a droving dog; its small size enabled it to dodge in and bite the lower legs of cattle, forcing them to move where required.

• **REMARK** Until the 1850s, the Cardigan Welsh Corgi was the only dog known to be kept in some Welsh communities.

erect, rounded ears

wide skull and fox-like head

powerful, muscular neck

long body in relation to height

COLOUR TYPES

ight 27–32cm (10½–12½in)	Weight 11–17kg (25–38lb)	Temperament Active, obedient

untry of origin Great Britain	First use Droving cattle	Origins 1000s

PEMBROKE WELSH CORGI

In spite of its size, this bold, inquisitive dog is still powerful, and has a surprisingly loud bark. Unlike the Cardigan (above), the Pembroke has only a short tail, and it is bred in a more restricted colour range.

• **HISTORY** The Welsh Corgi may be related to the Swedish Vallhund (see p.132), but its precise origins are not known. Its presence has been recorded in Wales since the Domesday Book of 1086.

• **REMARK** This breed is now internationally known as the favourite pet of Queen Elizabeth II.

pricked, medium-sized ears

powerful neck

flat skull

slightly tapering muzzle

round, brown eyes

short tail and strong hind-quarters

COLOUR TYPES

ght 25–31cm (10–12in)	Weight 10–12kg (20–26lb)	Temperament Active, obedient

Country of origin Australia	First use Herding cattle	Origins 1800s

AUSTRALIAN CATTLE DOG

This strong, compact dog was first developed in Australia to drive herds of cattle on long, arduous treks to market. Its key qualities are its amazing stamina, versatility, and endurance. It is essentially silent when working, controlling cattle with precision and the minimum of effort.

• **HISTORY** A number of different breeds contributed to its ancestry. The most significant of these was the dingo, the feral dog of the Aboriginal settler, which was too unruly to perform the task of cattle-driving competently.

• **REMARK** This breed holds the record for canine longevity – 29 years.

• **OTHER NAMES** Australian Queensland Heeler, Blue Heeler.

broad, erect ears

prominent black nose

thick-set neck

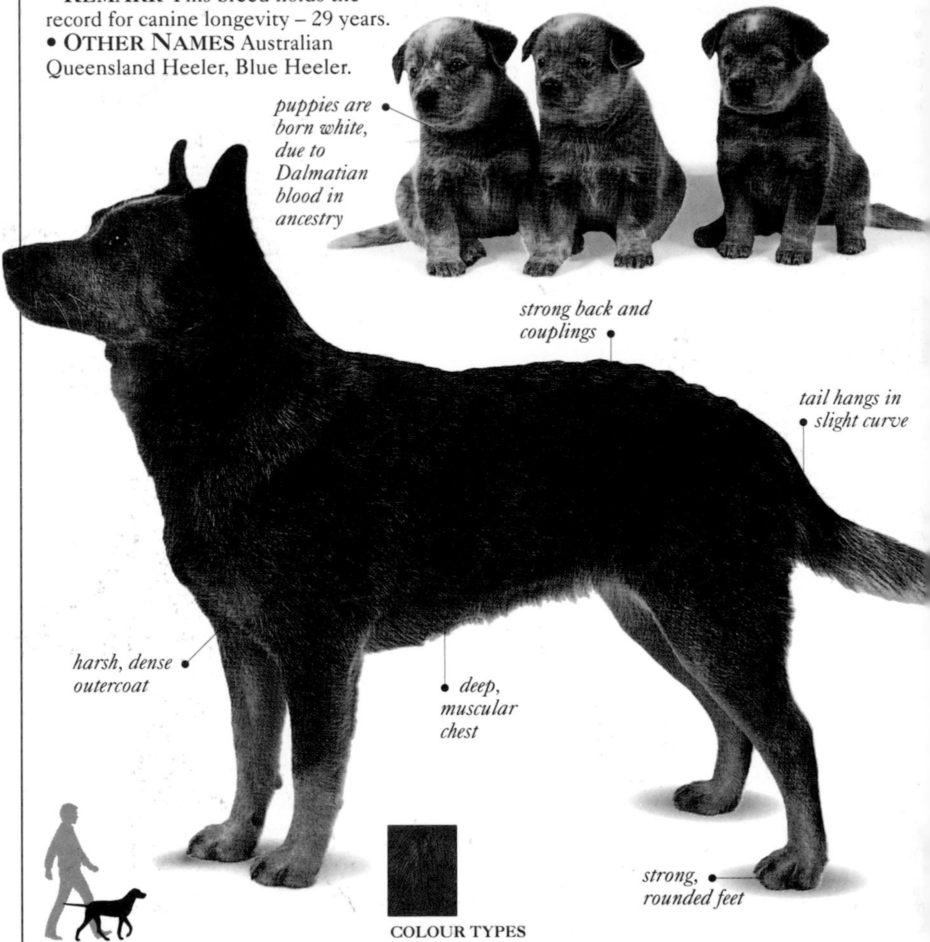

puppies are born white, due to Dalmatian blood in ancestry

strong back and couplings

tail hangs in slight curve

harsh, dense outercoat

deep, muscular chest

strong, rounded feet

COLOUR TYPES

Height 43–51cm (17–20in)	Weight 16–20kg (35–45lb)	Temperament Bold, determined

Country of origin	Australia	First use	Herding livestock	Origins	1800s

AUSTRALIAN KELPIE

The work rate of this tough little sheepdog has become a legend in its native Australia. An economical, compact body, well-muscled but lean, is supported on strong, firm-boned legs. The Kelpie has a tough, weather-resistant outercoat and a short, dense undercoat. A wide range of coat colours is seen; black dogs are sometimes known as barbs.

• **HISTORY** A New South Wales grazier called Allen imported a pair of English collies into Australia in 1870. These dogs mated on board ship and one of the offspring was bred with a local black-and-tan bitch named *Kelpie*. Her progeny became the basis of this breed, which was first exhibited in 1908.

• **REMARK** Australian Kelpies seem to have the ability to mesmerize and control sheep simply by staring at them.

• **OTHER NAMES** Kelpie, Barb.

very erect, pointed ears

lively, intelligent eyes

tough, glossy outercoat

fox-like face

small feet

well-developed hindquarters

powerful neck

broad chest

body slightly longer than dog is tall

COLOUR TYPES

Height	43–51cm (17–20in)	Weight	10–20kg (25–45lb)	Temperament	Keen, responsive

Country of origin Finland	First use Herding reindeer	Origins 1600s

FINNISH LAPPHUND

This medium-sized breed is typically spitz-like in appearance, with a beautiful, fluffy coat occurring in a large range of colours.
• **HISTORY** Originally kept by the Lapp people who have long inhabited northernmost Europe, it is probably related to the Samoyed evolved by the Samoyede tribes of the Urals.
• **REMARK** In the parti-coloured dog, the coloured area must predominate, with white markings small and symmetrical.
• **OTHER NAMES** Lapinkoira.

square-shaped skull

fox-like head

mane of longer hair evident on neck

muscular hindquarters

COLOUR TYPES

Height 46–52cm (18–20½in)	Weight 20–21kg (44–47lb)	Temperament Responsive, intelligent

Country of origin Finland	First use Herding reindeer	Origins 1600s

LAPINPOROKOIRA

This herding dog has a loosely curled tail, which may be held against the thigh rather than over the back. Its body is longer than that of the Finnish Lapphund (above).
• **HISTORY** Having been kept primarily as a working breed for many years, in the 1960s a standard was at last created for the Lapinporokoira by the Finnish Kennel Club.
• **REMARK** Working dogs from the north are brought south to mate with bitches; male offspring are then sent north to herd. This helps to maintain the breed's working instinct.
• **OTHER NAMES** Lapland Reindeer Dog.

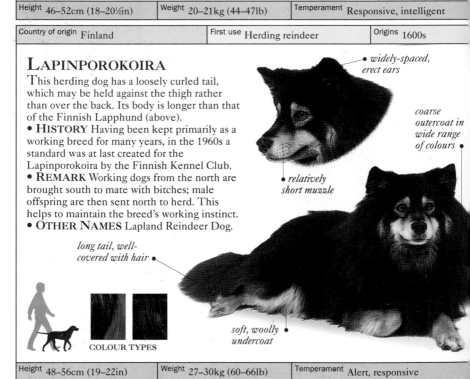

widely-spaced, erect ears

coarse outercoat in wide range of colours

relatively short muzzle

long tail, well-covered with hair

soft, woolly undercoat

COLOUR TYPES

Height 48–56cm (19–22in)	Weight 27–30kg (60–66lb)	Temperament Alert, responsive

Country of origin France	First use Hunting boar	Origins 1500s

BEAUCERON

One of the best-known sheepdogs in France, the Beauceron is somewhat reminiscent of the Dobermann (see pp.250–51) in overall appearance, but can be distinguished by its long tail and double dew-claws. In France, its ears are often cropped.
• **HISTORY** Originally used for hunting wild boar, its intelligent and adaptable nature was later employed for herding sheep, and even for carrying messages during wartime.
• **REMARK** The alternative name of Bas Rouge refers to the tan markings on the legs of this breed.
• **OTHER NAMES** Bas Rouge, Berger de Beauce.

black nose

long muzzle

reddish tan on lower legs

tail carried low

powerful neck

smooth, flat coat with fringes on flanks, legs, and tail

double dew-claws on hindlegs

rounded feet with black nails

COLOUR TYPES

Height 64–71cm (25–28in)	Weight 30–39kg (66–85lb)	Temperament Loyal, protective

Country of origin France	First use Guarding and herding stock	Origins 1200s

BRIARD

This large, muscular breed of French sheep-dog is one of the oldest of northern Europe. Although a fierce and protective guardian of its flock, it is an amiable giant, easy to train, affectionate, and patient with children. One of the most unusual features of the Briard is its double dew-claws, which must always be present on the hindlegs of show dogs. The muscular build of the Briard means that when running it should appear to have an effortless stride, seeming to glide over the ground. Its slightly wavy and very dry coat gives protection against the elements and needs little grooming.
• **HISTORY** The Briard is named after the French province of Brie, although the breed appears to have been kept all over France. They were used not only for herding stock, but also for guarding their charges against wolves.
• **REMARK** A number of Briards were taken to the USA after the First World War, but it was not until the 1970s that the breed started to become popular in Britain.
• **OTHER NAMES** Berger de Brie.

COLOUR TYPES

rectangular-shaped skull •

prominent, black nose •

strong, powerful forelegs •

• *coat not less than 7cm (3in) on body*

Height 57–69cm (23–27in)	Weight 34kg (75lb)	Temperament Lively, protective

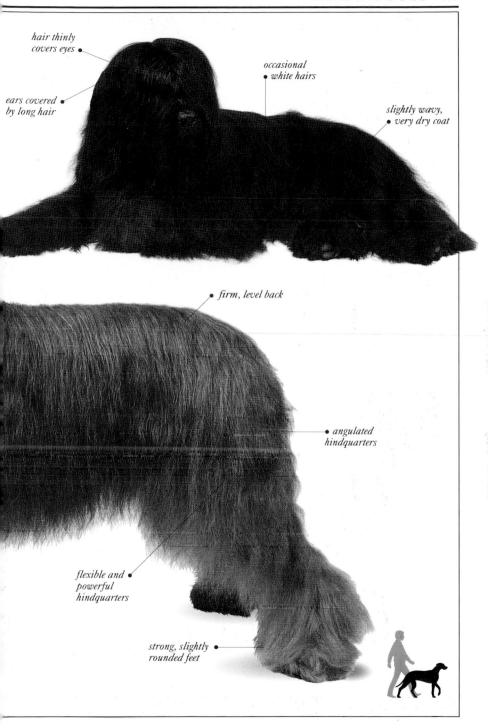

hair thinly
covers eyes •

ears covered •
by long hair

occasional
• white hairs

slightly wavy,
• very dry coat

• firm, level back

• angulated
hindquarters

flexible and •
powerful
hindquarters

strong, slightly •
rounded feet

Country of origin France	First use Herding sheep	Origins 800s

BERGER DE PICARD

This is the oldest of the French sheepdogs, and is thought to have been brought to northern France around the 9th century. In size, the Berger de Picard is about as tall as a German Shepherd, with a rough, durable outercoat and a thick, waterproof undercoat. The breed is usually fawn or grey in coloration, the white markings confined to the chest and legs.

• HISTORY The Celts are thought to have introduced the Berger de Picard into France. Its origins, however, are obscure, and the few that remain in France are largely working dogs. The breed is seen infrequently outside its native France.

• REMARK Members of this breed make excellent and affectionate housedogs. They tend, however, to be a little surly and defensive of their home territory.

• OTHER NAMES Picardy Shepherd.

large head with powerful muzzle

well-spaced, upright ears

tail slightly curled at tip

prominent chest

muscular thighs

rough, tousled coat, never curly

solid-boned legs

COLOUR TYPES

Height 55–66cm (21½–26in)	Weight 23–32kg (50–70lb)	Temperament Lively, adaptable

Country of origin Germany	First use Herding sheep	Origins 1800s

GERMAN SHEPHERD DOG

With a slightly elongated body and a strong, muscular build, the German Shepherd ranks among the most popular breeds in the world. A versatile and enthusiastic worker, it is used in many capacities, including search and rescue and guiding the blind. At one time, smooth-, long-, and wire-haired forms were recognized, but now only the short-haired form is accepted for show purposes. Occasionally, long-haired German Shepherds are still produced.

• **HISTORY** Although its working ancestry dates a great deal further back, the modern German Shepherd was first exhibited at a show in Hanover, Germany, in 1882.

• **REMARK** White coloration is not favoured in this breed, with only small light markings being permitted.

• **OTHER NAMES** Deutscher Schäferhund, Alsatian.

broad-based, pointed ears

black nose

hard, straight topcoat with dense undercoat

relatively long, muscular body

COLOUR TYPES

powerful thighs

muzzle is half the length of the head

straight, strong forelegs

rounded feet with short nails

Height 57–62cm (23–25in)	Weight 34–43kg (75–95lb)	Temperament Intelligent, responsive

Country of origin Germany	First use Guarding estates	Origins 1200s

HOVAWART

This breed has a long, thick, weatherproof coat, is lightly built, yet has a strong physique. In appearance, the breed is similar to the Flat-coated Retriever (see p.67), but there is no direct relationship between them. Indeed, the Hovawart is not a gundog, but a traditional guardian of sheep and other domestic stock. It exhibits a highly developed protective nature and displays great loyalty.

• **HISTORY** The recent development of the Hovawart is credited to the efforts of a German breeder, Kurt König. The breed was recognized by the German Kennel Club in 1936, and this dog was first seen in the USA during the 1980s.

• **REMARK** The name "Hovawart" comes from the German word, *hofe-wart*, meaning "guardian of the estate".

COLOUR TYPES

strong, straight back

tail extends past the hocks

feathering on back of foreleg

oval feet

powerful hindlegs

colour of claws matches that of coat

Height 58–70cm (23–28in)	Weight 25–41kg (55–90lb)	Temperament Alert, protective

pendulous ears

colour of nose
matches that of
coat

broad,
convex
forehead

long topcoat
with straight or
slightly wavy
undercoat

dark, oval-
shaped eyes

well-feathered
tail, held high
when excited

ightly
oping pasterns

a few white hairs are
permissible at end of tail

Country of origin Germany	First use Droving cattle	Origins 1400s

GIANT SCHNAUZER

This is the largest of the three breeds of schnauzer, and also the most recent addition to the group. The Giant Schnauzer is a powerful, muscular dog, whose height at the shoulders should match its body length, giving it a rather square shape when viewed in profile.

• **HISTORY** It is likely that the Giant Schnauzer was developed from rough-coated cattle dogs that were mated with smaller schnauzers. The breed was first exhibited at a show in Munich, Germany, in 1909, under the name of the Russian Bear Schnauzer. It was also known as the Munich Schnauzer for a brief period during its early development.

• **REMARK** The top coat of the Giant Schnauzer is especially important for show purposes. It must be harsh and wiry in texture, with no tendency towards softness. About twice a year, the coat needs to be stripped to remove dead hairs.

• **OTHER NAMES** Riesenschnauzer.

flat forehead

round feet with dark nails

chin whiskers and stubby moustache

deep chest

strong, rather square profile

muscular forelegs

COLOUR TYPES

Height 60–70cm (23½–27½in)	Weight 32–35kg (70–77lb)	Temperament Loyal, protective

Country of origin Poland	First use Herding sheep	Origins 1500s

POLISH LOWLAND SHEEPDOG

This breed looks a little like the Bearded Collie (see p.106), but it is smaller. Some are born tailless, but if a pup is born with a tail, it is docked.
- **HISTORY** After the Second World War, the breed was saved from extinction by a Polish veterinarian who had two dogs and six bitches that survived the war.
- **REMARK** This dog is said to have an excellent memory.
- **OTHER NAME** Polski Owczarek Nizinny.

medium-sized head

COLOUR TYPES

thick, shaggy coat

dark nose with wide nostrils

rectangular profile

Height 41–51cm (16–20in)	Weight 14–16kg (30–35lb)	Temperament Alert, affectionate

Country of origin Netherlands	First use Herding sheep	Origins 1700s

SCHAPENDOES

The Schapendoes, a native of Holland, has a long, straight, powerful back. A dense, shaggy coat gives it a friendly appearance, although as a working dog it is a hardy and fearless herder and guardian of its flock.
- **HISTORY** There is now no record of the early origins of this dog. It is believed to be a very old breed with a similar descent to that of the Briard (see pp.116–17) and the Bergamasco (see p.135).
- **REMARK** The decline in sheep herding has seen this dog's numbers fall.
- **OTHER NAMES** Dutch Sheepdog.

broad skull

ears flat to head

tail raised when dog is alert

broad, deep chest

COLOUR TYPES

Height 43–51cm (17–20in)	Weight 15kg (33lb)	Temperament Active, friendly

Country of origin Netherlands	First use Herding stock	Origins 1700s

DUTCH SHEPHERD DOG

A keen, alert expression graces the finely chiselled face of this hard-working and agile herding dog. The Dutch Shepherd is officially recognized as having three distinctly different coat types: long-haired, rough-haired, and short-haired. It occurs in various shades of brindle, such as yellow, red, and blue, and its coloration lightens as it grows older.

• **HISTORY** It is likely that this dog is descended from the Groenendael, one of the Belgian shepherd dog breeds (see p.126), and, apart from coloration, the two breeds are judged by the same standard.

• **REMARK** Short-tailed pups often occur, but these are not acceptable for show purposes.

• **OTHER NAMES** Hollandse Herdershond.

• medium-length muzzle with prominent nostrils

• triangular, erect ears, set high on head

long, parallel, well-muscled forelegs

• slightly sloping rump

• broad, deep chest

• when resting, tail hangs down with tip slightly upwards

• arched toes with rounded shape to forefeet

COLOUR TYPES

Height 58–64cm (23–25in)	Weight 30kg (66lb)	Temperament Alert, obedient

untry of origin Netherlands	First use Improving dog stocks	Origins 1900s

SAARLOOS WOLFHOUND

Unmistakably similar to a wolf in appearance, this dog still retains a strong pack instinct and needs firm handling as a result, due in particular to its large size and strong-willed nature.
• **HISTORY** This powerful breed was developed in the Netherlands by Leendert Saarloos, who felt that contemporary dogs had become weakened with hip dysplasia and similar conditions. He resolved to rectify the situation, and created this breed by crossing a German Shepherd Dog back to a wolf.
• **REMARK** Saarloos died in 1969, just six years before his breed was accepted by the Dutch Kennel Club.

erect ears, broad at base and pointed at tips

almond-shaped, intelligent eyes

long, well-muscled back

ruff of longer hair may be evident around neck

short and very dense coat

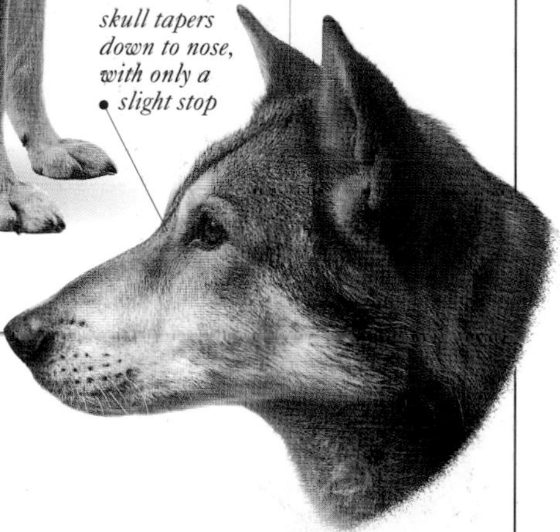

slightly domed skull

skull tapers down to nose, with only a slight stop

prominent, dark nose

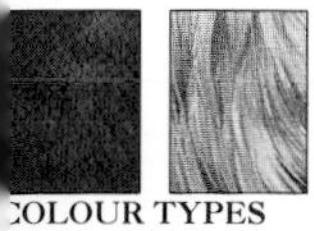

COLOUR TYPES

ght 70–75cm (27½–29½in)	Weight 36–41kg (79–90lb)	Temperament Shy, independent

Country of origin Belgium	First use Herding stock	Origins 1200s

GROENENDAEL

Its characteristic black coat easily distinguishes the Groenendael from the other three breeds typically grouped under the general heading of Belgian shepherd dogs (see pp.126–29). These dogs are all of a similar type, differing only in terms of their coloration and coat length.

• HISTORY The breeding of the Groenendael began by chance in about 1890. Nicholas Rose, owner of the Belgian Café du Groenendael, bred a black puppy, and obtained another. This pair formed the basis of the breed.

• REMARK In the USA, the Groenendael is the only dog considered to be a Belgian shepherd: the Tervuren and Malinois are recognized as separate breeds under their own names.

• OTHER NAMES
Chien de Berger Belge.

long head

slightly elongated neck

moderately harsh, long, straight outercoat

round forefeet

ruff around neck

males have longer coats than females

thick, springy soles

strong, short pasterns

Height 56–66cm (22–26in)	Weight 28kg (62lb)	Temperament Obedient, loyal

Country of origin Belgium	First use Herding and guarding stock	Origins 1200s

LAEKENOIS

This is considered to be the rarest of the Belgian shepherds, and it is still not widely recognized outside of its homeland. It can be immediately identified by its coat, which is rough and wiry, although not actually curly.
• **HISTORY** This breed was the favourite of Queen Henrietta of Belgium, and was named after the Château de Laeken where she lived. The breed was recognized in Belgium in 1897.
• **REMARK** The Laekenois served not only to guard sheep, but also linen. Linen-making was an important industry in the vicinity of Bloom, near Antwerp, where the breed originated, the linen being left in the fields to be bleached by the sun.
• **OTHER NAMES** Lackense, Chien de Berger Belge.

black shading on muzzle

erect, triangular-shaped ears

dark shading on tail

long, well-muscled forelegs

coat length averages about 6cm (2¼in)

oval-shaped hindfeet with arched toes

round front feet

Height 56–66cm (22–26in)	Weight 28kg (62lb)	Temperament Obedient, loyal

Country of origin Belgium	First use Herding stock	Origins 1890s

TERVUREN

This member of the Belgian shepherd
dog group is identical to the better-known
Groenendael (see p.126) apart from its coat
coloration. As a distinguishing feature, much
emphasis is placed on the coloration – each of
the Tervuren's hairs has a dark tip, creating an
impression of blackening on the back, ribs, and
shoulders, especially on a mature male. The
bitch has a shorter coat than the dog.

- **HISTORY** The Tervuren was developed
under the guidance of Professor Reul at the
Belgian School of Veterinary Science in 1891.
- **REMARK** Sharing the same origins as all
the Belgian shepherds, this robust breed's
particularly close relationship with the
Groenendael is demonstrated when
the mating of two Groenendaels
occasionally results in the birth
of a Tervuren pup.
- **OTHER NAMES** Belgian
Tervuren, Chien de Berger Belge.

*brownish
eyes and
black eyelids*

scissor bite

*hair shorter
on face than
on body*

*long, straight
topcoat; dense
undercoat*

*long, well-
muscled forelegs*

*well-muscled,
powerful
hindquarters*

COLOUR TYPES

Height 56–66cm (22–26in)	Weight 28kg (62lb)	Temperament Obedient, loyal

untry of origin Belgium	First use Herding stock	Origins 1200s

MALINOIS

The Malinois is the only Belgian shepherd dog with a short coat. It is also reputedly the oldest form, originating from the vicinity of Malines in Belgium.

• **HISTORY** Rather ironically, it was only when the working value of this hardy dog declined, at the end of the last century, that interest was rekindled in it.

• **REMARK** The breed obtains its full adult coloration by the time that it is 18 months old.

• **OTHER NAMES** Belgian Malinois, Chien de Berger Belge.

slightly tapering muzzle

thicker hair on neck

neck broadens close to shoulders

black shading on ears and muzzle preferred

hindquarters fringed with longer hair

deep, low chest

medium-length tail

short hair on lower legs

front feet round in shape

COLOUR TYPES

ight 56–66cm (22–26in)	Weight 28kg (62lb)	Temperament Obedient, loyal

Country of origin Belgium	First use Herding cattle	Origins 1600s

BOUVIER DES FLANDRES

The protective nature of this breed is reflected in its formidable appearance, and accentuated by its very impressive eyebrows, beard, and moustache. Despite this rugged appearance, the Bouvier des Flandres makes an excellent pet, being good with children and always vigilant. Although by no means lazy, this amiable giant is quite content with moderate exercise.

• **HISTORY** The ancestry of this breed is unclear, but by the 1800s several distinct types could be found on the Flanders plain. Three forms survived until 1965, when they were finally amalgamated under one standard. A breed club was founded in Belgium in 1922.

• **REMARK** Renowned for their bravery and loyalty, this dog was in active service during the First World War, carrying messages and locating wounded servicemen.

• **OTHER NAMES** Belgian Cattle Dog.

triangular-shaped ears

bushy eyebrows

harsh beard

large head

white star on chest permissible

beard and moustache

short, round, compact feet

coat length about 6cm (2½in), with unkempt appearance

Height 58–69cm (23–27in)	Weight 27–40kg (59½–88lb)	Temperament Alert, responsive

hair feels coarse to
the touch, and is
dry and matt •

powerful neck
muscles

• tail docked
here to second
or third joint

• deep chest and
powerful body

large, •
powerful
thighs

hocks well •
let down

COLOUR TYPES

Country of origin Sweden	First use Herding cows, ratting	Origins 500s

SWEDISH VALLHUND

Although small, the Swedish Vallhund is powerfully built with masses of energy. The breed bears a striking resemblance to the Welsh Corgi (see p.111), apart from its coat, which tends to be of more subdued coloration. In its native Sweden the main role of the Vallhund is herding.

- **HISTORY** The breed was recognized by the Swedish Kennel Club in 1948.
- **REMARK** There is some argument about whether the Vallhund is the ancestor or the descendant of the corgi breeds.
- **OTHER NAMES** Väsgötaspets.

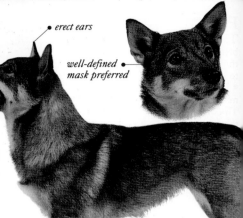

erect ears

well-defined mask preferred

harsh, medium-length coat

COLOUR TYPES

Height 31–35cm (12–14in)	Weight 11–15kg (25–35lb)	Temperament Responsive, affectionate

Country of origin Iceland	First use Herding, pulling sleighs	Origins 1800s

ICELAND DOG

This small dog has an elongated muzzle, a thick, medium-length coat, and carries its tail in a curve on its back. Although similar to other members of the spitz family, the Iceland Dog is more of a herder than a hunter.

- **HISTORY** It is thought that the Iceland Dog was introduced to Iceland by Norwegians, who refer to the breed as the Friaar Dog. It may share common ancestry with the Greenland Dog (see p.244).
- **REMARK** The breed came close to extinction at the turn of the century, due to an epidemic of distemper. It was saved by the efforts of Icelandic and English breeders.
- **OTHER NAMES** Icelandic Sheepdog, Friaar Dog.

black masking often present

widely spaced ears

thick coat carried close to body

slender legs

COLOUR TYPES

Height 31–41cm (12–16in)	Weight 9–14kg (20–30lb)	Temperament Lively, tough

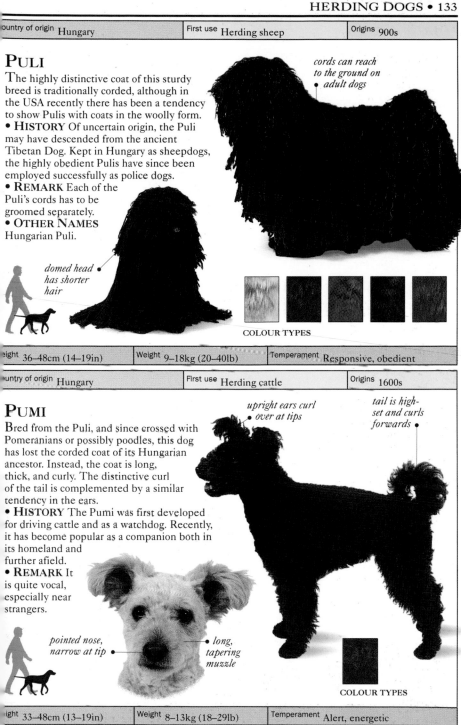

| Country of origin Hungary | First use Herding sheep | Origins 900s |

PULI

The highly distinctive coat of this sturdy breed is traditionally corded, although in the USA recently there has been a tendency to show Pulis with coats in the woolly form.
• **HISTORY** Of uncertain origin, the Puli may have descended from the ancient Tibetan Dog. Kept in Hungary as sheepdogs, the highly obedient Pulis have since been employed successfully as police dogs.
• **REMARK** Each of the Puli's cords has to be groomed separately.
• **OTHER NAMES** Hungarian Puli.

cords can reach to the ground on adult dogs

domed head has shorter hair

COLOUR TYPES

| Height 36–48cm (14–19in) | Weight 9–18kg (20–40lb) | Temperament Responsive, obedient |

| Country of origin Hungary | First use Herding cattle | Origins 1600s |

PUMI

Bred from the Puli, and since crossed with Pomeranians or possibly poodles, this dog has lost the corded coat of its Hungarian ancestor. Instead, the coat is long, thick, and curly. The distinctive curl of the tail is complemented by a similar tendency in the ears.
• **HISTORY** The Pumi was first developed for driving cattle and as a watchdog. Recently, it has become popular as a companion both in its homeland and further afield.
• **REMARK** It is quite vocal, especially near strangers.

upright ears curl over at tips

tail is high-set and curls forwards

pointed nose, narrow at tip

long, tapering muzzle

COLOUR TYPES

| Height 33–48cm (13–19in) | Weight 8–13kg (18–29lb) | Temperament Alert, energetic |

Country of origin Former Yugoslavia	First use Guarding flocks	Origins 1600s

ISTRIAN SHEEPDOG

The iron-grey coloration of this dog, offset with darker shadings, is quite striking. The coat itself is dense and harsh, offering good protection against the elements.
- **HISTORY** Originating in Karst, in the north of the former Yugoslavia, this flock guardian is related to the Illyrian Sheepdog (below).
- **REMARK** Although now scarce in its homeland, international interest in the breed started to develop in the late 1970s.
- **OTHER NAMES** Karst Sheepdog, Krasky Ovcar.

V-shaped ears lie flat to the head

tapering tail covered with hair

dark mask

powerful chest

straight back

compact, rounded feet

Height 51–61cm (20–24in)	Weight 26–40kg (58–88lb)	Temperament Loyal, reserved

Country of origin Former Yugoslavia	First use Herding sheep	Origins 1200s

ILLYRIAN SHEEPDOG

The Illyrian Sheepdog shares the main physical characteristics of the Istrian Sheepdog (above), but it has more variation in coat coloration than its near relative.
- **HISTORY** This breed developed in Illyria, the area that is present-day Bosnia and Albania. The dog's precise origins are unknown.
- **REMARK** The Illyrian was first exported to the USA in 1975 and has proved to be popular.
- **OTHER NAMES** Sarplaninac, Sar Planina.

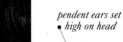

COLOUR TYPES

pendent ears set high on head

dense, medium-length coat

bushy, scimitar-shaped tail

powerful hindlegs

feathering on underparts and legs

powerful, straight leg

Height 56–61cm (22–24in)	Weight 25–37kg (55–80lb)	Temperament Reserved, independent

Country of origin Italy	First use Guarding livestock	Origins 100BC

BERGAMASCO

The distinctly corded coat of this sheepdog is not only effective protection against the elements, it also made it harder for wolves to inflict injury in the days when such attacks were likely in its native Italy. Coloration may be all shades of grey, with white markings (if present) comprising no more than 20 per cent of the entire coat area.

• **HISTORY** This breed is named after the Bergamo region of Italy, where the stock is believed to have originated as a working sheepdog. Its precise ancestry is unknown, but it began to win major Italian dog shows in 1949 and has since become internationally popular.

• **REMARK** A thick, naturally oily undercoat protects the skin.

• **OTHER NAMES** Cane da Pastore Bergamasco.

broad skull, slightly domed between the ears

triangular ears

hair forms long, wavy, strong flocks

tail tapers to a point

facial hair is finer textured

natural parting in middle of back

well-muscled body

thick tail, carried low

oval-shaped feet with well-arched toes

Height 56–61cm (22–24in)	Weight 26–38kg (57–84lb)	Temperament Loyal, intelligent

Country of origin Spain	First use Herding livestock	Origins 1700s

CATALAN SHEEPDOG

Bearing some similarity to the Bearded Collie (see p.106), the Catalan Sheepdog has a prominent beard and moustache, and is about the same size as an English Springer Spaniel (see p.66). Developed in the region of Catalonia, in northeast Spain, two distinct forms arose, differing in coat length. The short-coated version, sometimes described as Gos d'Atura Cerda, is now very scarce. Traditionally, the ears of this sheepdog were cropped to make it appear more ferocious.
• **HISTORY** The area in which the Catalan Sheepdog evolved has a strong French influence, and this suggests a possible relationship with French dog breeds. However, nothing certain has been recorded about its origins.
• **REMARK** Dogs of this adaptable breed acted as messengers and guard dogs in the Spanish Civil War.
• **OTHER NAMES** Gos d'Atura Catala.

long hair extends from top of head
• *down the face*

broad ribcage emphasizes muscular
• *body shape*

• *prominent, dark nose*

• *dark eyes*

• *large, thick tail set low on back*

• *straight muzzle*

• *broad, muscular chest*

• *wavy coat gives shaggy appearance*

COLOUR TYPES

Height 46–51cm (18–20in)	Weight 18kg (40lb)	Temperament Brave, forceful

Country of origin Portugal	First use Herding	Origins 1800s

PORTUGUESE SHEEPDOG

This medium-sized sheepdog can be variable in height, but the majority are taller than 45cm (18in). Its similarity to the Briard (see pp.116–17) is reflected by the presence of the hind dew-claws and a similar coat, although the Portuguese Sheepdog lacks an undercoat. Its facial expression has led to it being called the "monkey dog" in its homeland. It works not only with sheep, but is also used to guard horses, pigs, and other farm stock.

• **HISTORY** Dogs of this general type have been used for working purposes for many years, but only since 1930 has their appearance become standardized. They may have originated from crossings between Pyrenean Sheepdogs and Briards, or even Catalan Sheepdogs.

• **REMARK** With a reputation for intelligence and devotion to duty, these dogs are well able to locate stock that has strayed from the herd.

• **OTHER NAMES** Cão da Serra de Aires.

dark nostrils

ears hang straight down sides of head

well-defined stop

broad head

thick "eye-brows" above dark eyes

long, slightly wavy coat

beard and moustache of long hair

powerful, prominent chest

Height 41–56cm (16–22in)	Weight 12–18kg (26–40lb)	Temperament Active, independent

HOUNDS

O RIGINALLY BRED for hunting, these medium-sized dogs usually have short, bi- or tricoloured coats and an athletic build. Some are bred for stamina and some for pace. They may be divided broadly into sight hounds, such as the Afghan (see p.202), and scent hounds, such as the Bloodhound (see pp.166–67), depending on their hunting technique. Some breeds a▮ still kept solely for working purpose and may be unknown outside the local area. Hounds do not always adju▮ well to an urban lifestyle and nee▮ plenty of space for exercise. They a▮ friendly by nature, but their huntir▮ instincts are so strong that trainir▮ them to return can pose problems.

Country of origin USA	First use Hunting deer	Origins 1700s

CATAHOULA LEOPARD DOG

This compact, well-muscled, workman-like dog is used for a variety of purposes besides hunting. Its general appearance substantiates its affirmed hound ancestry. As a stock animal, it excels at rounding up and driving unruly cattle and pigs.

• **HISTORY** Named after the Parish of Cata-houla, Louisiana, USA, its precise ancestry is not known. It is, however, highly valued for herding semi-wild cattle and pigs found in the region.

• **REMARK** The Catahoula Leopard Dog was adopted as the state dog of Louisiana in 1979.

• **OTHER NAMES** Catahoula Hog Dog.

ears set well back on head

longish, muscular neck

eyes may be differen▮ colours

rounded tips to ears

short, dense coat

mottled, spotted patterning gives rise to its name

straight, well-boned forelegs

strong feet with webbed toes

COLOUR TYPES

Height 51–66cm (20–26in)	Weight 18–23kg (40–50lb)	Temperament Affectionate, protective

Country of origin USA	First use Hunting bears	Origins 1700s

PLOTT HOUND

The long, curving, high-held tail and outsize ears characterize this sturdy breed. Tenacious and strong, this hound tracks game over considerable distances. Since it occasionally finds itself pitched against a cornered bear at the end of the trail, its bravery is as much prized as its tremendous stamina.
• **HISTORY** This hound is named after the Plott family, who developed the breed over several generations from their home in the USA, after emigrating from Germany in 1750.
• **REMARK** Today, this hardy hound is still kept for hunting.

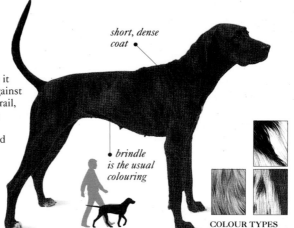

short, dense coat

brindle is the usual colouring

COLOUR TYPES

Height 51–61cm (20–24in)	Weight 20–25kg (45–55lb)	Temperament Responsive, active

Country of origin USA	First use Hunting raccoons	Origins 1900s

BLUETICK COONHOUND

The distinctive blue appearance of this hound results from the presence of heavy black ticking in white areas of its coat. The Bluetick is actually tricoloured, its coat being a combination of black, tan, and white.
• **HISTORY** Development of the Bluetick Coonhound began in the early 1900s. It is descended from French hounds such as the Grand Bleu de Gascogne (see pp.170–71) which were brought to the USA during the early days of colonization. These were crossed with other hunting breeds, such as the Bloodhound.
• **REMARK** The Bluetick is described as having a "cold nose", referring to its ability to follow an old trail left by the animal being pursued.

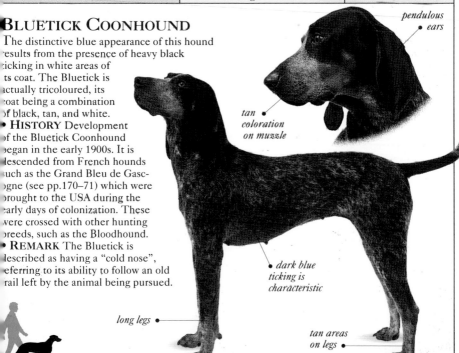

pendulous ears

tan coloration on muzzle

dark blue ticking is characteristic

long legs

tan areas on legs

Height 51–69cm (20–27in)	Weight 20–36kg (45–80lb)	Temperament Active, alert

Country of origin USA	First use Hunting bears	Origins 1800s

ENGLISH COONHOUND

This tenacious, medium-sized hound has a hard, short coat which gives it some protection outdoors during cold weather and when it is hunting in undergrowth. The majority of English Coonhounds have a red and white coat, described as red tick, but other colours are also recognized. This hardy breed is used primarily for hunting raccoons, from which the description of "coonhound" originates. It may, however, pursue other creatures, including foxes and even bears.

- **HISTORY** A number of divisions have occurred in coonhound breeds, with the English category coming into being by the early 1900s.
- **REMARK** The English Coonhound is still kept primarily for hunting, and rarely just as a companion, even though it possesses a friendly nature.
- **OTHER NAMES** Redtick Coonhound.

large, black nose

long, pendulous ears

elongated head

tail curves upwards

strong neck

muscular shoulders

ticked areas apparent in coat

hocks well let down

powerful, straight forelegs

COLOUR TYPES

Height 53–69cm (21–27in)	Weight 18–30kg (40–65lb)	Temperament Active, lively

Country of origin USA	First use Hunting raccoons	Origins 1700s

REDBONE COONHOUND

Immediately distinguishable by its mainly red coat, this is the only solidly coloured coonhound. Some individuals do have small traces of white, either on the feet or chest, but this is not penalized in show dogs. This good-natured, medium-sized hound is becoming increasingly popular throughout the USA.
• HISTORY Hounds with this coloration have been documented in the USA for more than 200 years. Earlier examples of this breed had larger areas of white on their coats than are seen in dogs today.
• REMARK This type of hound was probably named after an early breeder, Peter Redbone, who lived in Tennessee.

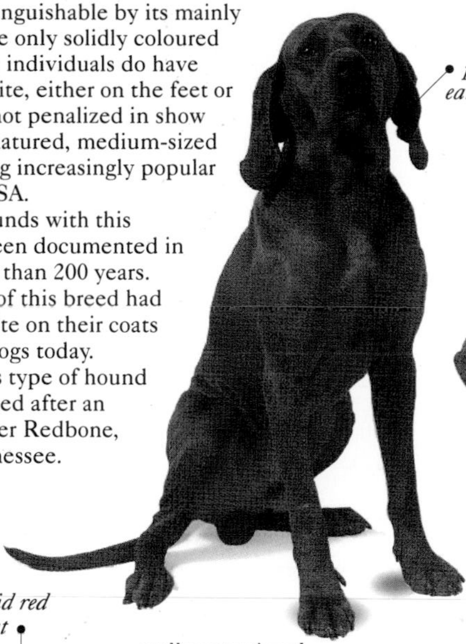

light-coloured iris

pendulous ears

broad muzzle

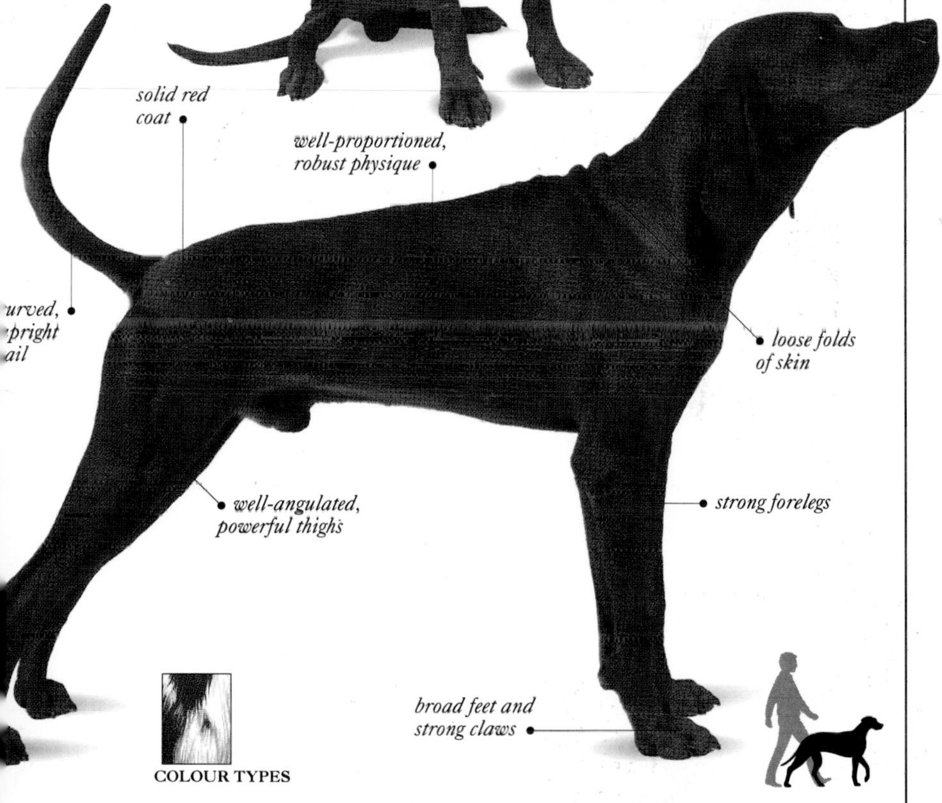

solid red coat

well-proportioned, robust physique

curved, upright tail

loose folds of skin

well-angulated, powerful thighs

strong forelegs

broad feet and strong claws

COLOUR TYPES

Height 53–66cm (21–26in)	Weight 23–32kg (50–70lb)	Temperament Determined, affectionate

Country of origin USA	First use Hunting raccoons	Origins 1700s

BLACK AND TAN COONHOUND

This breed was developed from foxhound and, probably, bloodhound stock. It is predominantly black in colour, with tan markings comprising 10 to 15 per cent of the coat. Occasional white areas around the chest are also still seen. Although good-natured, the Black and Tan Coonhound is a tenacious tracker once it is on the scent. Hunters recognize their dogs by their individual calls.

• **HISTORY** The origins of this dog lie in the USA, and can be traced back to the 1700s. In 1900, it was the first of the coonhounds to be recognized as a distinctive breed.

• **REMARK** It is often referred to as a "treeing hound", since it forces the raccoon to take refuge in a tree.

• **OTHER NAMES** American Black and Tan Coonhound.

long, drooping ears

small tan area above each eye, shaped like a pumpkin seed

skin fits loosely over body

black nails

powerful toes

Height 58–69cm (23–27in)	Weight 25–35kg (55–75lb)	Temperament Determined, lively

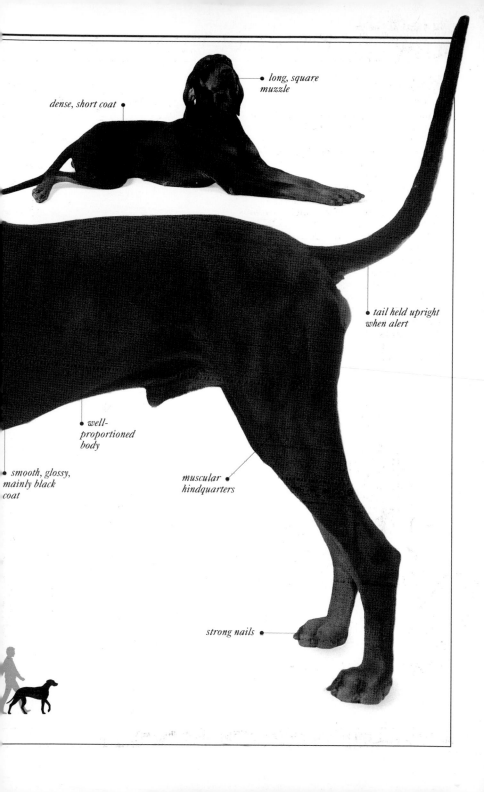

long, square muzzle

dense, short coat

tail held upright when alert

well-proportioned body

smooth, glossy, mainly black coat

muscular hindquarters

strong nails

Country of origin USA	First use Hunting raccoons	Origins 1800s

TREEING WALKER COONHOUND

This coonhound is lighter and faster than other similar breeds. The tricoloured dog is preferred, although bicolours do exist. Tan-and-white Treeing Walkers are not described as "red" to avoid confusion with the Redbone Coonhound (see p.141).

• **HISTORY** Descended from English Foxhounds, the development of this coonhound involved a dog stolen in the 1800s. This dog, named Tennessee Lead, added speed and treeing ability.

• **REMARK** This dog is still used for hunting raccoons and opossums.

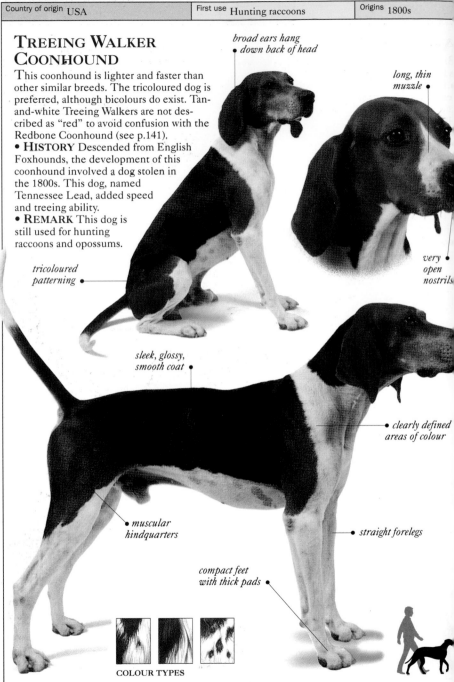

broad ears hang down back of head

long, thin muzzle

very open nostrils

tricoloured patterning

sleek, glossy, smooth coat

clearly defined areas of colour

muscular hindquarters

straight forelegs

compact feet with thick pads

COLOUR TYPES

Height 51–69cm (20–27in)	Weight 23–32kg (50–70lb)	Temperament Lively, intelligent

| Country of origin USA | First use Hunting foxes | Origins 1700s |

AMERICAN FOXHOUND

Bred for greater pace, the American Foxhound is lighter-boned than its English relative (see p.147), is lighter in weight, and has a keener sense of smell. Its short coat is close and hard and is acceptable in any colour combination, although the tricoloured form is the one most often seen in the show ring.

HISTORY The ancestry of the American Foxhound can be traced back to English hounds imported to North America in 1650 by Mr. Robert Brooke. A century later, these were crossed with French hounds sent by General Lafayette to George Washington.

REMARK The song-like voice of the American Foxhound has been recorded and incorporated into some popular music.

medium-length ears, broad and straight

sloping, muscular shoulders

deep chest

slightly domed skull

tail carried erect and slightly curved

medium-length, clean neck

well-sprung ribs

straight, medium-boned forelegs

strongly muscled thighs

COLOUR TYPES

| Height 53–64cm (21–25in) | Weight 30–34kg (65–75lb) | Temperament Active, friendly |

| Country of origin Great Britain | First use Hunting rabbits and hares | Origins 1800s |

BASSET HOUND

The Basset Hound and bassets in general are characterized by their short legs. Relative to its size, however, the Basset Hound is the heaviest-boned dog of any breed. Both bi- and tri-colour markings are acceptable.
• **HISTORY** Ironically, whereas most basset breeds originated in France, the Basset Hound itself was developed in Britain towards the end of the last century.
• **REMARK** The name is derived from the French word *bas*, meaning "low".

domed head

wrinkled skin above eyes

slightly curved tail

long ears extending down sides of face

wrinkles on lower legs

large feet

COLOUR TYPES

| Height 33–38cm (13–15in) | Weight 18–27kg (40–60lb) | Temperament Independent, active |

| Country of origin Great Britain | First use Hunting rabbits and hares | Origins 1300s |

BEAGLE

This sturdy and compact hound has medium-length legs, and is traditionally used to hunt hares. Working in packs, it pursues its quarry by scent, and displays remarkable stamina and tenacity.
• **HISTORY** The Beagle probably evolved from small foxhounds. Today it is still kept for hunting purposes, although it also makes an affectionate and playful pet.
• **REMARK** A miniature form, the Pocket Beagle, standing about 25cm (10in) high, was popular up to the First World War.
• **OTHER NAMES** English Beagle.

slightly domed sku

long ears

straight forelegs

clearly defined markings

compact feet, with thick pads

COLOUR TYPES

| Height 33–41cm (13–16in) | Weight 8–14kg (18–30lb) | Temperament Lively, friendly |

| Country of origin Great Britain | First use Hunting foxes | Origins 1700s |

FOXHOUND

The traditional Foxhound is a solid, well-built animal, with stamina an essential ingredient in its development. Foxhounds live in packs, the members of the pack always being counted in pairs, known as couples, rather than singly. This breed is still kept almost entirely for hunting, and is unlikely to be seen regularly at shows.

• **HISTORY** This dog was bred from the St. Hubert Hound, originally brought to Great Britain by the Normans after the invasion of 1066. The records of the Association of Masters of Foxhounds reveal that in 1880 there were 140 packs and 7,000 Foxhounds in Great Britain.

• **REMARK** Although kept in kennels, this breed is invariably friendly and affectionate.

• **OTHER NAMES** English Foxhound.

broad skull

level back

colour and markings highly variable between individuals

long, but never thick, neck

solid base to tail

deep girth giving plenty of room for heart

very powerful hindquarters

large space from end of ribs to hindquarters to give good stride length and pace

strong, straight forelegs

rounded, cat-like feet with toes close together

COLOUR TYPES

| Height 58–69cm (23–27in) | Weight 25–34kg (55–75lb) | Temperament Active, friendly |

Country of origin Great Britain	First use Hunting deer	Origins 800s

DEERHOUND

Although similar to the Irish Wolfhound (see pp.162–63), the Deerhound is of a sleeker, lighter build, reflecting the contribution of greyhound stock to its ancestry. This is perhaps most obviously apparent in terms of its head shape, the muzzle clearly tapering along its length. Dark blue-grey tends to be the colour most favoured today, but one of the oldest colours still seen is sandy red, with black areas on both the muzzle and the ears.

• HISTORY The Deerhound was originally developed in Scotland to hunt deer. However, the introduction of the gun for hunting led to a decline in numbers, but it is still valued today as a companion dog.

• REMARK The Deerhound's shaggy coat offers excellent protection against the elements.

• OTHER NAMES Scottish Deerhound.

head broadest at the ears

dark eyes with black rims

small ears preferred, kept folded back at rest

harsh, wiry, shaggy coat

tapering muzzle

ears have a soft, glossy appearance, and feel like a mouse's coat

softer coat on underparts and head

long, tapering tail almost reaching the ground

COLOUR TYPES

Height 71–76cm (28–30in)	Weight 36–45kg (80–100lb)	Temperament Gentle, active

Country of origin Great Britain	First use Otter hunting	Origins 1000s

OTTER HOUND

The coat, with its two distinct layers, is the chief feature of this breed. There is a rough outercoat, which feels hard to the touch, and a much shorter, woolly undercoat, which offers the dog protection when it enters the water.

• **HISTORY** This ancient breed probably evolved from foxhounds and other hunting dogs. It was formerly a pack hound.

• **REMARK** Like its traditional quarry, the otter, the Otter Hound has declined in numbers since the last half of the 19th century.

• *large, hairy head*

• *long, pendulous ears*

long, square muzzle •

high-set tail •

• *well-muscled, lean physique*

coat up to 15cm (6in) long over back

• *straight, solid-boned legs*

• *coat has slightly oily texture*

large feet • with webbing between toes

COLOUR TYPES

Height 58–69cm (23–27in)	Weight 30–55kg (65–120lb)	Temperament Athletic, independent

Country of origin Great Britain	First use Coursing hares	Origins 3000BC

GREYHOUND

The Greyhound kept for the show ring tends to be slightly larger and heavier than its famous racing counterpart, but it is, nevertheless, still built for acceleration and speed. Both forms are muscular and athletic in build, with a deep chest which provides excellent lung capacity. Few other breeds today are available in such a wide range of coat colours, including parti-coloured combinations.

• **HISTORY** The best evidence is that Greyhound stock originated in the Middle East, for similar dogs are represented on Egyptian tombs dating back nearly 5,000 years. An early British manuscript confirms that the breed had reached Britain by AD900.

• **REMARK** Although gentle dogs by nature, they do have a tendency to chase cats and small dogs, so they are best muzzled if allowed off the lead. They do not require a lot of exercise, a brief run being ideal.

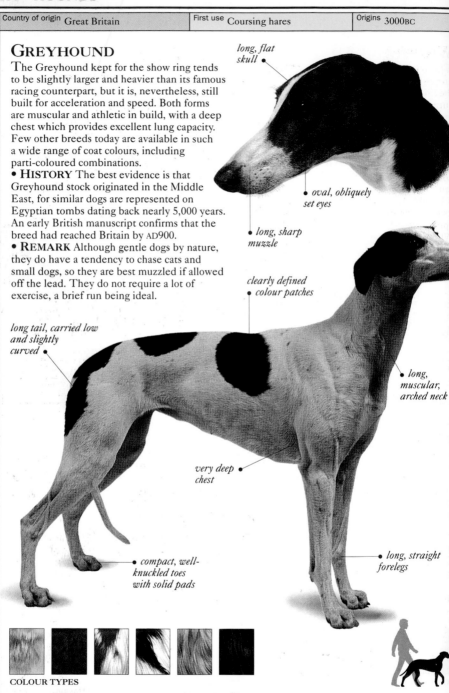

long, flat skull

oval, obliquely set eyes

long, sharp muzzle

clearly defined colour patches

long, muscular, arched neck

long tail, carried low and slightly curved

very deep chest

compact, well-knuckled toes with solid pads

long, straight forelegs

COLOUR TYPES

Height 69–76cm (27–30in)	Weight 27–32kg (60–70lb)	Temperament Lively, friendly

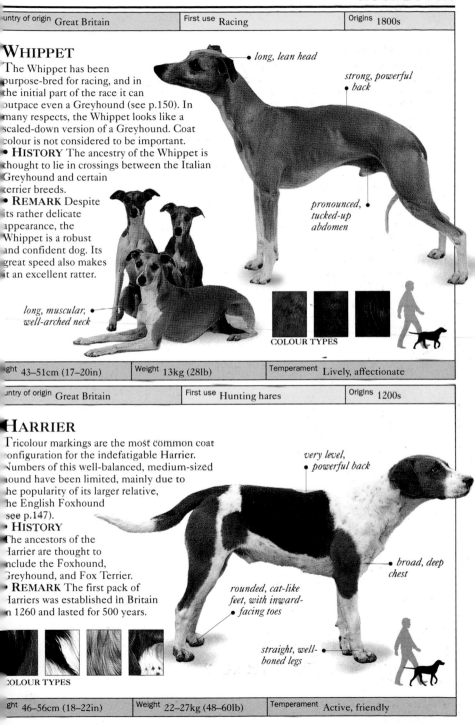

| untry of origin Great Britain | First use Racing | Origins 1800s |

WHIPPET

The Whippet has been
purpose-bred for racing, and in
the initial part of the race it can
outpace even a Greyhound (see p.150). In
many respects, the Whippet looks like a
scaled-down version of a Greyhound. Coat
colour is not considered to be important.
• **HISTORY** The ancestry of the Whippet is
thought to lie in crossings between the Italian
Greyhound and certain
terrier breeds.
• **REMARK** Despite
its rather delicate
appearance, the
Whippet is a robust
and confident dog. Its
great speed also makes
it an excellent ratter.

long, lean head

strong, powerful back

pronounced, tucked-up abdomen

long, muscular, well-arched neck

COLOUR TYPES

| ight 43–51cm (17–20in) | Weight 13kg (28lb) | Temperament Lively, affectionate |

| untry of origin Great Britain | First use Hunting hares | Origins 1200s |

HARRIER

Tricolour markings are the most common coat
configuration for the indefatigable Harrier.
Numbers of this well-balanced, medium-sized
hound have been limited, mainly due to
the popularity of its larger relative,
the English Foxhound
see p.147).
• **HISTORY**
The ancestors of the
Harrier are thought to
include the Foxhound,
Greyhound, and Fox Terrier.
• **REMARK** The first pack of
Harriers was established in Britain
in 1260 and lasted for 500 years.

very level, powerful back

broad, deep chest

rounded, cat-like feet, with inward-facing toes

straight, well-boned legs

COLOUR TYPES

| ight 46–56cm (18–22in) | Weight 22–27kg (48–60lb) | Temperament Active, friendly |

Country of origin Norway	First use Hunting rabbits	Origins 1800s

DUNKER

This sleek, lightly built, yet powerful hound has a poised, elegant appearance. Its thick, short coat is usually tan-coloured with a unique blue-marbled or black splodgy saddle. It is an extremely hardy breed, able to withstand extremes of cold, and adapts well to any terrain.

• **HISTORY** To create the Dunker, Norwegian breeder Wilhelm Dunker crossed a Russian Harlequin Hound with various reliable scent hounds, producing a dog that could hunt rabbit by scent rather than sight. It has yet to become popular outside of its homeland.

• **REMARK** A merle gene from the Harlequin Hound gave the Dunker its distinctive mottled saddle marking.

• **OTHER NAMES** Norwegian Hound.

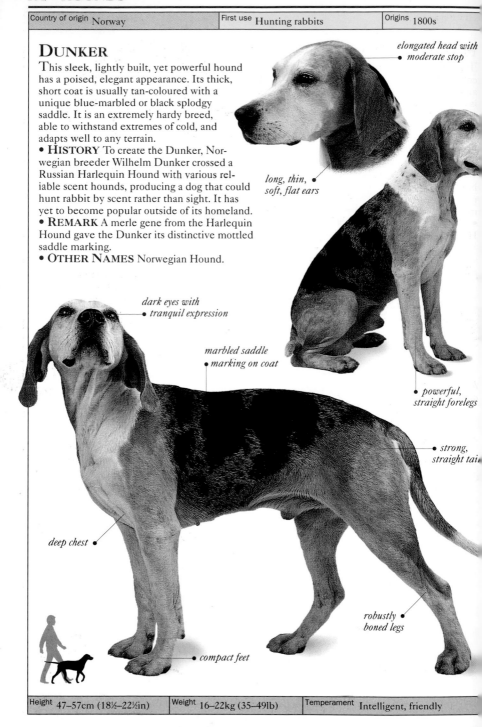

elongated head with moderate stop

long, thin, soft, flat ears

dark eyes with tranquil expression

marbled saddle marking on coat

powerful, straight forelegs

strong, straight tail

deep chest

robustly boned legs

compact feet

Height 47–57cm (18½–22½in)	Weight 16–22kg (35–49lb)	Temperament Intelligent, friendly

Country of origin Norway	First use Tracking game	Origins 1800s

HALDENSTÖVARE

This Norwegian scent hound has a distinctive tri-colour coat which is predominantly white, with black and tan markings on particular areas of the body. It is the largest of the four recognized stövare breeds.
• **HISTORY** Named after the city of Halden in southeastern Norway, not far from the Swedish border, it resulted from crossing local hounds with Swedish, German, and British hound stock.
• **REMARK** Like other Norwegian hounds, it is not a pack dog and makes a fine pet.
• **OTHER NAMES** Halden Hound.

pendent ears

straight muzzle with black nose

dome-shaped skull

long, thick tail carried low

long, curved neck

deep chest

oval-shaped feet with strong toes

Height 51–64cm (20–25in)	Weight 23–29kg (51–64lb)	Temperament Active, affectionate

Country of origin Norway	First use Hunting small game	Origins 1800s

HYGENHUND

This solid breed is often described as being "short-coupled" because it has a relatively short, compact body. The Hygenhund has been bred in several coat colours, but the yellow variety with white markings tends to be most common.
• **HISTORY** The Hygenhund was developed by a Norwegian enthusiast, F. Hygen, using Hölsteiner hounds from Germany crossed with various Scandinavian hounds.
• **REMARK** Developed for stamina, the Hygenhund tends to hunt singly with its owner.
• **OTHER NAMES** Hygenhound.

COLOUR TYPES

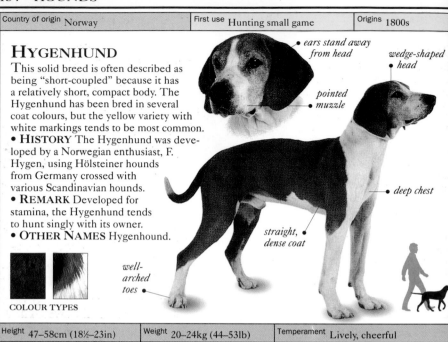

ears stand away from head

wedge-shaped head

pointed muzzle

deep chest

straight, dense coat

well-arched toes

Height 47–58cm (18½–23in)	Weight 20–24kg (44–53lb)	Temperament Lively, cheerful

Country of origin Finland	First use Hunting small game	Origins 1700s

FINNISH HOUND

This relatively large hound is longer than it is tall. It has a narrow head with a prominent nose, and large, pendulous ears which give it a rather charming appearance. It is also a nimble and very energetic hunter.
• **HISTORY** This breed has a mixed ancestry. A variety of English, Swiss, German, and Scandinavian hounds have contributed to its development.
• **REMARK** The Finnish Hound is a keen hunter in summer, but prefers the hearth in winter.
• **OTHER NAMES** Suomenajokoira.

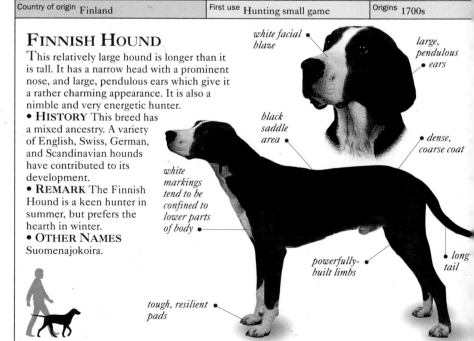

white facial blaze

large, pendulous ears

black saddle area

dense, coarse coat

white markings tend to be confined to lower parts of body

long tail

powerfully-built limbs

tough, resilient pads

Height 56–62cm (22–24½in)	Weight 25kg (55lb)	Temperament Friendly, active

Country of origin Sweden	First use Scenting and hunting game	Origins 1900s

DREVER

The long body and relatively short legs of the Drever give this breed a distinctly rectangular shape. White markings are an important feature and should be present on the face, neck, chest, and feet, as well as on the tip of the tail. The Drever can be recognized by its loud bark, which enables it to be tracked, even through woodland where its stature may conceal its presence.
• **HISTORY** Crossings of Westphalian and Danish Dachsbrackers gave rise to the Drever.
• **REMARK** These dogs have become popular in Canada.
• **OTHER NAMES** Swedish Dachsbracker.

expressive, chestnut-coloured eyes

white muzzle

short legs

COLOUR TYPES

Height 29–41cm (11½–16in)	Weight 15kg (33lb)	Temperament Alert, affable

Country of origin Sweden	First use Hunting foxes and hares	Origins 1200s

SCHILLERSTÖVARE

The light build of this hound gives it considerable pace, and it is regarded as the fastest of all Swedish breeds. The Schillerstövare has a thick undercoat which provides insulation, allowing it to work in deep snow, hunting foxes and snow hares.
• **HISTORY** This breed was developed by Per Schiller from a combination of Swedish hounds and recent hounds from Switzerland, Germany, and Austria.
• **REMARK** The Schillerstövare was represented at the first Swedish dog show, held in 1886.
• **OTHER NAMES** Schiller Hound.

soft ears

chestnut-coloured eyes

lips fit tightly to jaw

tail carried in slight sabre fashion

characteristic black saddle area

short, dense coat

long, straight forelegs

Height 53–57cm (21–22in)	Weight 18–24kg (40–53lb)	Temperament Active, enthusiastic

Country of origin Sweden	First use Tracking game	Origins 1800s

HAMILTONSTÖVARE

This well-built hound has plenty of stamina and will follow a scent with single-minded determination, no matter what the terrain or weather conditions. Well able to hunt in the thick snow of its native Sweden, the Hamilton-stövare's baying call indicates its position to the hunters when it is out of sight.

• HISTORY A.P. Hamilton, founder of the Swedish Kennel Club, was responsible for the development of this hound. His breeding programme was based on Foxhounds and Harriers from England, which were crossed with German hounds, including the now-extinct Holstein Hound, and Hanover Hounds.

• REMARK When this sturdy breed was first introduced into Britain in 1968 it was initially referred to simply as the Swedish Foxhound.

• OTHER NAMES Hamilton Hound.

long, rectangular head •

black • nose

short, dense, • double coat

white tip t tail •

ears lie flat against sides • of head

powerful body •

deep chest •

tail carried low

white markings on feet, as well as on • muzzle and chest

Height 51–61cm (20–24in)	Weight 23–27kg (50–60lb)	Temperament Courageous, active

Country of origin Sweden	First use Hunting foxes and hares	Origins 1200s

SMÅLANDSSTÖVARE

This compact, fox- and hare-hunting dog is the shortest and most heavily built of all the Swedish stövare breeds. Docking of the tail is not permitted in this breed, but many Smålandsstövares are born with tails that are unusually short for a hound. Coat colour is invariably black with tan markings on the muzzle, eyebrows, and lower parts of the legs, and occasionally with white flashes on the tips of the tail and feet. The coat itself is thick, smooth, and glossy and needs very little attention in terms of grooming.

• HISTORY Originating in Småland, central Sweden, this breed of hound was recognized by the Swedish Kennel Club in 1921. An early breeder, Baron von Essen, had a preference for the short-tailed individuals that were sometimes born, and helped to establish this characteristic in the breed. The basic form of this dog may date back to the Middle Ages.

• REMARK This dog requires lots of exercise.

• OTHER NAMES Smålands Hound.

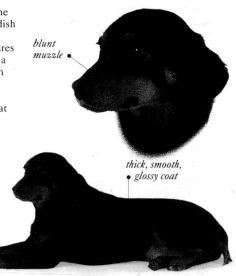

blunt muzzle

thick, smooth, glossy coat

dark, tranquil eyes

unusually short, undocked tail

tan markings on muzzle

prominent breastbone

well-boned, muscular legs

muscular, retracted abdomen

white markings permitted on feet, but not desirable anywhere

large feet, with well-arched toes

Height 46–50cm (18–20in)	Weight 15–18kg (33–40lb)	Temperament Active, enthusiastic

Country of origin Germany	First use Flushing badgers	Origins 1900s

MINIATURE DACHSHUND

Noticeably smaller than its standard-sized counterparts, this breed is seen here in three different forms. The Smooth-haired Miniature has a short, dense coat lying close to the body. The Long-haired Miniature also has a flat coat, but it is much longer, with some feathering. The wire-haired form has a harsh-textured coat of even length all over its body.

• HISTORY These miniatures, like the standard-sized version, are descended from the Teckel. The division between dachshund breeds was initially made on the basis of weight, and this still holds true today.

• REMARK The Wire-haired Miniature form was the last of the dachshunds to receive official recognition in Britain, in 1959.

• OTHER NAMES Zwergteckel.

SMOOTH-HAIRED
MINIATURE DACHSHUND

long, muscular
body

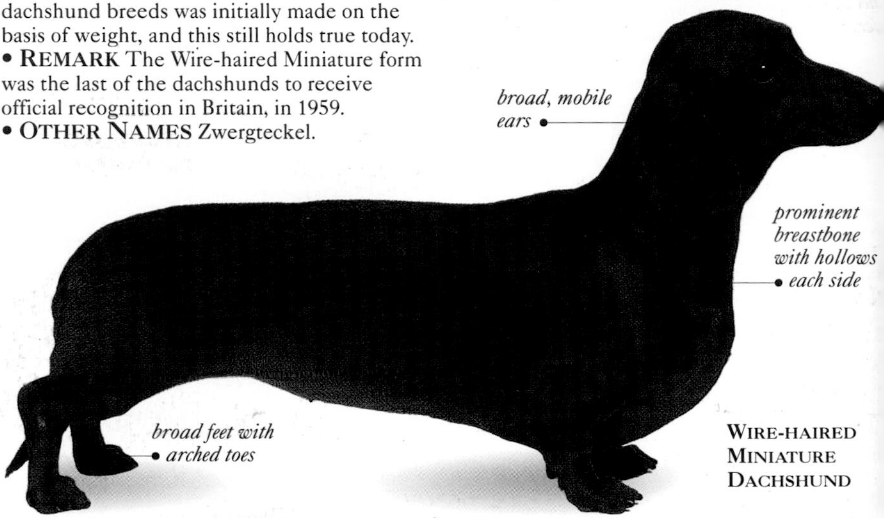

broad, mobile
ears

prominent
breastbone
with hollows
each side

broad feet with
arched toes

WIRE-HAIRED
MINIATURE
DACHSHUND

expressive,
oval eyes

bushy eyebrows

long,
muscular neck

front feet directed
slightly inwards

Height 13–23cm (5–9in)	Weight 4–5kg (9–10lb)	Temperament Active, determined

**LONG-HAIRED
MINIATURE
DACHSHUND**

COLOUR TYPES

*feathering
on tail*

*...t longest
...neck and
...derparts*

*hindfeet smaller
than front feet*

*restricted amount
of hair on feet*

*• wide mouth
opening behind
level of eyes*

*...ounded, broad
...ump •*

*relatively smooth
hair on ears*

long neck

Country of origin Germany	First use Tracking game	Origins 1700s

HANOVERIAN MOUNTAIN HOUND

Relatively heavy in build, with short legs, this hound is often used to track an animal that has been wounded but not killed outright. It often sports a distinctive black mask.
- **HISTORY** Developed by gamekeepers around Hanover in Germany, this breed descends from heavy tracking hounds crossed with lighter ones, such as the Haidbracke.
- **REMARK** This breed is still mainly kept as a working dog, and is highly valued for its fine nose.
- **OTHER NAMES** Hannoverscher Schweisshund.

dark mask is sometimes present

streaks of black create brindled effect

straight forelegs

very prominent nose with broad nostrils

COLOUR TYPES

Height 51–61cm (20–24in)	Weight 38–44kg (84–99lb)	Temperament Calm, loyal

Country of origin Germany	First use Tracking game	Origins 1800s

BAVARIAN MOUNTAIN HOUND

Rather shorter and lighter in build than similar breeds (above), this hound is highly valued for its tracking ability. It will continue on the trail until a wounded animal is found, rather than leaving it injured.
- **HISTORY** As its name suggests, this hound evolved in Bavaria in Germany, probably from crossings between Hanoverian and Tyrolean hounds.
- **REMARK** The group to which this hound belongs is described as *schweisshunden*, meaning "bloodhounds".
- **OTHER NAMES** Bayrischer Gebirgs-schweisshund.

slightly domed skull

long, pendent ears set well back on head

short, straight forelegs

powerful, well-muscled body

COLOUR TYPES

Height 51cm (20in)	Weight 25–35kg (55–77lb)	Temperament Active, intelligent

| Country of origin Poland | First use Hunting large game | Origins 1700s |

POLISH HOUND

This large, heavy hound has a well-wrinkled face, a rectangular head, and powerful jaws. It is a dedicated tracker with a prominent nose and a fine voice.
• HISTORY The breed's origins are unknown, but it is probably related to Austrian and German breeds. The Polish Hound declined in numbers during the Second World War, but has since recovered.
• REMARK There used to be a smaller version of the Polish Hound, known as the Gonczy Polski.
• OTHER NAMES Ogar Polski.

noble, rectangular-shaped head

large ears hang down close to head

thick tail

deep, muscular chest

black saddle marking

wrinkles of skin on forehead

prominent black nose

| Height 56–66cm (22–26in) | Weight 25–32kg (55–71lb) | Temperament Determined, friendly |

Country of origin Ireland	First use Hunting wolves	Origins 100BC

IRISH WOLFHOUND

A true giant, the Irish Wolfhound is the tallest dog in the world. It is somewhat similar in appearance to the Deerhound (see p.148), but it is larger in overall size. Despite its size, this is a graceful dog, with a rough, wiry coat and a muscular build. The long tail is surprisingly powerful, and can cause havoc in the home when swinging back and forth. The Irish Wolfhound's temperament is excellent, but because of its size it requires training from a young pup. Minimal grooming is needed.

• **HISTORY** The Irish Wolfhound's ancestry dates back many centuries, originating from an ancient lineage of royal dogs. The extinction of the wolf in Ireland during the 1800s almost resulted in the loss of this breed. It was saved only through the efforts of a Scot, Captain George Graham.

• **REMARK** An Irish Wolfhound pup should not be taken on long walks, as these can damage its joints. Instead, it should be encouraged to run and play at its own chosen pace.

long hair over eyes

long, slightly pointed muzzle

coat longer and more wiry under jaw

small ears

powerful thighs

rough and hardy coat

Height 71–90cm (28–35in)	Weight 40–55kg (90–120lb)	Temperament Gentle, friendly

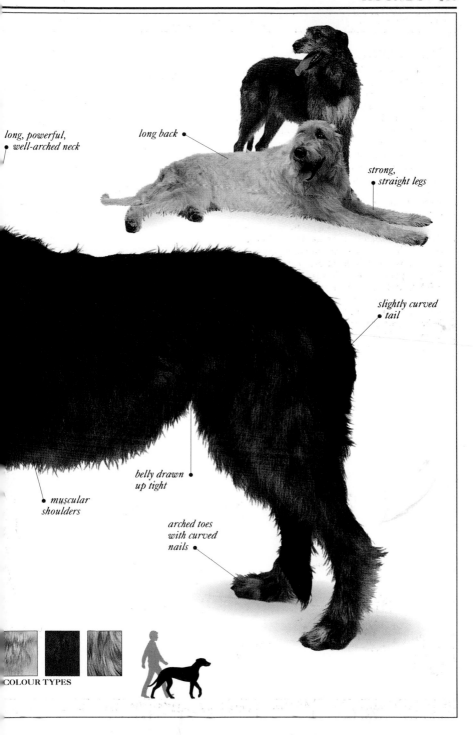

long, powerful,
well-arched neck

long back

strong,
straight legs

slightly curved
tail

muscular
shoulders

belly drawn
up tight

arched toes
with curved
nails

COLOUR TYPES

Country of origin Ireland	First use Hunting hares	Origins 1500s

KERRY BEAGLE

Mostly black and tan in coloration, although mottled and tricolour forms are not unknown, the Kerry Beagle is a substantially larger animal than the Beagle (see p.146). This dashing hound is close-coated, has a deep muzzle, and medium-length, unfolded ears. Essentially a pack dog, the Kerry Beagle is as yet unrecognized as a breed, even in Ireland, in spite of its long history and unmistakeable appearance.

• **HISTORY** Although the ancestry of the Kerry Beagle is obscure, it is thought the breed descended from a larger, deer-hunting hound. Its appearance also suggests that its development could have involved the Bloodhound.

• **REMARK** The breed is now used mainly for hunting small game and fowl.

• **OTHER NAMES** Pocadan.

broad skull

long, straight ears

heavy muzzle

long, tapering tail

medium-length neck

strong, well-boned limbs

close-fitting coat

COLOUR TYPES

Height 56–66cm (22–26in)	Weight 20–27kg (45–60lb)	Temperament Active, friendly

Country of origin Ireland	First use Coursing hares	Origins 1600s

LURCHER

There is considerable variation in the appearance of Lurchers, because they are not bred to conform to any standard. However, in general, the Lurcher has an athletic build and a wiry coat, and is now usually the result of cross-breeding involving deerhounds.

• HISTORY Traditionally, this dog has been bred for speed and responsiveness, often by gypsies in Ireland, who used collie and Greyhound crosses, as well as other breeds, to suit their purpose.

• REMARK The dark coat of the Lurcher provides good camouflage when out with poachers at night.

bright,
intelligent
eyes

long, narrow
head

ears tend to be
small

very powerful
hindquarters

long,
muscular,
arched neck

deep,
strong chest

long body

strong hindlegs

well-knuckled
toes with strong
pads

COLOUR TYPES

Height 69–76cm (27–30in)	Weight 27–32kg (60–70lb)	Temperament Responsive, quiet

Country of origin Belgium	First use Tracking scent	Origins 800s

BLOODHOUND

The best-known scent hound in the world, the
Bloodhound is also the largest. The folds of loose
skin apparent on its face and neck create the
famous mournful expression, which belies the
breed's lively and active nature. In spite of its
ferocious image, this dog is very friendly towards
people. It has a very distinctive, melodious voice,
which cannot be ignored.

• **HISTORY** The likely ancestor of today's
Bloodhound is the ancient St. Hubert's Hound,
which was supposedly brought back to Europe by
soldiers who had been fighting the Crusades.

• **REMARK** This indomitable hound has
incredible tracking skills. It has proved itself
capable of following a trail over 14 days
old, and has been known to pursue a
scent with its relentless, swinging
stride for 220 kilometres (138
miles). Evidence discovered
by a Bloodhound has been
used in courts of law.

• **OTHER NAMES** St.
Hubert Hound.

*dark brown or
hazel eyes •*

*thin, soft ears
tend to curl
inwards and
backwards*

*long, narrow
head with
pronounced
occipital peak •*

*characteristic •
dewlap*

*long tail tapers
• to a point*

Height 58–69cm (23–27in)	Weight 36–41kg (80–90lb)	Temperament Determined, responsive

waterproof coat

folds of loose skin
form wrinkles
above eyes

smooth, short
hair

powerful,
muscular body

thighs very
muscular

large, straight
forelegs

hocks well
let down

strong, well-
knuckled feet

COLOUR TYPES

Country of origin France	First use Tracking large game	Origins 1800s

BILLY

A large hound, with distinctive pale coloration, the Billy has a surprisingly musical call, which is often heard when packs are in pursuit of their quarry. The head is fine and lean, with a square muzzle and a prominent stop. Although not a heavy dog, a pack of Billys is nevertheless powerful enough for their favourite quarry, deer, and more than a match for wild boar, which they still track in France today.

• **HISTORY** The Billy is named after the home of the breeder who created them – Monsieur Gaston Hublot de Rivault, who lived at the Château de Billy, in Poitou. He used mainly bicoloured Céris hounds and the now-extinct Montemboeuf, another bicoloured breed. Foxhounds and the Larye, with its keen nose, have also contributed to its lineage.

• **REMARK** Just two Billys survived the Second World War. These were used by the son of the breed's founder to save these hounds from extinction.

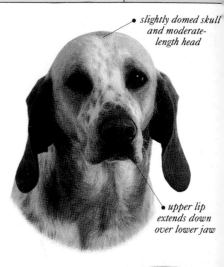

slightly domed skull and moderate-length head

upper lip extends down over lower jaw

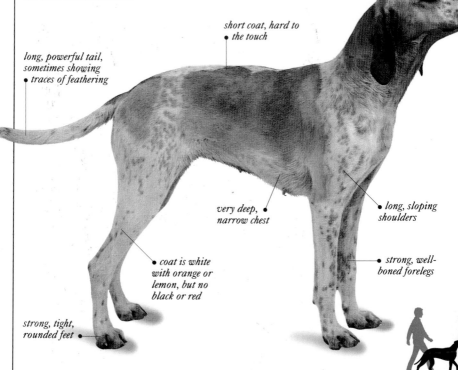

short coat, hard to the touch

long, powerful tail, sometimes showing traces of feathering

very deep, narrow chest

long, sloping shoulders

coat is white with orange or lemon, but no black or red

strong, well-boned forelegs

strong, tight, rounded feet

Height 61–66cm (24–26in)	Weight 25–30kg (55–66lb)	Temperament Intelligent, active

Country of origin France	First use Hunting small game	Origins 1800s

BASSET FAUVE DE BRETAGNE

Overall, the body shape of the Basset Fauve de Bretagne is typical of basset breeds – long, relative to its height, with slightly crooked legs and a long face. The coat, however, is quite different, having neither the rough texture of the Basset Griffon-Vendéen (see p.175), nor the smoothness of the Basset Artésian Normand (see p.173).

• **HISTORY** This breed was developed from the larger Griffon Fauve de Bretagne crossed with other bassets. It retains the solid coloration of its relative, sometimes with a single white spot on the chest or neck, although this is not encouraged.

• **REMARK** Traditionally, these dogs hunted small game in packs of four.

• **OTHER NAMES** Tawny Brittany Basset.

dark, open nose

shortish, muscular neck

oval-shaped ears set level with eyes and pleated at base

lively eyes

shortish, flat coat, hard and coarse

any white mark on chest to be discouraged

thick tail, tapering towards point

prominent breastbone

typical, slightly crooked legs, but can be straight

COLOUR TYPES

Height 33–38cm (13–15in)	Weight 16–18kg (36–40lb)	Temperament Lively, friendly

Country of origin France	First use Hunting deer and wild boar	Origins 1300s

GRAND BLEU DE GASCOGNE

Considered by many hound enthusiasts to
be the most majestic and aristocratic of the
French breeds, the Grand Bleu de Gascogne
is large and powerful. Developed in the dry
and hot Midi region in the southwest of
France, it is not especially quick in terms
of pace, but it displays prodigious stamina.
Its characteristic mottled appearance is
shared with other hounds from the area.

• HISTORY The origins of the Grand
Bleu de Gascogne are not known for
sure, but it is certainly an ancient breed.
It was developed in the old French provinces
of Guyenne and Gascony and was originally
used to hunt wolves, a task it performed until
the latter years of the last century. The breed
first appeared in the USA in the late 1700s.

• REMARK This hound is found in the USA
more often than anywhere else in the world,
including France itself.

• OTHER NAMES Large Blue
Gascony Hound.

*large, black
nose*

*folds of skin on
the cheeks, and
pendent lips*

*prominent
and well-
muscled thighs*

*long, oval,
well-knuckled feet*

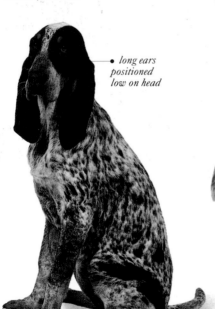

*long ears
positioned
low on head*

Height 64–71cm (25–28in)	Weight 32–35kg (71–77lb)	Temperament Active, friendly

light tan markings
above both eyes,
creating a "four-eyed"
impression

elongated head
with convex skull

ears
curl
inwards

long, powerful
forelegs

dense mottling
on weather-
resistant coat

slightly
sloping pasterns

strong,
black claws

Country of origin France	First use Hunting hares	Origins 1500s

CHIEN D'ARTOIS

This small, well-muscled, tricoloured scent hound is one of the original breeds of French hunting dog. It is the forerunner of many of the later breeds of hound still seen today.

• **HISTORY** This dog is named after the French province of Artois, where it was developed by crossing hounds and pointing breeds. Later infusions of British gundog blood almost resulted in the original breed's total disappearance. However, the numbers of pure Artois are now slowly recovering in France.

• **REMARK** This breed specializes in small game animals such as hares.

• **OTHER NAMES** Briquet.

broad skull

long, broad, flat ears set on level with eyes

long, powerful neck

long tail carried in sickle-like curve

fine, short hairs make up a close-fitting coat

slightly creased facial skin

square muzzle and black nose

distinct saddle-like marking

Height 52–58cm (20½–23in)	Weight 18–24kg (40–53lb)	Temperament Lively, friendly

| untry of origin France | First use Hunting dog | Origins 1600s |

BASSET BLEU DE GASCOGNE

This smallest member of the Bleu de Gascogne group retains the distinctive coloration of its larger relatives. It is a tri-coloured dog, being mostly white with black spots on its head and body, with tan markings on its head.

- **HISTORY** This basset is essentially a re-creation, by M. Alain Bourbon, of the original breed, which had died out by 1911.
- **REMARK** An enthusiastic hunting dog, the Basset Bleu de Gascogne is also a charming pet.

OTHER NAMES Blue Gascony Basset.

domed skull

dark brown eyes

relatively long tail

strong, oval-shaped feet

| ght 30–36cm (12–14in) | Weight 16–18kg (35–40lb) | Temperament Friendly, active |

| untry of origin France | First use Hunting dog | Origins 1600s |

BASSET ARTÉSIAN NORMAND

Although smaller in stature, this breed is sometimes confused with the Basset Hound (see p.146). The tri-coloured form, with black predominating, is preferred. Areas of white tend to be confined to the extremities.

HISTORY This is the survivor of breeds from Artois and Normandy.

REMARK There is a curled area of hair over each hip joint.

OTHER NAMES Artesian Norman Basset.

wide, black nose

ears set below level of eyes

short, well-boned legs

| ght 25–36cm (10–14in) | Weight 15kg (33lb) | Temperament Active, gentle |

Country of origin France	First use Hunting roe deer	Origins 1800s

GRAND GASCON-SAINTONGEOIS

Compared with hounds seen in other countries, the Grand Gascon-Saintongeois is a large dog, with exaggeratedly long ears. It has loose folds of skin around the head and neck. Ticking is evident in its fine, short, white coat. This dog has a black mask and head, with black often extending down on to its shoulders. A smaller version of this breed, the Petit Gascon-Saintongeois, is identical in all respects except height.

• **HISTORY** This breed was created by Baron de Virelade as a result of crossing the Gascon Bleu, Saintongeois, and Ariègeois breeds.

• **REMARK** Although a popular pack hound in France, the breed is unknown in other countries.

• **OTHER NAMES** Virelade.

very pronounced occipital peak

clear tan markings restricted to head

long, conical, pendulous ears

long, strong back

deep chest

typical black saddle marking

long, straight, well-boned forelegs

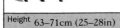

Height 63–71cm (25–28in)	Weight 30–32kg (66–71lb)	Temperament Affectionate, gentle

Country of origin France	First use Coursing hares	Origins 1700s

GRAND BASSET GRIFFON VENDÉEN

This form of the Basset Griffon Vendéen differs from its smaller relative only in size. White is often the predominant colour in bi- and tricolour forms. It is an active dog, and is valued for hunting rabbits and hares.
• **HISTORY** Both basset forms are descended from the Grand Griffon Vendéen (see p.176).
• **REMARK** The Grand Basset Griffon Vendéen can be very affectionate, yet has an independent nature.
• **OTHER NAMES** Large Vendéen Griffon.

GRAND BASSET GRIFFON VENDÉEN

PETIT BASSET GRIFFON VENDÉEN

ears attach below eye level

solid-boned forelegs

tail tapers along its length

wide, deep chest with rounded ribs

legs straighter than most bassets

large, powerful feet

COLOUR TYPES

Height 38–42cm (15–16½in)	Weight 18–20kg (40–44lb)	Temperament Affectionate, independent

Country of origin France	First use Hunting boars	Origins 1400s

GRAND GRIFFON VENDÉEN

The Grand Griffon Vendéen is either white or
wheaten, with various other colour markings. This
dog adapts well to land or water, having a rough,
wiry outercoat and a thick undercoat. Its head is
slightly elongated and its nose is well developed.
It has a moustache of longer hair above its lips.

• **HISTORY** Originating in the district of Vendée
in France, its ancestors are the St. Hubert Hound
(see pp.184–85), the Bracco Italiano (see p.101),
and the Griffon Nivernais (see p.177).

• **REMARK** Excitable at the start of a hunt, this
hound may tire before the quarry is in the bag.
It is an excellent dog for the part-time hunter.

• **OTHER NAMES** Large Vendéen Griffon.

large, dark eyes

large black nose and moustache

straight, well-muscled back

tail carried in a sabre-like curve

ears shaped like an elongated oval

firm, well-boned legs

strong chest

wiry coat must never be woolly

long hair covers feet

COLOUR TYPES

Height 60–66cm (23½–26in)	Weight 30–35kg (66–77lb)	Temperament Lively, friendly

ntry of origin France	First use Hunting small game	Origins 1600s

BRIQUET GRIFFON VENDÉEN

large, black nose with facial whiskers

COLOUR TYPES

This smaller relative of the Grand Griffon Vendéen (left) has a short head and low-set ears. It has a dense, bushy double coat, in solid or mixed colours.

HISTORY This hound shares a common ancestry with the Grand Griffon Vendéen but, instead of hunting boars and wolves, the Briquet's more likely quarry will be rabbits.

REMARK This breed works either in a pack or as a solitary hunter.

OTHER NAMES Medium Vendéen Griffon.

narrow, pendulous ears

solid bone structure

thick-soled feet

ht 48–56cm (19–22in)	Weight 24kg (53lb)	Temperament Energetic, lively

ntry of origin France	First use Hunting large game	Origins 1200s

GRIFFON NIVERNAIS

long, slightly conical ears

The Griffon Nivernais is a tall, light-framed dog, not unlike the Spinone (see p.100) and the Otter Hound (see p.149). It has a bushy, slightly unkempt appearance. The coat hair is long and hard, and usually grey or brown in colour.

HISTORY This is an ancient breed descended from the now-extinct Chien Gris de St. Louis.

REMARK This hound was developed specifically to hunt wild boar and bear.

OTHER NAMES Chien de Pays.

shaggy, coarse-textured coat

long hair covering legs

broad, prominent muzzle

COLOUR TYPES

ht 53–62cm (21–24in)	Weight 23–25kg (50–55lb)	Temperament Active, lively

Country of origin France	First use Hunting rabbits	Origins 1500s

PETIT BLEU DE GASCOGNE

In spite of its name, the Petit Bleu de Gascogne is a relatively large breed of hound. Although a relative of the Petit Griffon Bleu de Gascogne (right), it can be distinguished by its ears, which are folded rather than flattish, and larger in size. It is also slightly taller in the leg and of a heavier build, and has a smoother, shorter coat.

• HISTORY Selective breeding, essentially from the Grand Bleu de Gascogne (see pp.170–71), which led to a reduction in its size, underlies the development of this breed of dog. It originated in the province of Gascony, close to the Pyrenees, in the southwest of France.

• REMARK The Petit Bleu de Gascogne is highly prized in its homeland for its ability to hunt rabbits and hares.

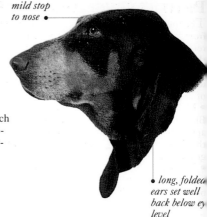

mild stop to nose

long, folded ears set well back below eye level

characteristic tan markings above eyes

straight, well-muscled back

refined, narrow head

tail tapers along its length, finishing in a point

oval feet

Height 48–58cm (19–23in)	Weight 18–21kg (40–46lb)	Temperament Proud, tenacious

Country of origin	France	First use	Hunting hares	Origins	1700s

PETIT GRIFFON BLEU DE GASCOGNE

The rough, wiry nature of the coat of this breed sets it apart from the other Bleu de Gascogne breeds. However, it still retains the characteristic coloration of the group, with the tan areas confined essentially to the head, as is the solid black coloration. The rest of the body should ideally appear bluish, resulting from the roaning of black and white hairs in the coat.

• HISTORY Of uncertain origin, the Petit Griffon Bleu de Gascogne is described as having a "rustic appearance", which reflects the involvement of the Petit Bleu de Gascogne and wire-haired griffons in its ancestry.

• REMARK This good-natured breed is considered to rank among the rarest of all of today's French hounds.

eyebrows must not obscure eyes

long ears lying unfolded, close to face

long, straight back

close, harsh coat – never curly or woolly

oval feet with firm toes

coat denser on thighs

Height	43–52cm (17–21in)	Weight	18–19kg (40–42lb)	Temperament	Diligent, friendly

Country of origin France	First use Hunting small game	Origins 1970s

ANGLO-FRANCAIS DE PETITE VÉNERIE

This is the smallest of the three Anglo-Francais breeds. Generally, this scent hound's coat is coloured tan and white, black and white, or a combination of white, black, and tan. Although compact, it has an athletic, well-muscled body, a head that is slightly small in relation to its body size, low-set ears, and a well-developed nose.

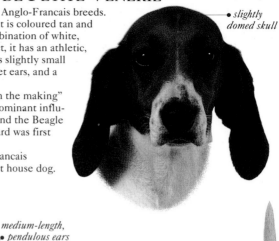

slightly domed skull

• **HISTORY** This is a "hound in the making" so its line is not yet fixed. The dominant influences so far are French hounds and the Beagle (see p.146). A preliminary standard was first drawn up in 1978.

• **REMARK** Of all the Anglo-Francais breeds, the Petite makes the best house dog.

• **OTHER NAMES** Small French-English Hound.

medium-length, pendulous ears

tail carried erect when dog is alert

compact, well-muscled neck

broad chest

short, smooth coat, but wire-haired individuals are not unknown

straight forelegs

Height 46–56cm (18–22in)	Weight 16–20kg (35–44lb)	Temperament Reserved, willing

untry of origin France	First use Hunting wolves	Origins 1200s

GRIFFON FAUVE DE BRETAGNE

The Griffon Fauve de Bretagne is mainly distinguished by its coat, which is very coarse-textured without being too long. Coloration varies through shades of fawn to brownish red; black is not a permitted colour. This well-muscled dog has a slightly elongated muzzle, either a black or a brown nose, and long, pendulous ears terminating in a point. This is an excellent pack hound, but it is virtually unknown outside its native France.

• **HISTORY** This ancient breed of hound was very well known during the Middle Ages in France. It reached its peak of popularity during the 1800s.

• **REMARK** In recent years, fears were expressed that the breed standard was becoming diluted. Very strict qualifications are now set for all show dogs.

• **OTHER NAMES** Tawny Brittany Griffon.

• narrow skull

COLOUR TYPES

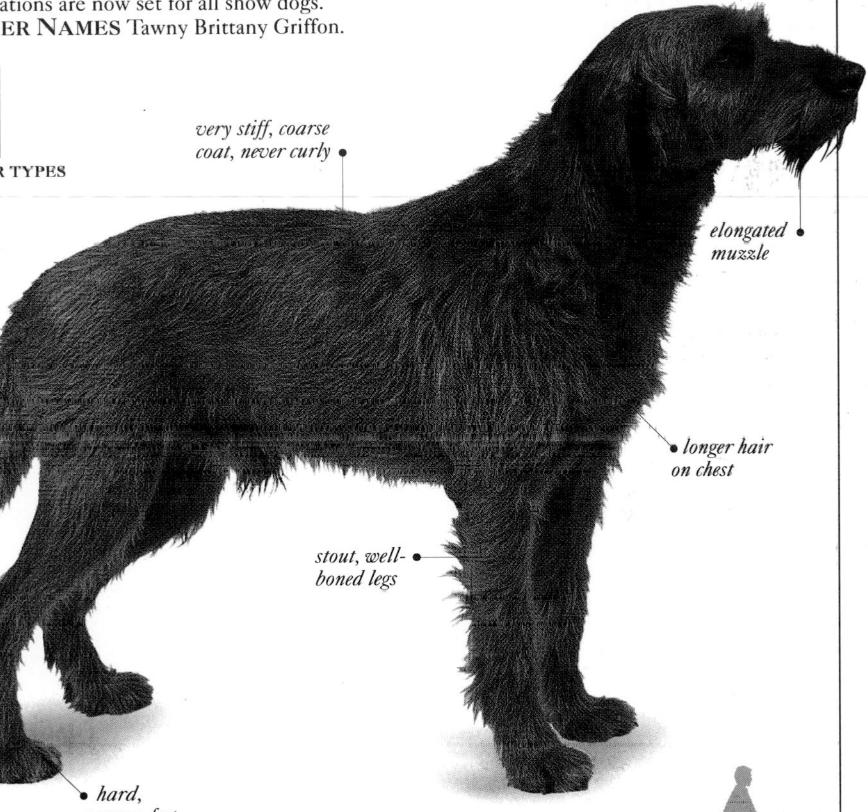

very stiff, coarse coat, never curly •

elongated • muzzle

long tail •

• longer hair on chest

stout, well- • boned legs

• hard, narrow feet

ight 51–56cm (20–22in)	Weight 20kg (44lb)	Temperament Active, courageous

Country of origin France	First use Hunting deer and hares	Origins 1600s

PORCELAINE

The magnificent white coat of the Porcelaine is
the inspiration for this breed's name, which in
French means literally "porcelain". It is a solid
white coat consisting of very short, fine-textured
hairs, although orange-coloured markings may be
present, especially on the ears. Its head is finely
formed, its ears are long, and its build is light
but well-muscled.

• **HISTORY** This is thought to be the oldest of
the French scent hounds, evolved from the now-
extinct Montaimboeuf. The breed died out
during the French Revolution but was re-
created in the mid-1800s by Swiss enthusiasts.

• **REMARK** The Porcelaine has an excellent
sense of smell and a fine, musical voice.

• **OTHER NAMES** Chien de Franche-Comte.

finely chiselled head

black nose with very open nostrils

tail is thick at base, carried in a slight curve

long, folded ears may have orange markings

fine-textured, very short hair with a high sheen

long, slender neck

broad feet with well-arched toes

Height 56–58cm (22–23in)	Weight 25–28kg (55–62lb)	Temperament Active, friendly

ntry of origin Switzerland	First use Hunting small game	Origins 1500s

JURA LAUFHUND: BRUNO

This hound, from the Jura region of western Switzerland close to the French border, is characterized by the absence of white markings in its coat. Otherwise, the Bruno Jura is similar to laufhunds from other regions. It can be distinguished immediately from the St. Hubert form (see pp.184–85) by its less massive head and generally more refined appearance.

HISTORY The laufhund is thought to descend from the old, heavier, French breeds, of which only smooth-haired forms survive.

REMARK This breed retains a strong hunting instinct and requires plenty of exercise in order to remain in good condition.

OTHER NAMES Jura Hound.

• broad, round skull

large, black, saddle-shaped marking on • back

long, broad back •

ears set low on • head, and folded

• rounded feet with hard pads

• large, black nose with broad nostrils

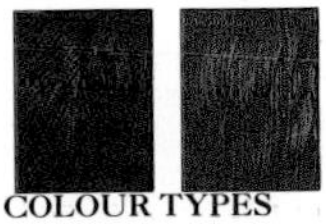

COLOUR TYPES

ght 46–58cm (18–23in)	Weight 15–20kg (34–44lb)	Temperament Lively, determined

Country of origin Switzerland	First use Hunting game	Origins 1500s

JURA LAUFHUND: ST. HUBERT

Although the black-and-tan coloration of this hound suggests a close affinity with the Bruno Jura Laufhund (see p.183), it is somewhat different in appearance. It tends to be of heavier build, with wrinkled skin on its forehead, reminiscent of a Bloodhound. The black markings may take the form of a saddle over the back, or they may be more widespread, typically on the head and legs, contrasting with tan areas.

• **HISTORY** The St. Hubert is thought to have a close relationship with the now-extinct St. Hubert Hound of France. This Swiss breed is certainly derived from French stock.

• **REMARK** The word *laufhund* means "walking dog". A keen tracker, it bays loudly when following a scent. This laufhund has plenty of stamina and is used to hunt a variety of game, ranging from small hares and foxes to larger animals such as deer.

• **OTHER NAMES** Jura Hound.

tail carried high, without a marked curve

powerful thighs

relatively long, straight back

rounded feet

Height 46–58cm (18–23in)	Weight 15–20kg (34–44lb)	Temperament Active, friendly

wrinkled skin
on forehead •

prominent black nose
with wide nostrils •

folds of loose skin
evident on back •

• long,
pendent ears

heavy, massive,
domed skull •

deep •
ribcage

strong, •
straight forelegs

pronounced •
dewlap

strong, dark •
nails

Country of origin Hungary	First use Hunting small game	Origins 800s

HUNGARIAN GREYHOUND

This breed of greyhound is long-legged, lean, and elegant, and closely resembles the Greyhound proper (see p.150), although it is somewhat smaller in stature. The head and muzzle are wide for a dog that relies on sight rather than scenting ability. Its coat is short and coarse, and solid colours and brindles are acceptable.

• **HISTORY** This is an ancient breed which accompanied the fierce Magyar people into central Europe in the 10th century.

• **REMARK** This breed is not well-known outside its native Hungary and is rarely seen at shows.

• **OTHER NAMES** Magyar Agár.

ears folded back

elongated head

wide muzzle

long, thin tail, curled at end

short, sleek, coarse-textured coat

prominent breastbone

long, fine-boned limbs

COLOUR TYPES

Height 64–70cm (25–27½in)	Weight 22–31kg (49–68lb)	Temperament Active, affectionate

Country of origin Switzerland	First use Hunting in Alpine regions	Origins 1000s

BERNER LAUFHUND

This breed of hound has a narrow head and long, folded ears. Its body is long but not heavy, with strong, well-boned legs. The Berner Laufhund's soft undercoat is covered with a harder, tricoloured outercoat.

• **HISTORY** These hounds have been used by Swiss Alpine hunters for about 900 years.

• **REMARK** The formation of the Swiss Hound Club in 1931 is largely responsible for the pres-ervation of this breed.

• **OTHER NAMES** Bernese Hound.

strong muzzle

tan markings on face

black and white body markings

long, conical ears

soft undercoat, abundant outercoat

thick, powerful neck

well-boned legs may show tan markings

Height 46–58cm (18–23in)	Weight 15–20kg (34–44lb)	Temperament Active, responsive

Country of origin Switzerland	First use Hunting small game	Origins 1500s

SCHWEIZER LAUFHUND

The bicoloured appearance of this hound serves to distinguish it from other related Swiss breeds. White predominates in the coat, offset against yellowish orange, orange, or even red markings, which are large in extent, although occasional small spots of colour are not penalized in the show ring. The Schweizer Laufhund is a talented tracker and has a powerful voice, which is invariably heard whenever a scent trail is located.

• **HISTORY** This breed originated close to the Franco-Swiss border and is related to the French breeds found in that region.

REMARK The shorter-legged version of this breed, known as the Schweizer Neider-laufhund, has identical coat coloration.

OTHER NAMES Swiss Hound.

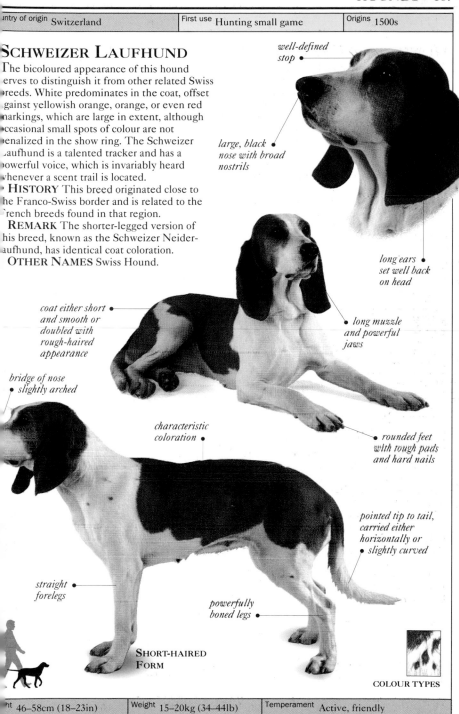

well-defined stop •

• large, black nose with broad nostrils

long ears • set well back on head

coat either short and smooth or doubled with rough-haired appearance •

• long muzzle and powerful jaws

bridge of nose • slightly arched

characteristic coloration •

• rounded feet with tough pads and hard nails

straight • forelegs

powerfully boned legs •

pointed tip to tail, carried either horizontally or • slightly curved

SHORT-HAIRED FORM

COLOUR TYPES

Height 46–58cm (18–23in)	Weight 15–20kg (34–44lb)	Temperament Active, friendly

Country of origin Switzerland	First use Hunting large game	Origins 1500s

LUZERNER LAUFHUND

The Luzerner Laufhund is generally similar to the other four breeds of laufhund that have been developed in Switzerland. This breed, however, is characterized by a distinctive tri-coloured appearance. The pronounced black ticking over the white areas of the coat gives rise to an impression of blue coloration. There is a short-legged form of this breed, known as the Luzerner Neiderlaufhund, which stands no more than 42cm (16½in) tall.

• **HISTORY** The similarity between the Luzerner and French breeds, as well as their geographical proximity, indicates a close ancestral relationship. Its precise origins are, however, unknown.

• **REMARK** This breed has excellent tracking abilities, and it gives voice with a very distinctive bark whenever a fresh scent is located.

• **OTHER NAMES** Lucernese Hound.

narrow skull

prominent black nose

long, pendulous, folded ears

heavy ticking in coat, offset against black and tan areas

thick, hard, short coat

deep ribcage

straight, powerful forelegs

tapering tail never held erect

rounded feet

Height 46–58cm (18–23in)	Weight 15–20kg (34–44lb)	Temperament Active, friendly

untry of origin Former Yugoslavia	First use Tracking and hunting game	Origins 1000BC

BALKAN HOUND

This obedient hound is black and
tan, typically with a distinctive
black saddle, flat head, and
black marks over the eyes.
It is particularly muscular
in the shoulders and limbs.
A diligent, determined hunter,
the Balkan Hound works in packs,
and is used to hunt game ranging
from hares to wild boars.
• HISTORY The Balkan hound's
ancestors are thought to have been
brought to the Balkan region from
Egypt by Phoenicians in about 1000BC.
• REMARK Despite its undoubted
tracking skills in many
different terrains, the
Balkan Hound is still
not widely known.
• OTHER NAMES
Balkanski Gonic.

*flat top to skull
and relatively
• long head*

*rounded,
pendulous
ears*

*distinctive
markings*

*rounded, powerful
• feet with dark nails*

ght 43–53cm (17–21in)	Weight 20kg (44lb)	Temperament Active, responsive

untry of origin Former Yugoslavia	First use Hunting small game	Origins 1700s

POSAVAC HOUND

The coat of this stocky hound tends
to be predominantly red in colour.
Other colours, such as yellow and
fawn, are less common.
• HISTORY The Posavac
probably shares a common origin
with other similar breeds that have
originated in the former Yugoslavia,
their ancestors having been introduced via the ports of the
Adriatic coast.
• REMARK Exercise
is absolutely essential for
this active hound.
• OTHER NAMES
Posavski Gonic.

*thick, hard,
coat •*

*pendulous ears
• with rounded tips*

COLOUR TYPES

*white markings
tend to be confined
to underparts*

*relatively
short legs*

ght 43–59cm (17–23in)	Weight 16–20kg (35–45lb)	Temperament Active, alert

Country of origin Former Yugoslavia	First use Hunting	Origins 1700s

YUGOSLAVIAN MOUNTAIN HOUND

This particular breed of hound, of the many breeds that
have originated within the borders of the former country of
Yugoslavia, can be recognized by its black-and-tan coloration. The Yugoslavian Mountain Hound has a smooth,
coarse-textured, thick outercoat and a very full undercoat,
making it ideal for the harsh mountain terrain and thick
bushland in which it normally hunts.

• **HISTORY** This is certainly an old
breed, whose ancestors may have
been brought to the Adriatic
by the Phoenicians. Selective
breeding in different parts of
the region has given rise to the
diversity of hound breeds seen
there today.

• **REMARK** A keen sense of smell,
an athletic build, and a good voice
make this an excellent hunting dog.

• **OTHER NAMES** Jugoslavenski
Planinski Gonic.

• *broad head*

powerful • muzzle

long, tapering • tail

long, pendulous ears with • rounded tips

relatively long body • creates rectangular profile

clearly • defined areas of black and tan

strong, • relatively short legs

flat, coarse, • thick outercoat

Height 46–56cm (18–22in)	Weight 20–25kg (44–55lb)	Temperament Active, friendly

Country of origin Former Yugoslavia	First use Hunting small game	Origins 1800s

YUGOSLAVIAN TRICOLOURED HOUND

The coloration of this short-haired breed of hound distinguishes it from the Yugoslavian Mountain Hound (opposite). Tan markings are prominent here, offset against black; a white area is evident at the front of the dog, sometimes extending down to its underparts. This breed is very localized in its distribution, and is most common in the southern parts of what was formerly Yugoslavia. Even here, however, it has become quite a rare sight in recent years.

• HISTORY A combination of sight and scent hound stock, as has been used in other Yugoslavian hounds, underlies this dog's breeding history.

• REMARK Although a devoted hunter, this breed is very adaptable and enjoys human companionship.

• OTHER NAMES Jugoslavenski Tribarvni Gonic.

white facial blaze

prominent black nose

muscular ears hang down sides of face

black tends to dominate in coat

white tip on tail

prominent white area on front

powerful thighs

white areas on feet and legs

solid, thick pads

Height 46–56cm (18–22in)	Weight 20–25kg (44–55lb)	Temperament Active, obedient

Country of origin Italy	First use Hunting game	Origins 100s

ITALIAN HOUND

Strong and powerfully built, this hound has a long, tapering muzzle, which is convex when seen in profile, sloping downwards to the nose. Its lips are black at the edges.

• **HISTORY** This breed is descended from the early sight hounds, which were probably introduced to Italy by the Phoenicians, and scent hounds from Europe. During the Renaissance it was a popular hunting dog and has recently undergone a further revival in Italy.

• **REMARK** A rough-coated form, known as Segugio Italiano a Pelo Forte, is identical in all respects other than coat type.

• **OTHER NAMES** Segugio Italiano.

low-set, long, folded ears

sickle-shaped tail

thick, very short, shiny coat

COLOUR TYPES

Height 52–58cm (20½–23in)	Weight 18–28kg (40–62lb)	Temperament Docile, active

Country of origin Italy	First use Hunting small game	Origins 1000BC

CIRNECO DELL'ETNA

This elegant, athletic Sicilian sight hound also hunts by scent. It is smaller than similar Mediterranean island breeds.

• **HISTORY** The Cirneco dell'Etna is probably descended from ancestral sight-hound stock acquired in Egypt and traded in the Mediterranean by the Phoenicians.

• **REMARK** Surprisingly, this breed is internationally less well known than either the similar Ibizan Hound (see p.194) or the Pharaoh Hound (see p.193).

• **OTHER NAMES** Sicilian Greyhound.

broad, stiff, triangular ears

long, straight forelegs

short, smooth coat

white marking permitted

Height 42–50cm (16½–19½in)	Weight 8–12kg (18–26lb)	Temperament Friendly, alert

| untry of origin Malta | First use Hunting rabbits | Origins 1000BC |

PHARAOH HOUND

The large, upright ears and the tan coloration of this hound immediately attract attention. It bears a striking likeness to depictions of the Egyptian god Anubis, whose task it was to act as guide for the souls of the dead. Although it is a sight hound, it also tracks its quarry by scent.
• **HISTORY** Ancestors of the Pharaoh Hound are thought to have been brought to Malta by Phoenician traders. Here they remained in a relatively pure state, first attracting attention overseas only during the late 1960s.
• **REMARK** Without adequate exercise, these dogs rapidly become overweight.
• **OTHER NAMES** Kelb Tal-fenek.

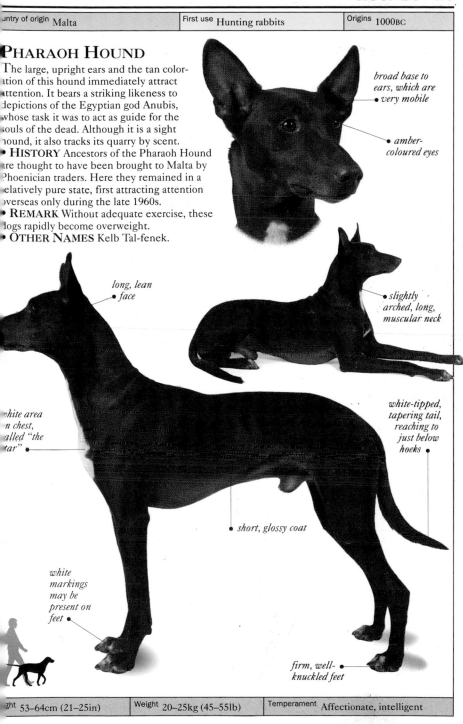

broad base to ears, which are
• very mobile

• amber-coloured eyes

long, lean
• face

• slightly arched, long, muscular neck

white-tipped, tapering tail, reaching to just below hocks •

white area
n chest,
alled "the
ar"

short, glossy coat

white markings may be present on feet •

firm, well-knuckled feet

| ght 53–64cm (21–25in) | Weight 20–25kg (45–55lb) | Temperament Affectionate, intelligent |

Country of origin Spain	First use Hunting rabbits	Origins 3000BC

IBIZAN HOUND

Using large ears, this hound hunts by means of sound as well as sight. It is quite tall and, compared with other fast-paced hunting dogs, relatively stocky. Variable coloration helps distinguish it from Pharaoh Hounds (see p.193).
• HISTORY Images of hounds similar to the Ibizan have been found in Egypt, and date back some 5,000 years. Some were probably taken from there to the island of Ibiza.
• REMARK This is a sensitive and loyal dog.
• OTHER NAMES Podenco Ibicenco.

ears erect when
• alert

long, slightly
• arched neck

base of ears
level with
eyes •

back slopes
slightly to rump •

thin tail set •
low on back

deep chest •
and flat ribcage

• long,
straight
legs

• powerful
hindquarters

COLOUR TYPES

Height 57–70cm (22½–27½in)	Weight 19–25kg (42–55lb)	Temperament Alert, adaptable

Country of origin Spain	First use Tracking game	Origins 500s

SABUESO ESPAÑOL

The similarity in appearance of the Sabueso Español and the mastiff breeds indicates that this is an ancient dog. There are two forms of this breed: the de Monte (shown here) weighs about 25kg (55lb), stands 56cm (22in) high, and has a hard, white coat with red or black patches; the Lebrero form is smaller, standing no more than 51cm (20in) high, and is usually of a more uniform red colour.

• HISTORY Thought to have been introduced to the region by the Phoenicians, this breed has changed little within the confines of the Iberian Peninsula.

• REMARK This is still a hunting dog and does not generally make a good house dog or pet.

• OTHER NAMES Spanish Hound.

prominent, pigmented nose

large dewlap

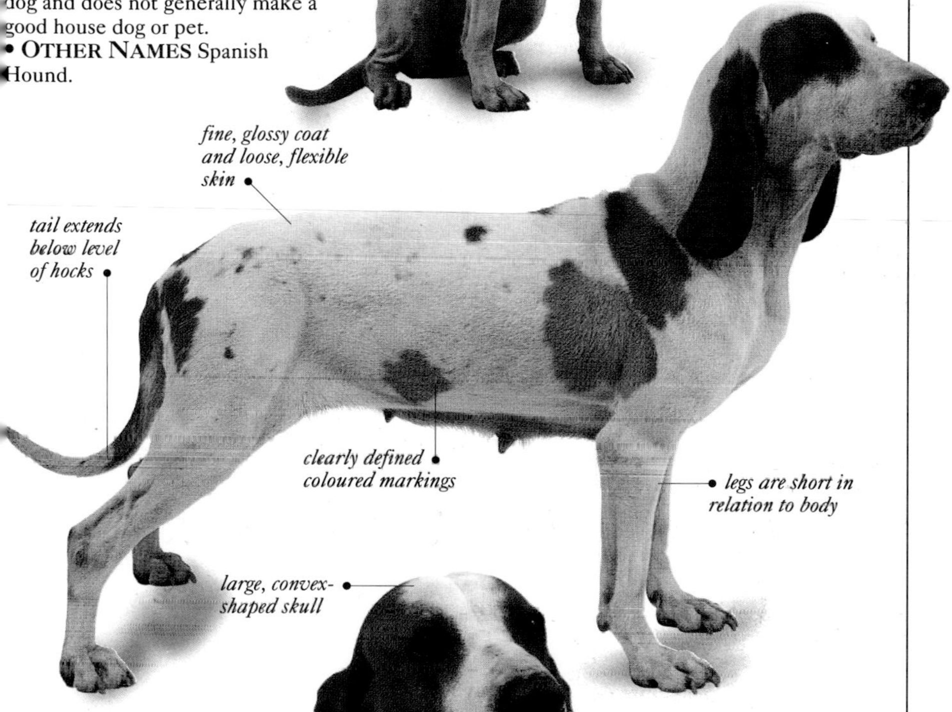

fine, glossy coat and loose, flexible skin

tail extends below level of hocks

clearly defined coloured markings

legs are short in relation to body

large, convex-shaped skull

very long, soft, folded ears

COLOUR TYPES

Height 46–56cm (18–22in)	Weight 20–25kg (45–55lb)	Temperament Energetic, loyal

Country of origin Spain	First use Hunting game, racing	Origins 600BC

SPANISH GREYHOUND

With the unmistakable outline of a greyhound, this dog is built for speed. It is a little smaller than the Greyhound itself, however (see p.150), which it otherwise resembles in appearance. The stop is also more pronounced and its build generally sturdier. Crosses with Greyhounds have occurred to produce a breed known locally in Spain as the Galgo Inglés-Español, which is used for racing.

• HISTORY The early origins of the Spanish Greyhound are not clear, but it is of ancient lineage and was documented in Roman times.

• REMARK As a racing dog, this breed is not as swift as the Greyhound itself.

• OTHER NAMES Galgo Español.

SMOOTH-HAIRED FORM

dark, expressive, oval eyes

rose ears falling backwards

WIRE-HAIRED FORM

long, narrow head

slightly arched, powerful loin

long, muscular, elegantly arched neck

tall, straight forelegs

well-bent stifles

very long, relatively slender tail carried low

COLOUR TYPES

Height 66–71cm (26–28in)	Weight 27–30kg (60–66lb)	Temperament Active, friendly

Country of origin Portugal	First use Flushing game, ratting	Origins 1800s

PODENGO PORTUGUESO PEQUEÑO

The Pequeño is sometimes described as
resembling a sturdy Chihuahua (see p.41),
but there seems to be no ancestral link
between the two breeds. The Pequeño
is in fact a miniature sight hound, a well-
proportioned little dog, with a body longer
than it is tall, a convex skull, a straight
muzzle, and a lively, intelligent expression.
• **HISTORY** It appears that this breed was
derived from the Podengo Portugueso Medio,
and it, too, is bred in both wire-
and smooth-haired forms.
• **REMARK** This enthusiastic
breed sometimes works
with its larger cousins.
It enters warrens and
flushes out rabbits,
leaving them to be
captured by the other
dogs. It is also a very
talented ratter and an
affectionate and popular
house pet.
• **OTHER NAMES** Small
Portuguese Hound.

*triangular,
mobile ears*

*tail carried
erect when
dog is alert*

*short,
coarse coat*

*convex
skull*

**SMOOTH-HAIRED
FORM**

*medium-
length, shaggy
coat*

*straight
muzzle*

**WIRE-HAIRED
FORM**

COLOUR TYPES

Height 20–31cm (8–12in)	Weight 5–6kg (11–13lb)	Temperament Lively, affectionate

| Country of origin Portugal | First use Hunting small game | Origins 1600s |

PODENGO PORTUGUESO MEDIO

Both smooth- and wire-haired forms of the Medio are bred, with fawn and white coloration tending to predominate, although yellow and black forms with white markings are also seen. This medium-sized hound is powerful for its size, muscular, agile, and an extremely efficient hunter of small game, either singly or working in conjunction with other dogs.

- **HISTORY** The sight hounds of northern Africa were probably used in the development of the Podengo breeds, although it is thought that this medium-sized version descended directly from the Podengo Portugueso Grande, and is, therefore, of more recent origin.
- **REMARK** Of all the Podengo breeds, the Medio is the most popular in Portugal, being thought of as neither too small nor too large, and able to adapt readily to a softer, domestic lifestyle.
- **OTHER NAMES** Medium Portuguese Hound.

ears naturally upright and directed forwards

WIRE-HAIRED FORM

powerful, muscular neck

tail erect when dog is alert

arched eyebrows

straight muzzle

coat is coarse-textured in both forms

SMOOTH-HAIRED FORM

COLOUR TYPES

| Height 39–56cm (15–22in) | Weight 16–20kg (35–44lb) | Temperament Lively, alert |

Country of origin Iran	First use Hunting gazelle	Origins 3000BC

SALUKI

In terms of appearance, the Saluki is unmistakable – slim, high-stepping, and elegant. It has a relatively short coat with significantly longer hair on both its ears and tail. Feathering is also present on the thighs and at the back of the legs. For all its elegance, the Saluki possesses devastating acceleration, which, in its homeland, enables it to outpace gazelles, one of the fastest of all antelopes.
• **HISTORY** Images of dogs similar to the contemporary Saluki have been found on ancient Egyptian tombs dating back more than 5,000 years, but the breed's name is thought to derive from the city of Saluk, which is now part of Yemeni territory.
• **REMARK** Care should be taken when exercising these hounds in areas where they could encounter cats or small dogs.
• **OTHER NAMES** Gazelle Hound.

long, narrow head

long, mobile ears hang close to sides of head

black or liver-coloured nose

smooth, silky coat

powerful hips

long, naturally curved tail

long, muscular and supple neck

well-boned, straight forelegs

feathering present on backs of legs

inner toes longer than outer toes

COLOUR TYPES

Height 56–71cm (22–28in)	Weight 20–30kg (44–66lb)	Temperament Active, friendly

Country of origin Russia	First use Hunting wolves	Origins 1200s

BORZOI

Built on lines of speed and grace, this beautiful sight hound was traditionally used to course wolves. This required not only pace, but also intelligence and considerable bravery on the part of the dog. These qualities are clearly reflected in the Borzoi's proud, aristocratic bearing. Sensitive and aloof in temperament, it is, nevertheless, faithful and protective towards its owner.

• **HISTORY** The ancestry of the Borzoi is inextricably linked with Russian royalty. Popular as gifts, they were sent to Britain's Princess Alexandra in 1842, and were exhibited at the first Crufts Dog Show in 1891.

• **REMARK** The name "Borzoi" derives from the Russian word *borzii*, meaning swift.

• **OTHER NAMES** Russian Wolfhound.

long, powerful jaws

hair is longer over chest, neck, and thighs

gracefully curved back

long, elegant neck

deep chest

oval front feet, with hindfeet more hare-like

strong forelegs

very powerful hindlegs

COLOUR TYPES

Height 69–79cm (27–31in)	Weight 35–48kg (75–105lb)	Temperament Active, intelligent

Country of origin Mali	First use Hunting gazelles	Origins 1000s

AZAWAKH

With an exceedingly athletic appearance, the Azawakh is exceptionally fast, being able to reach speeds of 64km/h (40mph), and displays considerable stamina. The breed's slender head is characterized by the presence of distinctive swellings on the sides of its face.

• **HISTORY** The Azawakh was developed by the Tuareg people of the southern Sahara to slow down gazelles and other game animals, thus allowing riders to overtake and kill them.

• **REMARK** This breed is slowly finding homes in other countries throughout the world.

• **OTHER NAMES** Tuareg Sloughi.

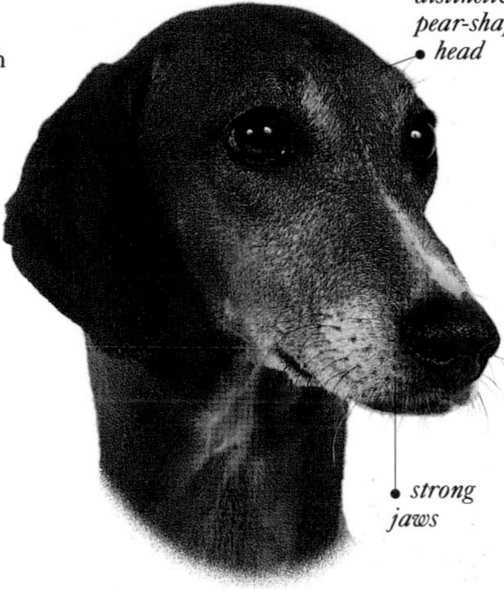

distinctive, pear-shaped head

strong jaws

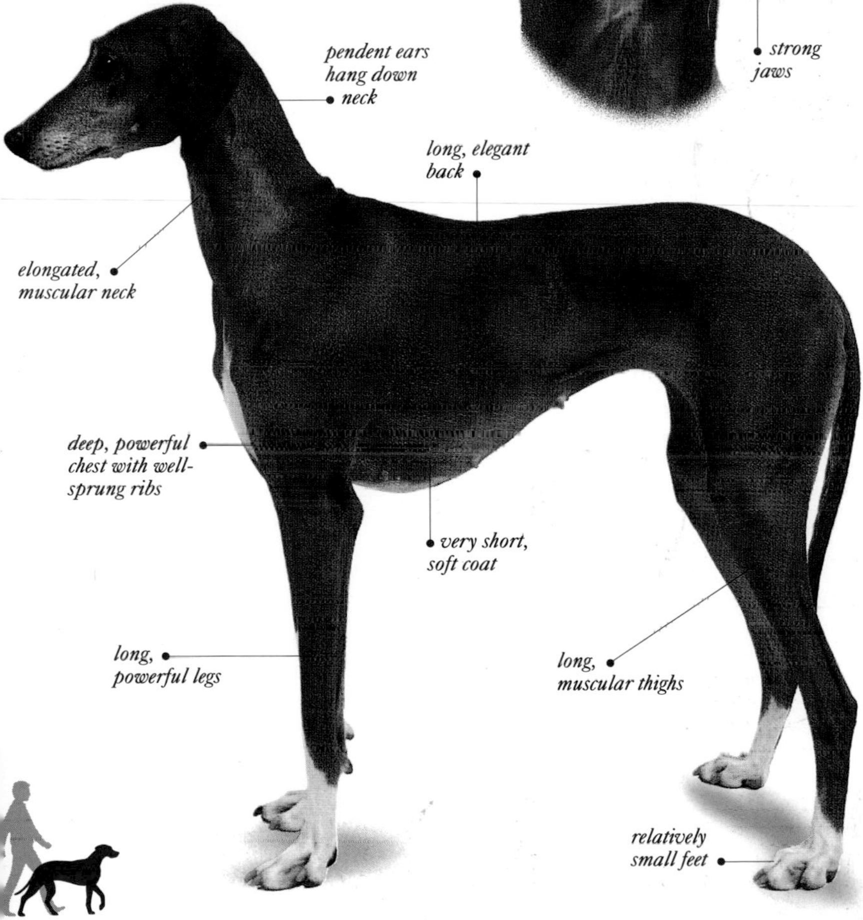

pendent ears hang down neck

long, elegant back

elongated, muscular neck

deep, powerful chest with well-sprung ribs

very short, soft coat

long, powerful legs

long, muscular thighs

relatively small feet

Height 58–74cm (23–29in)	Weight 17–25kg (37–55lb)	Temperament Independent, alert

Country of origin Afghanistan	First use Hunting gazelles and wolves	Origins 1600s

AFGHAN HOUND

The elegant appearance of the Afghan, with its long, silky coat, has attracted many people to this breed. Such styling, however, is possible only by dedicated grooming. The length of the coat has been greatly developed by selective breeding over about the last 50 years. In motion, the Afghan Hound is high-stepping, giving the impression of springing over the ground with its coat flowing behind.

• **HISTORY** This hound was first seen in Europe in the late 1800s, when it was brought back by soldiers returning from the Afghan War. At that time there were a number of localized forms – some were larger, for example – but such distinctions have disappeared in contemporary bloodlines.

• **REMARK** This athletic hound requires plenty of exercise. It may tend to run off too readily – perhaps a reflection of its hunting past.

• **OTHER NAMES** Tazi.

long skull

long, silky hair covering eyes

prominent hip bones

dense covering of long hair on feet

long, straight legs

large, strong forefeet

COLOUR TYPES

Height 64–74cm (25–29in)	Weight 23–27kg (50–60lb)	Temperament Lively, active

Country of origin Morocco	First use Guarding flocks	Origins 6000BC

SLOUGHI

The build of the Sloughi has led to debate that it is merely a smooth-coated form of Saluki (see p.199), modified by crossings with other similar breeds. That aside, the Sloughi is a striking dog, slenderly built, with fine, well-defined musculature and rather sad, dark eyes.

• HISTORY This breed's origins lie in North Africa where ancient drawings and carvings depict similar dogs. Earlier, its ancestors probably came from the region of present-day Saudi Arabia.

• REMARK Although used as a flock guardian and hunter in its homeland, it can occasionally be seen in the show ring in Britain and the USA.

• OTHER NAMES Arabian Greyhound.

large, dark eyes

well-defined bone structure

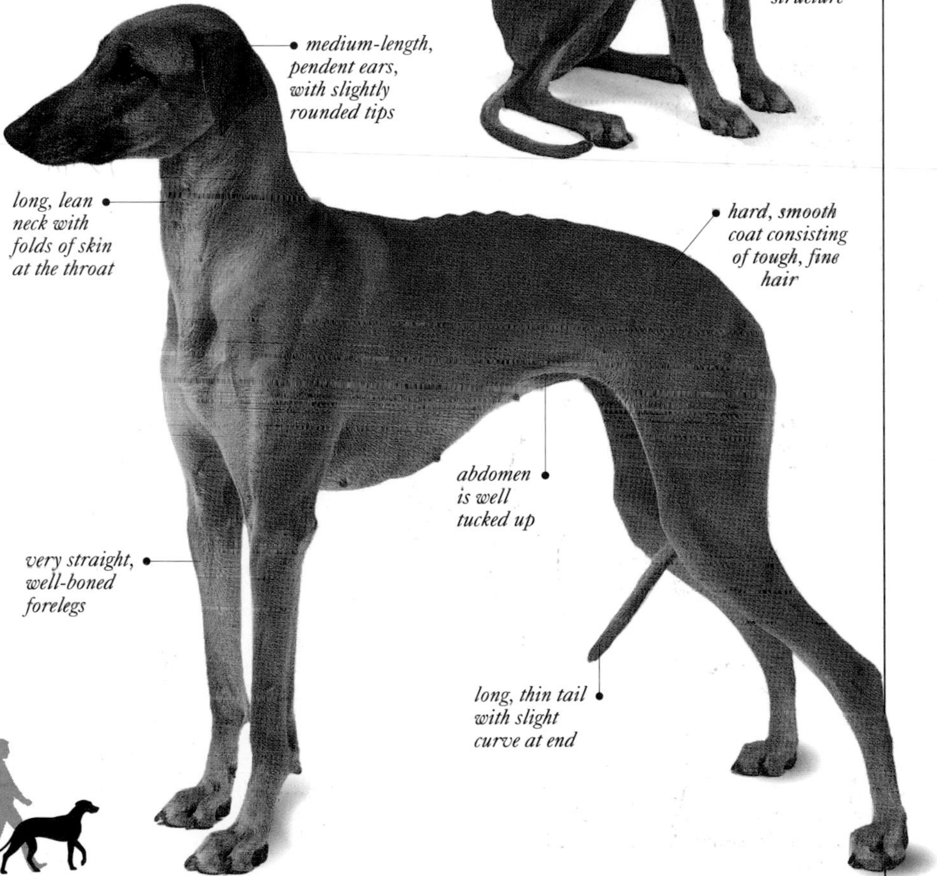

medium-length, pendent ears, with slightly rounded tips

long, lean neck with folds of skin at the throat

hard, smooth coat consisting of tough, fine hair

very straight, well-boned forelegs

abdomen is well tucked up

long, thin tail with slight curve at end

Height 61–72cm (24–28½in)	Weight 20–27kg (45–60lb)	Temperament Active, friendly

Country of origin Japan	First use Hunting boar and deer	Origins 1700s

KAI DOG

The fiercely loyal Kai Dog is a powerfully
built animal with strong legs which makes it
well suited to hunting in its mountainous Japanese homeland. It is invariably brindled in
coloration. The red form is known as Aka-Tora,
the medium is called Chu-Tora, and the black
brindle form is Kuro-Tora.

• **HISTORY** The name of this breed
originates from part of central Japan that is now
in the prefecture of Yamanashi. The Kai was
first seen in the USA in 1951, but it did not
become established here at this stage.

• **REMARK** Kai Dog pups are usually born
solid black in colour. Their
distinctive brindle colouring
develops only as they grow
and mature.

• **OTHER NAMES**
Tora Dog.

*triangular
pricked
ears directed
slightly
forwards*

*thick tail set high
and curled over
the back*

thick, muscular neck

*ears are larger
than on other
medium-sized
Japanese breeds*

*deep, muscular
chest*

*straight, well-
muscled forelegs*

*small, dark
brown eyes*

*well-arched, tightly
closed toes*

*harsh, straight
outercoat with soft,
thick undercoat*

COLOUR TYPES

Height 46–58cm (18–23in)	Weight 16–18kg (35–40lb)	Temperament Determined, independent

untry of origin South Africa	First use Hunting lions	Origins 1800s

RHODESIAN RIDGEBACK

Dignified and formidable, the Ridgeback derives its name from the distinctive ridge of hair which grows, contrary to the direction of the rest of the coat, in a tapering line along the middle of its back. It shares the colour as well as the heart of the lion which was once its quarry.

• **HISTORY** Developed by the Boers in the late 19th century, its standard was fixed in Rhodesia (now Zimbabwe) in 1922. In the hunt for lions it was renowned for its great stamina and surprising agility. Nowadays it is used as a guard dog and makes a loyal and affectionate family pet.

• **REMARK** The breed's unique ridge of hair is thought to have been inherited from the now extinct Hottentot Dog.

• **OTHER NAMES** African Lion Hound.

broad, flat skull

clearly defined ridge

strong, tapering tail

short, sleek coat

long, muscular neck

trace of white permitted on chest

powerful hindquarters

strong, deep chest

compact, well-arched toes

ght 61–69cm (24–27in)	Weight 30–39kg (65–85lb)	Temperament Friendly, obedient

TERRIERS

MOST OF THE DOGS in this group are relatively small in size, but, despite this, they can be quite spirited and independent. Although many terriers were originally kept on farms, often as rat catchers, they have made the transition to household pets quite readily, to the extent that a number of them are among the best-known breeds in the world. Their alert and curious nature, and their tendency to explore underground, mean that they are m[o] inclined to dig than other breeds, a[n] have an alarming tendency to disapp[ear] down rabbit holes when out for a wa[lk]. As a result, they are not true [gun] dogs although they do make lo[yal] companions. Terriers are usually live[ly], alert, and extremely plucky. They [do] not always get on well togeth[er], however, and enjoy every opportun[ity] to run about on their own.

Country of origin USA	First use Hunting rats	Origins 1930s

AMERICAN TOY TERRIER

This small, attractive terrier shows a clear relationship to the Smooth Fox Terrier (see p.216). The tricoloured form with white predominating in the coat is favoured in the show ring. A popularizing feature is the American Toy Terrier's smooth, short coat, which is extremely easy to care for and groom.
- **HISTORY** The American Kennel Club recognized this breed in 1936. Crosses with English Toy Terriers and Chihuahuas have refined its features.
- **REMARK** These terriers have been trained to assist handicapped people around the home.
- **OTHER NAMES** Toy Fox Terrier, Amertoy.

white blaze often present

close-set ears

tail is traditionally docked

square body shape

straight, lightly boned forelegs

oval, compact feet

Height 25cm (10in)	Weight 2–3kg (4½–7lb)	Temperament Lively, alert

Country of origin USA	First use Dog fighting	Origins 1800s

AMERICAN PIT BULL TERRIER

This is probably the most feared and legislated against dog in the world today. The breed exudes power, with a broad, slab-like head, immensely strong jaws, and a thickly muscled neck and body. To house the Pit Bull's fearsome jaws the face is particularly wide between its cheeks.

• **HISTORY** This terrier was bred specifically for dog fighting and it is still used for this purpose today, often illegally. The breed descends from Staffordshire Bull Terriers crossed with bulldogs.

• **REMARK** In the UK, ownership is legally restricted to registered, neutered dogs only.

• **OTHER NAMES** Pit Bull Terrier, American Pit Bull.

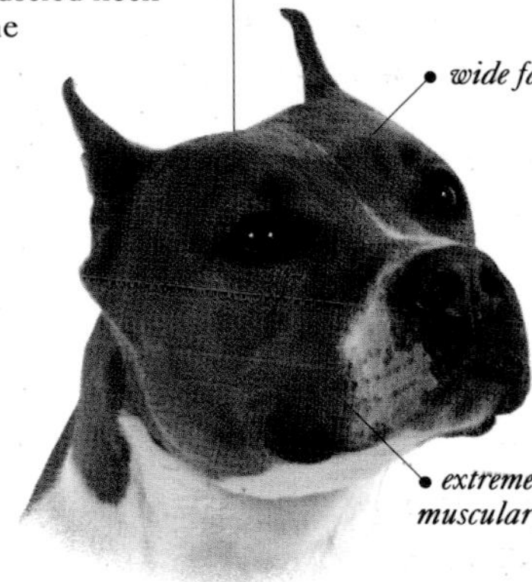

thick-boned, slab-like head

wide face

extremely muscular jaws

small ears

slightly long back in relation to height

powerful hindquarters

round, often black, eyes

very broad, muscular chest

thick, hard, short coat

white markings typically cover less than 80 per cent of body

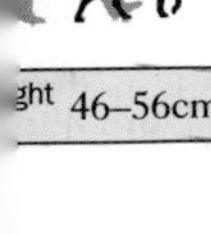

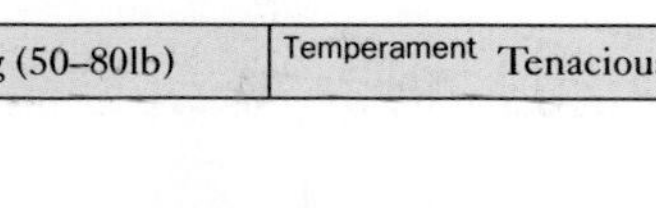

COLOUR TYPES

Height 46–56cm (18–22in)	Weight 23–36kg (50–80lb)	Temperament Tenacious, fearless

Country of origin USA	First use Baiting bulls	Origins 1800s

AMERICAN STAFFORDSHIRE TERRIER

broad head with powerful jaw muscles

ears may be cropped

This breed resembles its English ancestor, the Staffordshire Bull Terrier (see p.212), although it is taller, heavier, and generally more substantial. This dog is very powerful, but not usually ill-disposed towards people.

• **HISTORY** The American Kennel Club first granted recognition of the American Staffordshire Terrier as a separate breed in 1936.

• **REMARK** The close similarity in appearance of this breed to the notorious American Pit Bull Terrier (see p.207) has not served to enhance its reputation recently.

tail appears short in relation to body

smooth, short coat

COLOUR TYPES

Height 43–48cm (17–19in)	Weight 18–23kg (40–50lb)	Temperament Intelligent, determined

Country of origin USA	First use Baiting bulls, ratting	Origins 1800s

BOSTON TERRIER

Although descended from bull-baiting dogs, the Boston Terrier today, with its broad, flat head without wrinkles, large, round eyes, and sweet expression, is a well-tempered and patient companion dog. Brindle and white are the preferred coat colours. The breed is grouped into three categories depending on weight.

• **HISTORY** The Boston Terrier can be traced back to crosses involving bulldogs and terriers in the city of Boston some time in the 1800s.

• **REMARK** The broad head of this dog can lead to problems, pups sometimes becoming trapped in the birth canal.

COLOUR TYPES

small, thin ears set at corners of skull

large, round, dark, intelligent eyes

small, rounded feet with well-arched toes

Height 38–43cm (15–17in)	Weight 4.5–11.5kg (10–25lb)	Temperament Intelligent, lively

| ntry of origin Great Britain | First use Hunting badgers and otters | Origins 1800s |

AIREDALE TERRIER

The largest of all the terriers, the Airedale is a distinctive combination of black and tan in colour. Its wiry coat is dense and waterproof.

HISTORY This hardy breed evolved in southern Yorkshire, England. It is descended from an old type of terrier crossed with an Otter Hound.

REMARK The coat is shed twice a year and should be stripped on these occasions.

OTHER NAMES Waterside Terrier, Bingley Terrier.

long, flat skull

tops of ears extend above line of skull

deep chest

black saddle extends over top of tail and neck

small, rounded feet

| ght 56–61cm (22–24in) | Weight 20–23kg (44–50lb) | Temperament Intelligent, responsive |

| ntry of origin Great Britain | First use Hunting badgers and rats | Origins 1800s |

BEDLINGTON TERRIER

Lithe and graceful, with a lamb-like appearance, the Bedlington Terrier is unlikely to be confused with any other breed. In spite of its gentle appearance, however, it is tough and hardy.

HISTORY Wire-coated terriers crossed with Whippets (see p.151) and Dandie Dinmonts (see p.213) laid the foundations for the breed.

REMARK The coat requires regular trimming.

OTHER NAMES Rothbury Terrier.

COLOUR TYPES

silky "top-knot"

roached (sloping) back

long, hare-like feet

| ght 38–43cm (15–17in) | Weight 8–10kg (17–23lb) | Temperament Alert, affectionate |

Country of origin Great Britain	First use Ratting and rabbiting	Origins 1800s

ENGLISH TOY TERRIER

A miniature form of the Manchester Terrier (below), it can be distinguished primarily by its size and the erect carriage of the ears. Coloration is a vital feature of this breed, comprising jet-black and rich chestnut markings. Thin black lines, described as "pencilling", are present on the toes and pasterns.

- **HISTORY** This compact breed was developed from crossing the now extinct Black and Tan Terrier with the Italian Greyhound (see p.50).
- **REMARK** The ears are never cropped.
- **OTHER NAMES** Toy Manchester Terrier.

"candle flame" ears

strong, level bite

narrow, deep chest

dainty, arched feet

Height 25–30cm (10–12in)	Weight 3–4kg (6–8lb)	Temperament Lively, alert

Country of origin Great Britain	First use Ratting and rabbiting	Origins 1500s

MANCHESTER TERRIER

Evidence of Whippet (see p.151) is visible in this breed's elegant, roach back and the relatively straight shape of the nose.

- **HISTORY** The Manchester Terrier used to show great variation in size, and miniature versions became popular in the latter part of the last century, when the breed was first introduced to North America.
- **REMARK** A Manchester Terrier, called Billy, took just 6 minutes and 13 seconds to kill 100 rats in a contest held during the late 1800s.
- **OTHER NAMES** Black and Tan Terrier.

tan spots above eyes

tan markings should reach sides of nose

small, V-shaped ears

sleek coat

forelegs set well under dog

well-arched toes

tan markings on legs

Height 38–41cm (15–16in)	Weight 5–10kg (12–22lb)	Temperament Lively, attentive

Country of origin Great Britain	First use Hunting rats	Origins 1700s

BORDER TERRIER

The Border is one of the smallest of the terriers, standing only 25cm (10in) high. It is still able to keep up with horses when out fox-hunting, while its narrow body allows it to go to earth without difficulty. Its coat is durable enough to withstand the weather on the borders between Scotland and England. It is capable of confronting a fox or even the much tougher badger.

• **HISTORY** There is evidence of dogs similar to the Border Terrier in the 18th century, and the name is thought to come from the then-famous Border Hunt.

• **REMARK** A Border Terrier Club was established in 1921 and the breed is now widely distributed throughout the world.

small, V-shaped ears

otter-like head

powerful jaws

moderately short tail

deep, narrow body

muscular hindquarters

COLOUR TYPES

Height 25cm (10in)	Weight 5–7kg (11½–15½lb)	Temperament Plucky, alert

Country of origin Great Britain	First use Hunting rats	Origins 1800s

NORWICH TERRIER

This is one of the native terrier breeds of Norfolk, England, a region traditionally rich in game. The Norwich is readily distinguishable from the Norfolk Terrier (see p.214) by its alert, pricked ears. The coat is generally short and smooth on the head and ears. For its size it is a powerful dog, with a tight-lipped mouth and a scissor bite.

• **HISTORY** In the 19th century, the Norwich Terrier was the mascot of the students at Cambridge University, England.

• **REMARK** Tail docking is now optional in the case of this breed.

erect, pointed ears

slightly rounded, wide skull

strong neck

short, powerful legs and rounded feet

COLOUR TYPES

Height 25cm (10in)	Weight 5–5.5kg (11–12lb)	Temperament Alert, friendly

Country of origin Great Britain	First use Baiting bulls, ratting	Origins 1800s

MINIATURE BULL TERRIER

This breed is the smallest surviving version of the Bull Terrier (see p.239) and is still a strong reminder of its larger relative. The head is almost flat at the top of the skull and curves down to the tip of its powerful muzzle.

• **HISTORY** Common during the 1800s, its popularity waned until quite recently.

• **REMARK** The Miniature Bull Terrier delights in human company, but tends to be less tolerant towards other dogs.

small, thin ears

muscular neck

short, flat, glossy coat

powerful hindlegs

COLOUR TYPES

Height 25–35cm (10–14in)	Weight 11–15kg (24–33lb)	Temperament Fearless, determined

Country of origin Great Britain	First use Dog fighting, ratting	Origins 1800s

STAFFORDSHIRE BULL TERRIER

This smooth-coated breed gives the appearance of power and strength coupled with agility and athleticism. Coat coloration is very varied.

• **HISTORY** This powerful terrier originates from the county of Staffordshire, England, and its ancestry displays crossings with the Bulldog and a variety of terrier breeds.

• **REMARK** Although bred originally for dog fighting, its loyalty and devotion is legendary.

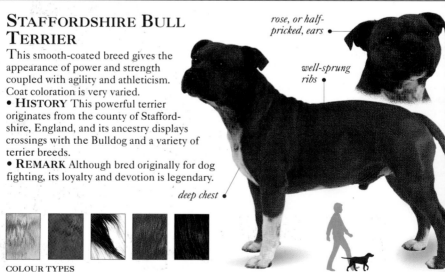

rose, or half-pricked, ears

well-sprung ribs

deep chest

COLOUR TYPES

Height 36–41cm (14–16in)	Weight 11–17kg (24–38lb)	Temperament Plucky, strong-willed

Country of origin Great Britain	First use Hunting badgers and rats	Origins 1600s

DANDIE DINMONT TERRIER

Distinguished by its "top-knot" of hair, this small terrier also has an unusual texture to its coat. This occurs because of a combination of hard and soft hair, which creates a crisp texture over much of the body. The underparts, however, are predominantly soft-haired.

• **HISTORY** This very old breed was probably developed by crossing Scottish and Skye Terriers.

• **REMARK** It is named after a character in Sir Walter Scott's book *Guy Mannering*.

very silky hair on head

pendulous ears

black nose

long, low body

COLOUR TYPES

Height 20–28cm (8–11in)	Weight 8–11kg (18–24lb)	Temperament Independent, lively

Country of origin Great Britain	First use Hunting foxes and rats	Origins 1500s

CAIRN TERRIER

Lively and fearless, this shaggy terrier is well adapted to working outdoors, and possesses a dense, double-layered, water-resistant coat. The head of a Cairn is broader and not as long as that of other terrier breeds, and the jaw is surprisingly powerful for a dog of this size.

• **HISTORY** The breed name was changed to Cairn Terrier only after 1909, before which it was called the Short-haired Skye Terrier. Cairn Terriers were originally used to drive foxes and other animals from rocky retreats. The breed was introduced into the USA in 1913.

• **REMARK** The Cairn Terrier is an excellent swimmer.

small, erect ears

strong, level jaw

front feet larger than hind feet

COLOUR TYPES

Height 25–30cm (10–12in)	Weight 6–7.5kg (13–16lb)	Temperament Bold, alert

| Country of origin Great Britain | First use Ratting, killing vermin | Origins 1700s |

LAKELAND TERRIER

Square-framed and solidly built, with a wiry, waterproof double coat, this sturdy terrier is equally content on the slopes of its Lake District ancestral home, in the north of England, as it is in the family home.

• **HISTORY** There used to be several strains of this terrier, known under a variety of names. They were grouped in 1912.

• **REMARK** Stingray of Derrybach, a Lakeland Terrier, was best in show at Crufts in 1967, and at the National Westminster Show, New York, in 1968.

small, V-shaped ears •

tail set high and usually docked •

• broad muzzle

• straight, well-boned forelegs

relatively • narrow chest

COLOUR TYPES

| Height 33–38cm (13–15in) | Weight 7–8kg (15–17lb) | Temperament Brave, hardy |

| Country of origin Great Britain | First use Ratting | Origins 1800s |

NORFOLK TERRIER

The Norfolk is distinguishable from its close relative, the Norwich Terrier (see p.211), by its drop ears, which are folded forwards. Its outercoat is hard and wiry and there is a thick undercoat beneath. White markings on the coat are considered an undesirable feature.

• **HISTORY** The Norfolk and Norwich Terrier breeds were inextricably linked until 1964, when the two breeds finally received separate recognition. They both seem to have developed as farm terriers in their East Anglian homeland in England.

• **REMARK** The British Kennel Club accepts "scars from fair wear and tear" in the breed's standard.

broad, and • slightly rounded skull

ears drop forwards close to • cheeks

tail can be docked, as • here

• wedge-shaped, strong muzzle

rougher and longer coat at shoulders

COLOUR TYPES

| Height 25–26cm (10–10¼in) | Weight 5–5.5kg (11–12lb) | Temperament Alert, friendly |

| untry of origin Great Britain | First use Going to ground and ratting | Origins 1800s |

PARSON JACK RUSSELL TERRIER

This active, robust, and well-known terrier has a predominantly white coat, which can occur in three forms: smooth-, broken-, and rough-coated. It is similar in appearance to the Fox Terrier (below).
• **HISTORY** The Reverend Jack Russell (nicknamed "the Hunting Parson"), from Devon, England, is credited with developing this breed.
• **REMARK** The Jack Russell Terrier often works with hounds, driving foxes from their lairs.

strong neck

tail docked to 10cm (4in)

muscular hindlegs

white blaze is common

COLOUR TYPES

| ight 23–38cm (9–15in) | Weight 5–8kg (12–18lb) | Temperament Alert, lively |

| untry of origin Great Britain | First use Hunting foxes | Origins 1700s |

WIRE FOX TERRIER

Similar to the smooth-coated breed (see p.216) in all but coat type, the Wire Fox Terrier should have a coat with a dense and wiry texture, without any traces of curls. It is actually double-layered, with a softer undercoat.
• **HISTORY** Breeds of terrier that are now extinct, notably the Wire-haired Terrier, contributed to the development of this dog.
• **REMARK** It takes considerable time to prepare the coat for show purposes.

short, level back

straight front legs

dark, round eyes

ears fold forward towards cheeks

COLOUR TYPES

| ight 39cm (15½in) | Weight 7–8kg (16–18lb) | Temperament Alert, determined |

| Country of origin Great Britain | First use Flushing foxes | Origins 1700s |

SMOOTH FOX TERRIER

Less well-known than its wire-haired relative (see p.215), the Smooth Fox Terrier is an easily recognized breed, with its short back and long, tapering muzzle. Its distinctive, short tail is set high and carried gaily. This dog is lively and alert, and will take any amount of exercise.
• **HISTORY** The origins of this terrier are not clear, although it was first recorded about 20 years after the appearance of the wire-haired form. The breed standard has not altered significantly in terms of type since 1876, except that today's dogs are somewhat lighter than their ancestors.
• **REMARK** White colouring should always predominate in the coat of this terrier.

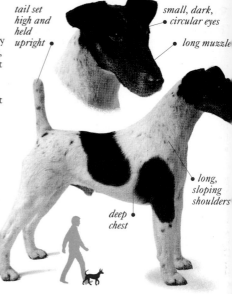

tail set high and held upright

small, dark, circular eyes

long muzzle

long, sloping shoulders

deep chest

COLOUR TYPES

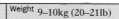

| Height 39cm (15½in) | Weight 7–8kg (16–18lb) | Temperament Alert, determined |

| Country of origin Great Britain | First use Hunting rats | Origins 1800s |

WELSH TERRIER

Often confused with the Lakeland Terrier (see p.214), the Welsh Terrier can be distinguished by its broader head and distinctive coloration. Black and tan is preferred, but black, grizzle, and tan is also permitted, provided there is no black pencilling on the toes.
• **HISTORY** The old Black and Tan Terrier contributed to the ancestry of this breed. It was first recognized by the Kennel Club in Britain in 1886, and was introduced to the USA two years later.
• **REMARK** It needs hand-stripping twice a year for show purposes.

flat top to head

small ears

long, sloping shoulders

powerful, muscular thighs

hard, wiry, thick coat

small, cat-like feet

COLOUR TYPES

| Height 36–39cm (14–15½in) | Weight 9–10kg (20–21lb) | Temperament Active, playful |

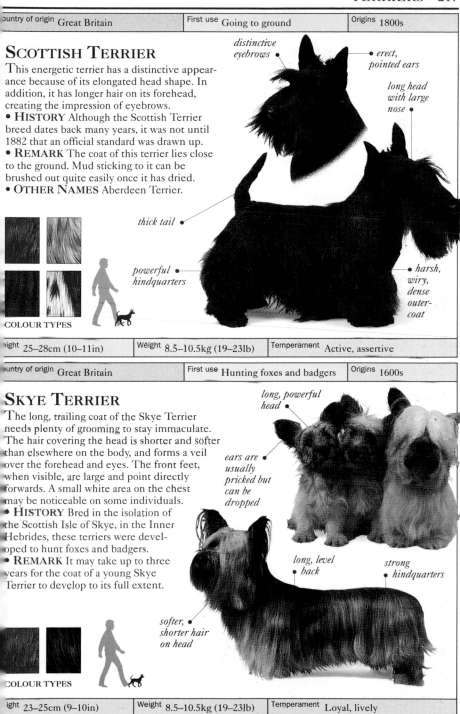

| Country of origin Great Britain | First use Going to ground | Origins 1800s |

SCOTTISH TERRIER

This energetic terrier has a distinctive appearance because of its elongated head shape. In addition, it has longer hair on its forehead, creating the impression of eyebrows.
• **HISTORY** Although the Scottish Terrier breed dates back many years, it was not until 1882 that an official standard was drawn up.
• **REMARK** The coat of this terrier lies close to the ground. Mud sticking to it can be brushed out quite easily once it has dried.
• **OTHER NAMES** Aberdeen Terrier.

distinctive eyebrows

erect, pointed ears

long head with large nose

thick tail

powerful hindquarters

harsh, wiry, dense outer-coat

COLOUR TYPES

| Height 25–28cm (10–11in) | Weight 8.5–10.5kg (19–23lb) | Temperament Active, assertive |

| Country of origin Great Britain | First use Hunting foxes and badgers | Origins 1600s |

SKYE TERRIER

The long, trailing coat of the Skye Terrier needs plenty of grooming to stay immaculate. The hair covering the head is shorter and softer than elsewhere on the body, and forms a veil over the forehead and eyes. The front feet, when visible, are large and point directly forwards. A small white area on the chest may be noticeable on some individuals.
• **HISTORY** Bred in the isolation of the Scottish Isle of Skye, in the Inner Hebrides, these terriers were developed to hunt foxes and badgers.
• **REMARK** It may take up to three years for the coat of a young Skye Terrier to develop to its full extent.

long, powerful head

ears are usually pricked but can be dropped

long, level back

strong hindquarters

softer, shorter hair on head

COLOUR TYPES

| Height 23–25cm (9–10in) | Weight 8.5–10.5kg (19–23lb) | Temperament Loyal, lively |

Country of origin Great Britain	First use Hunting rabbits	Origins 1700s

PATTERDALE TERRIER

Although only small in size, the Patterdale Terrier is a brave and tenacious working dog, with a short, coarse, weatherproof coat of black, black-and-tan, brown, or red coloration. This stocky, well-built dog retains the terrier's love of hunting.

• **HISTORY** Originating in the north of England, the breed is named after the Cumbrian village of Patterdale, where it was popular.

• **REMARK** These lively dogs need plenty of exercise.

• **OTHER NAMES** Black Fell Terrier.

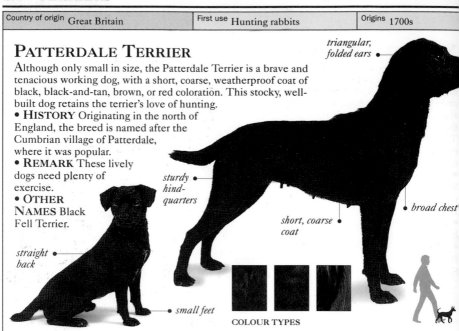

triangular, folded ears

sturdy hind-quarters

broad chest

short, coarse coat

straight back

small feet

COLOUR TYPES

Height 30cm (12in)	Weight 5–6kg (11–13lb)	Temperament Brave, enthusiastic

Country of origin Great Britain	First use Hunting rats	Origins 1800s

WEST HIGHLAND WHITE TERRIER

As its name implies, this terrier from the Western Highlands of Scotland is pure white in coloration. Its face is a little fox-like in appearance, and there is a pronounced stop to the nose

• **HISTORY** It is likely that all the Scottish terriers descended from a common ancestry in what was then a sparsely populated part of Great Britain. The dogs were first shown as Poltalloch Terriers – bred in a village of this name for over sixty years by a Colonel Malcolm.

• **REMARK** The thick coat needs a lot of attention.

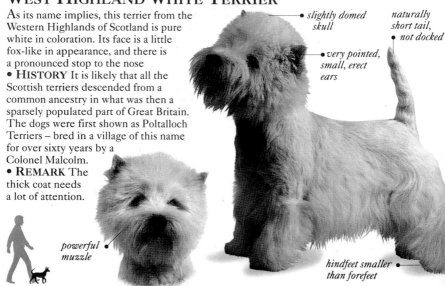

slightly domed skull

naturally short tail, not docked

very pointed, small, erect ears

powerful muzzle

hindfeet smaller than forefeet

Height 25–28cm (10–11in)	Weight 7–10kg (15–22lb)	Temperament Active, assertive

Country of origin	Great Britain	First use	Hunting rats	Origins	1800s

YORKSHIRE TERRIER

Apart from its diminutive size, the most
distinctive feature of this active little
terrier is its coat, which is steely blue in coloration with areas of golden tan on the head,
silky in texture, and sufficiently long to reach
the ground. When seen walking, the Yorkshire
Terrier can give the impression of being
mounted on wheels since its feet may
not be visible.

• HISTORY Developed by the miners of the
West Riding area of Yorkshire, this terrier is the
result of relatively recent crosses of the Skye,
Dandie Dinmont, and Maltese Terriers.

• REMARK New-born Yorkshire Terriers are
black in colour.

• OTHER NAMES
Broken-haired
Scottish Terrier.

small, flat-
topped head

dark,
sparkling eyes

short, level back

perfectly
straight, silky
body hair

rich, bright
tan-coloured
hair on chest

short, very rich,
deep-tan hair
on ears

medium-length
muzzle

very long
hair on
muzzle

round feet

straight limbs

Height	23cm (9in)	Weight	Less than 3kg (7lb)	Temperament	Intelligent, confident

Country of origin Great Britain	First use Hunting badgers and otters	Origins 1850s

SEALYHAM TERRIER

Although small, no more than 30cm (12in)
high, the Sealyham has powerful jaws, a
muscular neck, and strong legs. Its coat
is long and coarse, usually white or
yellowish-white in colour, and it must
be stripped by hand every six months
to remove dead hair.

• **HISTORY** This strong, determined
terrier is named after the village of
Sealyham, Wales, where it originated. The first breed club was
established there in 1908.

• **REMARK** Having been bred
to hunt badgers, the Sealyham
has kept its bold disposition
and active temperament.

long, powerful head

erect tail

deep, broad chest

rounded, cat-like feet

COLOUR TYPES

Height 25–30cm (10–12in)	Weight 8–9kg (18–20lb)	Temperament Strong-willed, active

Country of origin Australia	First use Working on farms	Origins 1800s

AUSTRALIAN TERRIER

This terrier used to be only blue
and tan in coloration, but shades of
red were introduced following crosses
with Cairn Terriers (see p.213).

• **HISTORY** Descended from
British terriers, it was originally
known as the Broken-coated Toy
Terrier. It was recognized by the
Kennel Club in 1936.

• **REMARK** Among
the smallest of the
working breeds, it
is still tough
enough to
tackle
snakes.

small ears

COLOUR TYPES

long body for its height

hard, straight hair

distinctive ruff

Height 25.5cm (10in)	Weight 4–7kg (12–14lb)	Temperament Feisty, dutiful

| untry of origin Australia | First use Companion | Origins 1800s |

AUSTRALIAN SILKY TERRIER

A compact and lightly built dog, the Australian Silky has typical terrier characteristics. Straight, silky body hair forms a natural parting along its moderately long, level back, and the ears are pricked and alert.
- **HISTORY** The Australian Silky was developed during the 1800s from British terriers, notably the Yorkshire Terrier (see p.219), and the Australian Terrier (see p.220).
- **REMARK** This dog was developed strictly as a companion dog.
- **OTHER NAMES** Silky Terrier, Sydney Silky.

skull broad between the ears

wedge-shaped skull

erect ears

moderately long, level back

silky hair may be 15cm (6in) long on the back

small cat-like feet

| ght 23cm (9in) | Weight 4–5kg (8–11lb) | Temperament Spirited, friendly |

| untry of origin Germany | First use Hunting rats and small game | Origins 1800s |

GERMAN HUNTING TERRIER

The cheeks of this relatively large terrier are full, the jaw powerful, and the teeth strong. Its dense coat is usually black or chocolate with tan markings, or t may be pure red. Both wire-haired and smooth-haired forms are found.
- **HISTORY** Despite being developed in Bavaria, its ancestry consists entirely of British terrier breeds, including Welsh and Fox Terriers.
- **REMARK** This breed is still strictly a working dog, renowned for its fine nose.
- **OTHER NAMES** Deutscher Jagdterrier.

triangular, folded ears

short, thick tail

powerful jaws and muzzle

well-muscled legs

large feet

COLOUR TYPES

| ght 41cm (16in) | Weight 9–10kg (20–22lb) | Temperament Keen, tenacious |

Country of origin Germany	First use Hunting rats	Origins 1800s

GERMAN PINSCHER

OFTEN bearing the black-and-tan markings of its relative, the
Doberman Pinscher (see p.250), the German, or Standard,
Pinscher is, however, also seen in dark brown and various shades
of fawn. It has the same elegance of bearing and cleanness of line
as the Doberman Pinscher, albeit without that dog's musculature
and aura of barely restrained power.

• HISTORY This native of Germany may be related to
the Black and Tan Terrier, as are the Doberman and
Miniature Pinschers (see p.223), although it has
never achieved the international popularity of the
other two breeds.

• REMARK This breed is large for a terrier and
so is most often used as a general farm hand.

• OTHER NAMES Standard
Pinscher.

cropped ears
are erect

well-arched
toes

natural, folded
position of ears

well-
muscled
neck

tail
traditionally
docked

deep chest

well-defined
colour markings

well-boned
forelegs

COLOUR RANGE

Height 41–48cm (16–19in)	Weight 11–16kg (25–35lb)	Temperament Alert, intelligent

| Country of origin Germany | First use Hunting rodents | Origins 1600s |

AFFENPINSCHER

A foreshortened muzzle, pronounced stop, large round eyes, erect ears, and fly-away head and facial hair all combine to give this little terrier a unique, rather impish appearance. The coat is variable in length, being longer on some parts of the body than others.
• **HISTORY** There is no precise record of the Affenpinscher's ancestry, although it contributed to the development of the better-known Brussels Griffon.
• **REMARK** Although small, this breed makes an excellent watch dog.

domed skull

blunt, short muzzle

straight, well-boned forelegs

distinct moustache

rough, harsh-textured coat

| Height 25cm (10in) | Weight 3–3¼kg (7–8lb) | Temperament Alert, quiet |

| Country of origin Germany | First use Hunting rats | Origins 1800s |

MINIATURE PINSCHER

This square-shaped, high-spirited terrier is sturdy and athletic and able to out-jump dogs far larger than itself. One of its most distinctive features is its hackney gait (characterized by pronounced flexion of the knee).
• **HISTORY** This ancient breed descended from traditional native German terriers. The German Pinscher Club was established in 1895 and the breed became standardized.
• **REMARK** This breed was known as the Reh Pinscher because of its resemblance to small roe deer (*reh* in German) living in German forests.
• **OTHER NAMES** Reh Pinscher, Zwergpinscher.

large, erect ears

narrow, tapering muzzle

very dark eyes

short, smooth coat, hard to the touch

powerful hindquarters

| Height 25–30cm (10–12in) | Weight 4–5kg (8–10lb) | Temperament Lively, alert |

Country of origin Germany	First use Ratting	Origins 1400s

MINIATURE SCHNAUZER

This dog has the general appearance and all the appealing features of its full-sized brethren (see p.122) – bushy eyebrows, bristly, stubby moustache, and chin whiskers. It is very nearly square in profile, with a straight and level back and well-developed thighs. The ears may be cropped in the USA.

• **HISTORY** This miniature form of schnauzer is thought to have evolved from crossings of the Standard Schnauzer and Affenpinschers. The breed was first seen in Britain in 1928. Its diminutive size makes it an excellent ratter.

• **REMARK** The coat of this terrier must be stripped at least twice a year, and regularly groomed to remove dead hairs. Its whiskers and longer hair should be combed every day.

• **OTHER NAMES** Zwergschnauzer.

prominent black nose and wide nostrils

strong, straight back, slightly higher at shoulders than hindquarters

dark, oval eyes set beneath bushy eyebrows

forelegs appear straight from every angle

V-shaped ears, high on head, hanging forwards to temples

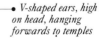

COLOUR TYPES

Height 33–36cm (13–14in)	Weight 6–7kg (13–15lb)	Temperament Lively, very friendly

Country of origin Germany	First use Watchdog, companion	Origins 1945

KROMFOHRLÄNDER

Of powerful build, this attractive terrier has been bred in a wire-coated form, which is the most common, and in a less popular, straight-haired form. Coloration is a significant feature, being a combination of white and tan in various shades. There is often a tan area on the head, and another on the back which forms a saddle-type patch.

• **HISTORY** At the end of the Second World War, American soldiers entering the town of Siegen in Westphalia, Germany, brought with them a tawny-coloured dog of griffon type. They gave it to a local resident called Frau Schleifenbaum, and it mated with a terrier. Frau Schleifenbaum decided to form a breed from the resulting puppies.

• **REMARK** The Kromfohrländer was first recognized by the German Kennel Club in 1953.

balanced markings are desirable

muzzle tapers along its length

STRAIGHT-HAIRED FORM

ears are positioned high on head

medium-length coat

dark, oval-shaped eyes

WIRE-HAIRED FORM

wedge-shaped head

deep chest

straight, sturdy front legs

strong hindlegs

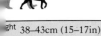

Height 38–43cm (15–17in)	Weight 12kg (26lb)	Temperament Affectionate, alert

Country of origin Ireland	First use Watchdog	Origins 1700s

IRISH TERRIER

Of unmistakable terrier appearance, with a harsh coat, the long-legged Irish Terrier is somewhat reminiscent of the larger Airedale (see p.209). It has an active, lively nature. Good-tempered towards people, it is not generally well-disposed towards other dogs.

• HISTORY Crossings involving the old Black and Tan and Wheaten Terriers may have laid the foundations of this breed, which originated in County Cork, Ireland. Standardization occurred only in 1879 when a breed club was established.

• REMARK Hand clipping of the coat is required to maintain the graceful outline of these terriers.

• OTHER NAMES Irish Red Terrier.

long head, and stop visible only in profile

small, V-shaped ears falling close to cheeks

long, powerful, muscular jaws

moderately long neck widening towards shoulders

tail traditionally docked to three-quarters of full length

deep, muscular chest

perfectly straight forelegs

dense, crisp hair on legs

small, dark eyes

arched toes with black nails

Height 46–48cm (18–19in)	Weight 11–12kg (25–27lb)	Temperament Determined, friendly

untry of origin Ireland	First use Herding cattle, ratting	Origins 1700s

SOFT-COATED WHEATEN TERRIER

This terrier has a distinctive coat, which is not shed. It needs thorough grooming daily to prevent matting. The coat colour is described as "wheaten", because it should match the colour of ripening wheat. Whitish or reddish tones are not acceptable. Pups may have darker markings on their coats, however, which should disappear by two years of age. The adult coat hangs either in loose waves or in large, light curls.

• **HISTORY** This is believed to be the oldest terrier breed in Ireland, most common in the vicinity of Kerry (where it gave rise to the Kerry Blue Terrier) and Cork, but its precise origins are unknown. When working, the Soft-coated Wheaten Terrier is an adept badger and otter hunter.

• **REMARK** Training requires a little effort, but the results are worth it.

long hair on head falls forwards • *over eyes*

tight, black lips •

large black nose •

V-shaped, folded ears •

moderately long, strong, • *muscular neck*

upright, docked tail, set high on back •

square-shaped muzzle with strong jaws •

strong, muscular thighs •

powerful feet with black toenails •

deep chest •

ight 46–48cm (18–19in)	Weight 16–20kg (35–45lb)	Temperament Lively, loyal, energetic

Country of origin Ireland	First use Hunting vermin	Origins 1700s

GLEN OF IMAAL TERRIER

The body of this terrier is relatively long compared with its height, and its coat is of medium length. It is both agile and silent when working, factors that allow it to strike its quarry unexpectedly.

• HISTORY This dog is named after the Glen of Imaal in County Wicklow, Ireland, where it was first recognized in 1933.

• REMARK This is a hardy, working terrier breed, well able to deal with badgers as well as the more typical terrier fare, such as rats.

round, brown eyes

harsh outercoat

ears back when relaxed

strong feet with rounded pads

front feet turn out slightly

Height 36cm (14in)	Weight 16kg (35lb)	Temperament Determined, brave

Country of origin Ireland	First use Hunting vermin	Origins 1800s

KERRY BLUE TERRIER

The appearance of pups of this breed differs greatly from that of adult dogs because they are born with black coats. It can take up to 18 months before young dogs acquire the characteristic blue adult coloration. Dark points may also be seen in adult dogs.

• HISTORY Originating in County Kerry, in the southwest of Ireland, this terrier is thought to be descended from Welsh, Bedlington, and Soft-coated Wheaten Terrier stock.

• REMARK The silky coat of these terriers is not shed, and needs daily attention.

V-shaped ears hang forward on head

tail set high and carried erect

long, lean head with powerful jaws

straight forelegs

small, rounded feet with black nails

Height 46–48cm (18–19in)	Weight 15–17kg (33–37lb)	Temperament Determined, friendly

untry of origin Belgium	First use Hunting vermin	Origins 1800s

GRIFFON BRUXELLOIS

There is considerable confusion over the nomenclature of this dog, which is shown as one breed in North America and the UK, but which is separated into three types in Europe. The Brussels Griffon can be distinguished from the Belgian Griffon by its red coloration, although both have long coats. In contrast, the Petit Brabancon has a short coat.
- **HISTORY** It is thought that the Affenpinscher may have been involved in the ancestry of this dog. Other breeds, such as the Pug, may also have played a part in its development.
- **REMARK** The ears of this dog are commonly cropped in North America, and its tail is docked.
- **OTHER NAMES** Griffon Belge.

PETIT BRABANCON

- *semi-erect, small, high-set ears*
- *short coat*

- *slight arch to neck*
- *very dark, large, round eyes*
- *tail set high and held erect*

BELGIAN GRIFFON

- *short, tight coat*
- *straight, medium-length legs*

- *head is large in relation to body*

- *harsh, wiry coat with no hint of a curl*

BRUSSELS GRIFFON

COLOUR TYPES

ght 18–20cm (7–8in)	Weight 2.5–5.5kg (6–12lb)	Temperament Lively, obedient

Country of origin Austria	First use Ratting, watchdog	Origins 1800s

AUSTRIAN PINSCHER

This small dog displays typical pinscher characteristics. Seen from the front, it has a very broad chest, suggesting greater width than height.

• **HISTORY** Although related to other European terrier breeds, it has never been particularly common outside Austria.

• **REMARK** The Austrian Pinscher proves to be an alert and noisy guardian, but is often given to persistent barking.

• **OTHER NAMES** Österreichischer Kurzhaariger Pinscher.

small ears sometimes pricked

very broad, powerful chest

fringes of hair on belly

muscular legs

COLOUR TYPES

Height 36–51cm (14–20in)	Weight 12–18kg (26–40lb)	Temperament Bold, alert

Country of origin Czechoslovakia	First use Watchdog	Origins 1940s

CESKY TERRIER

Sporting a distinctive, silky coat and a fine beard and eyebrows, this graceful little terrier is robust and agile. It has a long head with a large nose.

• **HISTORY** This loyal breed was developed by the Czechoslovakian geneticist, Dr. F. Horàk. It was officially recognized in 1963.

• **REMARK** The Cesky is good with children and makes a fine watchdog. It is now becoming popular in the USA.

• **OTHER NAMES** Czesky, Bohemian Terrier.

long head

coat is clipped

sturdy legs

profuse beard

silky coat

COLOUR TYPE

Height 25–36cm (10–14in)	Weight 5.5–8kg (12–18lb)	Temperament Good-natured, obedient

WORKING DOGS

THE DIVERSITY IN APPEARANCE of the many breeds of working dogs reflects the variety of tasks they have performed throughout history. For thousands of years, man has exploited the dog's powerful territorial instinct to protect his own property from intruders. This basic function was mythologized by the Ancient Greeks in the form of Cerberus, the fearsome guardian at the gates of Hades. But the dog has other, more specialized, functions: seeing for the blind; hearing for the deaf; rescuing the injured; transporting man and his cargo across Arctic terrain. As man made ready to enter the Space Age, it was the dog he sent before him to prepare the way.

Country of origin USA	First use Guarding farms, fighting	Origins 1700s

AMERICAN BULLDOG

This powerful dog is thought to be similar to the old form of 16th-century British bulldog, a breed used for bull-baiting. The head of the American Bulldog is large, and the neck and shoulders hugely muscled.
• **HISTORY** Settlers brought the original bulldog stock from Britain, and their versatility as hunters and farm dogs ensured their popularity in the USA.
• **REMARK** The American Bulldog is still very much a working dog and so there is a wider variation in height and weight than there is with its British counterpart which has become a companion and show breed.
• **OTHER NAMES** Old Country Bulldog.

long, square skull

very powerful jaws

thick, powerful neck and shoulders

short, shiny, hard coat

angulated, parallel hindlegs

straight, well-muscled forelegs

more than half the coat should be white, with patches of colour

COLOUR TYPES

Height 48–71cm (19–28in)	Weight 30–58kg (65–130lb)	Temperament Bold, lively

Country of origin USA	First use Baiting bulls, guard dog	Origins 1900s

OLDE ENGLISH BULLDOGGE

This powerfully built, medium-sized, mastiff-type dog is the result of American breeders' attempts to produce a traditional image of the old-style English Bulldog, while eliminating breed weaknesses such as breathing difficulties.
• **HISTORY** This form of dog is said to be the result of a breeding programme carried out by David Leavitt in Pennsylvania, USA, involving Bullmastiffs (see p.238), the Bulldog itself (see p.39), American Bulldogs (see p.231), and American Pit Bull Terriers (see p.207).
• **REMARK** Although a large, fierce-looking dog, the aim of the breeding programme has been to produce a determined and courageous dog, yet one that is not aggressive.

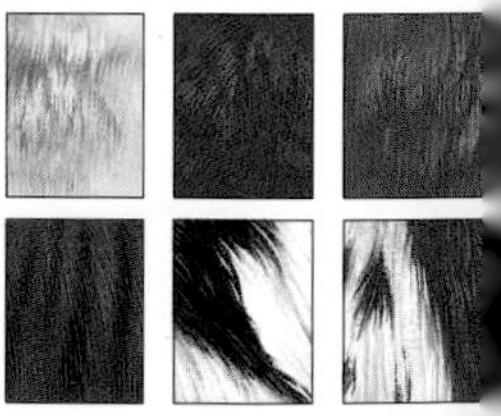

powerful, broad, mastiff-type head

double-folded dewlap

short, broad muzzle with prominent stop

semi-pendulous flews

thick, powerful neck

rose or button-style ears

well-boned, straight forelegs

short, close coat

COLOUR TYPES

Height 51–64cm (20–25in)	Weight 29.5–48kg (65–105lb)	Temperament Bold, friendly

Country of origin USA	First use Pulling sledges	Origins 1900s

CHINOOK

The tawny coloration is characteristic of this breed. Seen from the side it has a square profile, emphasizing its great strength. The thick, double coat of the Chinook becomes thinner during the hot summer months.

• **HISTORY** Developed as a sledge dog by breeder Arthur Walden, the Chinook was derived from crossings involving Eskimo Dogs (see p.239), smooth-coated St. Bernards (see p.273) and Belgian shepherd dogs (see pp.126–29).

• **REMARK** Fewer than 200 known individuals of this breed exist today.

pendent ears are preferred

heavily muscled hindquarters

broad, deep, strong chest

thickly cushioned pads on feet

Height 53–66cm (21–26in)	Weight 29.5–41kg (65–90lb)	Temperament Strong, determined

Country of origin USA	First use Herding, hunting	Origins 1000BC

CAROLINA DOG

This dog is similar in appearance to other pariah-type dogs, such as the Dingo, seen in other parts of the world. The Carolina Dog has a dense, yellowish gold coat and a strong, prominently boned head and face.

• **HISTORY** This breed could be similar to the earliest types of dog seen in North America. Formerly kept by American Indians, the Carolina Dog is now best known in the southern states of the USA.

• **REMARK** Some Carolina Dogs are semi-wild, but pups can easily be trained to herd stock or hunt small prey.

large, triangular-shaped ears

thick neck and broad chest

straight forelegs

tail reaches to level of hocks

Height 56cm (22in)	Weight 13.5–18kg (30–40lb)	Temperament Active, reserved

Country of origin USA	First use Pulling sledges	Origins 3000BC

ALASKAN MALAMUTE

Powerful and strong, this northern dog has been developed for stamina rather than speed, unlike some of the smaller breeds from this part of the world. Its dense, double-layered coat affords excellent protection from the often severe elements, having coarse outer guard hairs over a thick, oily, woolly undercoat. The length of the guard hairs varies, becoming longest over the shoulders and in the vicinity of the neck, as well as down the back. The colour ranges from light grey through intermediate shades to black, or from gold through shades of red to liver.

- **HISTORY** The breed is named after the Malhemut tribe, an Inuit people who lived in the northwest of Alaska. They were nomadic, and the dogs were used to haul their possessions between locations.
- **REMARK** Due to its size and considerable strength, firm training from an early age is essential. It still retains something of a pack instinct, which may lead to outbreaks of aggressive behaviour when it is in the company of other dogs. However, by nature it is friendly and affectionate to people.

powerful hindquarters •

large, prominent muzzle •

weather-resistant double coat •

• *moderately b stifles*

• *broad, strong hocks*

• *tough, thick pads*

Height 58–71cm (23–28in)	Weight 39–57kg (85–125lb)	Temperament Active, exuberant

ears are small
in relation to
size of head

brown, almond-
shaped eyes which
may be lighter in
red or white dogs

powerful neck

body is somewhat
longer than dog's
height

broad jaws with
large teeth

longer guard
hairs around
shoulders
and neck

white coloration
dominates lower
part of body

strong,
deep chest

large,
compact feet

Country of origin Great Britain	First use Guard dog	Origins 1000BC

MASTIFF

This grand, ancient breed is powerfully built, well-boned, and extremely muscular. The Mastiff is renowned for its great courage and guarding instincts. Its massive size is an important feature of this dog, combined with a symmetrical, well-knit frame. The head should appear square when viewed from any angle. In spite of its ferocious appearance, the Mastiff is responsive and docile in temperament, although it is a reliable guardian which does not take kindly to intruders.

• **HISTORY** Mastiffs were documented in Britain at the time of the Roman invasion: Julius Caesar acknowledged their bravery in battle. Later, at the Battle of Agincourt in 1415, Sir Peers Legh's body was guarded by his Mastiff as the battle raged. On returning to England, it reputedly started the famous Lyme Hall bloodline. Mastiffs nearly died out during the Second World War, but have since recovered in number.

• **REMARK** Renowned for its intelligence, this breed requires plenty of human contact. Potential owners should therefore have a great deal of time for their dog. The Mastiff also requires lots of space and exercise.

broad skull with flat forehead

large, rounded feet

high-set tail, wide at base and tapering along length

ears positioned at highest point on sides of skull

square head

short, close-lying coat

Height 70–76cm (27½–30in)	Weight 79–86kg (175–190lb)	Temperament Loyal, alert

very powerful
hindquarters

forehead wrinkles
when attention is
excited

ears lying flat and
close to cheeks

very muscular and
slightly arched neck

great depth in the
flanks, emphasizing
the powerful build

strong, straight
legs

black hair extends
over the muzzle,
nose, and around the
eyes, irrespective of
the dog's coloration

Country of origin Great Britain	First use Guarding estates	Origins 1800s

BULLMASTIFF

The powerful, active Bullmastiff can easily be distinguished from the Mastiff (see pp.236–37) by its smaller size and its more compact face. The American Bull-mastiff tends to be more Mastiff-like than its British counterpart. Originally, dark-coloured brindle was the favoured coloration, but today fawns and reds are popular.

• **HISTORY** Crossings between Mastiffs and bulldogs gave rise to the Bullmastiff, which is sometimes known as "the gamekeeper's dog". It was bred specifically to accompany gamekeepers on their rounds, being able to track well and having sufficient size and strength to tackle and overpower a poacher.

• **REMARK** As is the case with other large breeds, pups may seem clumsy and uncoordinated when very young. Once mature, there should be no evidence of awkwardness in the way they move.

large, square-shaped skull

short muzzle

short, hard coat lying close against body

muscular shoulders

black muzzle is essential

short, straight back

tail is set high on back and tapers along its length

wide, deep chest

well-spaced, powerful legs

well-arched, rounded toes

COLOUR TYPES

Height 64–69cm (25–27in)	Weight 41–59kg (90–130lb)	Temperament Loyal, fearless

ountry of origin Great Britain	First use Bull-baiting	Origins 1800s

BULL TERRIER

The most obvious features of this powerful breed are its very long, oval-shaped head with no stop; small, triangular eyes; thin, erect ears; and tight-fitting coat over a large-boned and muscular physique.
• **HISTORY** The Bull Terrier was developed from crosses with the bulldog and Old English Terrier.
• **REMARK** It may not get on well with other dogs.
• **OTHER NAME** English Bull Terrier.

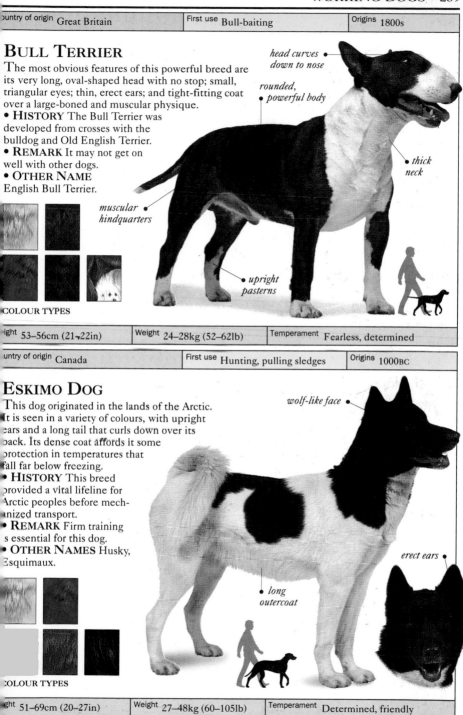

head curves down to nose

rounded, powerful body

thick neck

muscular hindquarters

upright pasterns

COLOUR TYPES

ight 53–56cm (21–22in)	Weight 24–28kg (52–62lb)	Temperament Fearless, determined

untry of origin Canada	First use Hunting, pulling sledges	Origins 1000BC

ESKIMO DOG

This dog originated in the lands of the Arctic. It is seen in a variety of colours, with upright ears and a long tail that curls down over its back. Its dense coat affords it some protection in temperatures that fall far below freezing.
• **HISTORY** This breed provided a vital lifeline for Arctic peoples before mech-anized transport.
• **REMARK** Firm training s essential for this dog.
• **OTHER NAMES** Husky, Esquimaux.

wolf-like face

erect ears

long outercoat

COLOUR TYPES

ght 51–69cm (20–27in)	Weight 27–48kg (60–105lb)	Temperament Determined, friendly

Country of origin Canada	First use Helping fishermen	Origins 1700s

NEWFOUNDLAND

THIS massive, imposing dog looks rather like a bear cub as a puppy.
In spite of its size, the adult Newfoundland is usually gentle and
affectionate. However, it can prove to be a loyal household guard
if necessary. Its distinctive, oily coat is highly water-resistant, and
falls back naturally into place if groomed against the lie of the fur.

• **HISTORY** The earliest Newfoundland originated
in northeastern Canada. It is thought to be descended
from dogs brought by European colonists, although
native Americans may have had
mastiff-type dogs.

• **REMARK** It was
originally used to
help fishermen
haul in nets.

coat is flat,
quite coarse,
and dense •

• very powerful
hindquarters

straight forelegs
with feathering
behind, right
down to paws •

large, powerful,
• webbed feet

Height 66–71cm (26–28in)	Weight 50–68kg (110–150lb)	Temperament Responsive, docile

small, dark brown,
wide-set eyes

dull black
coloration

short, square
muzzle

broad and
massive skull

small,
close-lying
ears

strong neck

Country of origin Argentina	First use Hunting pumas and jaguars	Origins 1920s

DOGO ARGENTINO

One of the few breeds developed in South
America, the Dogo Argentino is a powerful dog,
invariably white in colour. It has a strong, square-
shaped head, indicative of mastiff origins.
Notorious for its aggressive, fearless nature, it was
originally used to pursue big cats in its homeland.
It is, nevertheless, reputedly trustworthy with
people and is exceptionally loyal.

• **HISTORY** The breed is descended from the
Old Fighting Dog, which originated in Spain.
Crosses with other breeds, most notably the
Boxer (see p.255), took place under the guidance
of the breed's founder, Dr. Antonio Martinez, to
produce a more biddable temperament.

• **REMARK** This dog is banned in Great Britain
due to concerns about its temperament.

• **OTHER NAMES**
Argentinian Mastiff.

ears are
invariably
cropped

broad jaws

short, sleek
coat

relatively
long tail

long,
straight
forelegs

traces of
pigment on
skin may be
visible
through hair

powerful
hindlegs

Height 61–69cm (24–27in)	Weight 36–45kg (80–100lb)	Temperament Bold, brave

Country of origin Brazil	First use Hunting big game	Origins 1800s

FILA BRASILEIRO

The result of the combination of powerful mastiff stock with the Bloodhound (see pp.166–167), the Fila Brasileiro displays distinctive folds of skin on its huge head, which extend on to the neck. Further links with the Bloodhound can be detected from its unerring sense of smell and elongated muzzle.
• **HISTORY** Aggression was first bred into the Fila Brasileiro for bringing down wild cats and for controlling cattle.
• **REMARK** This fearsome breed was also used for tracking down escaped slaves.
• **OTHER NAMES** Brazilian Mastiff.

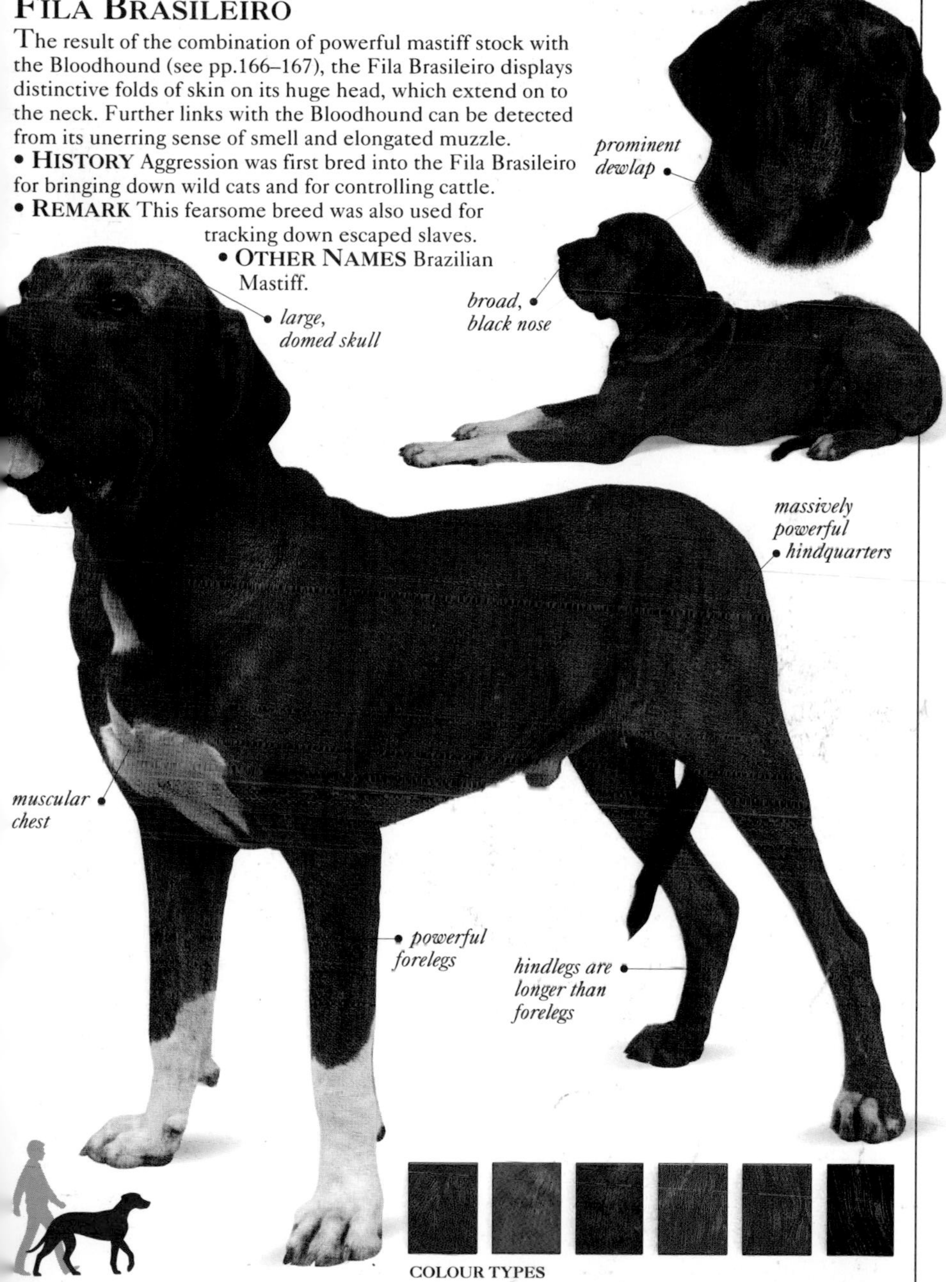

prominent dewlap

large, domed skull

broad, black nose

massively powerful hindquarters

muscular chest

powerful forelegs

hindlegs are longer than forelegs

COLOUR TYPES

ight 61–76cm (24–30in)	Weight 41–50kg (90–110lb)	Temperament Bold, aggressive

Country of origin Greenland	First use Pulling sledges	Origins 1500s

GREENLAND DOG

The Greenland Dog is generally taller than the Eskimo Dog (see p.239), but slightly lighter and shorter in the back. So close is the relationship between these breeds, however, that they are judged to the same standard in some countries.

• **HISTORY** Thought by some to be descended from Arctic wolves, this dog is superbly adapted to survival in the harsh conditions found in that region. Many local forms of this type of dog were bred in the Arctic regions before mechanized transport was introduced.

• **REMARK** As a hunter, the Greenland can track the breathing holes of seals in the ice.

• **OTHER NAMES** Grønlandshund, Grünlandshund.

broad, wedge-shaped head

strong jaws

small, triangular-shaped ears

large, well-spread feet

large, bushy tail curls to one side over back

broad chest

colour is highly variable between individuals

straight, powerful forelegs

COLOUR TYPES

Height 56–64cm (22–25in)	Weight 30–32kg (66–70lb)	Temperament Affectionate, independent

Country of origin Norway	First use Hunting elk	Origins 1000s

NORWEGIAN ELKHOUND

Bred as a specialist hunter of elk, this dog is large and powerfully built. Its heavily muscled body is compact, giving it a rather stocky appearance, an impression that is reinforced by a dense covering of grey hair. A black form also exists (below).
• **HISTORY** Skeletons of Stone Age dogs closely resembling Elkhounds have been unearthed in Scandinavia.
• **REMARK** This is a very friendly dog and makes an excellent companion.
• **OTHER NAMES** Norsk Elghund (Grå), Elkhound.

grey coat with black tips

tightly curled tail

powerful hindquarters

large, dark eyes

well-boned legs

darker hair on muzzle

Height 49–52cm (19–21in)	Weight 20–23kg (44–50lb)	Temperament Alert, friendly

Country of origin Norway	First use Hunting elk	Origins 1000s

BLACK NORWEGIAN ELKHOUND

This dog is the black form of the more common grey Norwegian Elkhound (above). Apart from its comparative rarity, it is essentially the same dog, except a little smaller and lighter.
• **HISTORY** The Norwegian Elkhounds are thought to have changed little since they first became human companions over a thousand years ago.
• **REMARK** It can scent an elk over a distance of several kilometres.
• **OTHER NAMES** Norsk Elghund (Sort).

pointed, mobile ears

glossy black coat

thick, coarse hair

straight forelegs

conical head

strong jaws

Height 46–51cm (18–20in)	Weight 18kg (40lb)	Temperament Alert, friendly

Country of origin Norway	First use Hunting puffins	Origins 1500s

LUNDEHUND

A neat, compact build characterizes this strong and industrious breed. Its specialized breeding has resulted in well-developed feet, additional toes, and extra joints to aid it in its traditional job of scaling cliff faces in search of puffins. This very agile dog can bend its head horizontally backwards almost to touch its back.

shortish, rough coat

• HISTORY The breed was used for centuries along the coasts of Norway. The Lundehund went into decline, however, along with the popularity of puffin hunting, and at one point there were only 50 individuals known to exist.

at least six toes on each foot

• REMARK The Lundehund can close its ears to keep out water.

• OTHER NAMES Norwegian Puffin Dog.

COLOUR TYPES

Height 31–39cm (12–15½in)	Weight 6kg (13–14lb)	Temperament Lively, alert

Country of origin Norway	First use Herding stock	Origins 800s

NORWEGIAN BUHUND

This dog shows typical spitz characteristics, as do many northern European breeds. It has erect, pointed ears, a powerful, stocky body, and a tail curling up and forwards over its body.

COLOUR TYPES

• HISTORY The Buhund was developed primarily for farm work, undertaking a variety of tasks. Its herding instinct is so ingrained that it will even round up chickens.

• REMARK The name comes from the Norwegian word *bu*, meaning "shed", or "stall".

• OTHER NAMES Norsk Buhund.

short, dense outercoat

tail set high on back

deep chest

quite small, oval feet

Height 43–46cm (17–18in)	Weight 24–26kg (53–58lb)	Temperament Brave, companionable

| Country of origin | Finland | First use | Hunting birds and game | Origins | 1800s |

FINNISH SPITZ

An alert, pointed face and a reddish brown or red-gold coloration give this member of the spitz family a distinctly fox-like appearance.
• **HISTORY** A standard for the Finnish Spitz was established in 1812. Originally the dog was used for hunting birds and small game.
• **REMARK** In contests, dogs bark to indicate the presence of game and are marked on the number of barks per minute, which can be as many as 160.
• **OTHER NAMES** Suomenpystykorva, Finsk Spets.

dark, almond-shaped eyes

plumed tail curves forwards and around the thigh

deep chest and strong, straight forequarters

outercoat is longer and coarser on shoulders

round feet

| Height | 38–51cm (15–20in) | Weight | 14–16kg (31–35lb) | Temperament | Lively, vocal |

| Country of origin | Finland | First use | Hunting large game | Origins | 1600s |

KARELIAN BEAR DOG

Robust and lively, this breed has a very distinctive coloration – predominantly black with white markings on its face, neck, chest, abdomen, feet, and tail.
• **HISTORY** This breed was named after the Karelia province of Finland. It was first recognized by the Finnish Kennel Club in 1935.
• **REMARK** After a decline in the 1960s, it is now increasing in numbers worldwide.
• **OTHER NAMES** Björnhund, Karjalankarhukoira.

wedge-shaped head

fully arched tail preferred, though bobtails do exist

characteristic white tip on tail

strong chest

white blaze on face

thick, tall, rounded paws

| Height | 48–58cm (18–23in) | Weight | 20–23kg (44–50lb) | Temperament | Brave, determined |

Country of origin Sweden	First use Hunting elk	Origins 1000s

SWEDISH ELKHOUND

This is the largest and most powerful of the elkhound-type breeds native to Scandinavia. The Swedish Elkhound has an elongated, rather narrow head, and this, combined with a straight muzzle, gives it a slightly fox-like appearance. The coat of this breed consists of a long, hard outercoat and a dense, woolly, much softer undercoat.

• HISTORY The forebears of the Swedish Elkhound may have accompanied Stone Age people in the Scandinavian region of the world. Certainly this specific breed has been known for centuries, even though it was not officially recognized by the Swedish Kennel Club until 1946.

• REMARK Best known in the Jämtland area of Sweden, the Swedish Elkhound is designed for living in cold climates.

• OTHER NAMES Jämthund.

• large, erect, pointed ears

• small, dark eyes

tail curls tightly over back and rests on one side

broad, muscular shoulders •

• deep, powerful chest

heavily • muscled hindlegs

hard, long • outercoat over woolly undercoat

Height 58–64cm (23–25in)	Weight 30kg (66lb)	Temperament Friendly, alert

Country of origin Sweden	First use Herding reindeer	Origins 1800s

SWEDISH LAPPHUND

This medium-sized dog shows typical spitz characteristics in terms of its fox-like facial appearance and dramatically curving tail. It is protected from the cold of its homeland by a dense, woolly, double coat.

• **HISTORY** The ancestors of this breed were kept by the Lapps to herd reindeer, although they have since been adapted to working sheep. The breed was officially recognized in Sweden in 1944.

• **REMARK** This dog tends to be solid in colour although individuals with white markings are seen and not penalized.

• **OTHER NAMES** Lapplandska Spets.

short, erect ears

dark, chestnut-coloured eyes

plumed tail hangs forwards

harsh, thick coat

feathering on legs and body

COLOUR TYPES

Height 17½–19½in (44–49cm)	Weight 20kg (44lb)	Temperament Lively, alert

Country of origin Sweden	First use Hunting birds	Origins 1600s

NORRBOTTENSPETS

The Norrbottenspets is one of the smaller spitz breeds, distinguishable from other spitzes by its relatively short coat, which is dense and stands away from the body. Its ears are pointed and erect, its muzzle is pointed, and its eyes are alert and lively.

• **HISTORY** The breed was close to extinction in 1948, but enthusiasts sought out the last few remaining dogs and bitches and started a successful breeding programme.

• **REMARK** The Norbottenspets was once widely kept in Sweden as a hunting dog.

• **OTHER NAMES** Pohjanpystykorva, Nordic Spitz.

erect, triangular ears

short, stand-off coat

any coloured areas must be well defined

straight, muscular forelegs

white is the dominant colour

COLOUR TYPES

Height 41–43cm (16–17in)	Weight 12–15kg (26–33lb)	Temperament Quiet, affectionate

Country of origin Germany	First use Guard dog	Origins 1800s

DOBERMANN

This medium-sized mastiff breed
has a sculpted, elegant appearance.
It is sleek, well-muscled, and powerful, and is usually black and tan in
coloration. The Dobermann is a bold,
alert dog with a great deal of stamina.
• **HISTORY** This breed of dog was developed by a German tax collector, Ludwig
Dobermann, to act as a deterrent against thieves
and muggers, as well as aggrieved tax-payers. He used
a variety of breeds, including the German Shepherd Dog,
Rottweiler, German Pinscher, and Manchester Terrier.
• **REMARK** The Dobermann once had a particular reputation
for aggression. Although this has now been curbed to a great
extent, firm training is still necessary from puppyhood.
• **OTHER NAMES** Doberman Pinscher.

flat top to skull

*lean,
relatively long
neck*

*almond-shaped eyes,
no lighter than coat
colour*

*powerful jaws
and well-filled
face*

Height 65–69cm (25½–27in)	Weight 30–40kg (66–88lb)	Temperament Bold, fearless

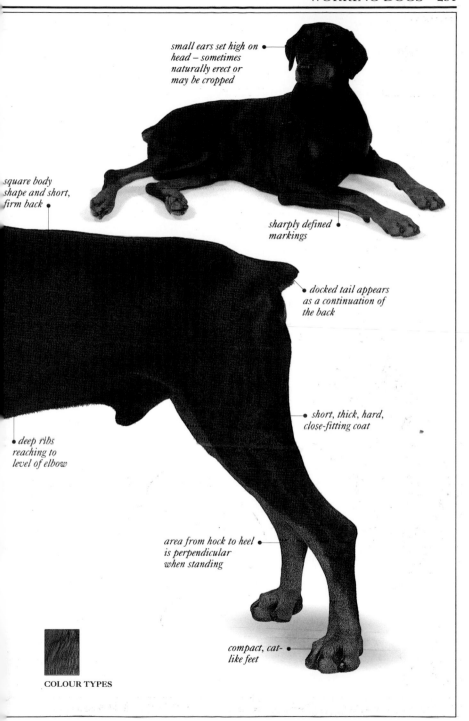

small ears set high on head – sometimes naturally erect or may be cropped

square body shape and short, firm back

sharply defined markings

docked tail appears as a continuation of the back

short, thick, hard, close-fitting coat

deep ribs reaching to level of elbow

area from hock to heel is perpendicular when standing

compact, cat-like feet

COLOUR TYPES

Country of origin Germany	First use Hunting large game	Origins 2000BC

GREAT DANE

A gentle giant, the Great Dane combines enormous size and strength with equal proportions of dignity and elegance. It has a long, well-chiselled face with a distinctive, intelligent expression. It comes in a variety of colours including black, blue, brindle, fawn, and a striking harlequin. The breed is often seen with cropped ears in North America, giving the dog a more fearsome appearance which belies its naturally affectionate disposition.

- **HISTORY** Of ancient origin, the Great Dane was developed in Germany and is believed to have inherited its grace and agility from crossings with greyhounds.

wide, blunt nose with characteristic ridge

- **REMARK** Renowned for its tolerance towards children, clean in its habits, and easy to groom, the Great Dane makes an excellent family pet for those who have the space and can afford to pay for this gigantic dog's equally huge food bill.
- **OTHER NAMES** Deutsche Dogge.

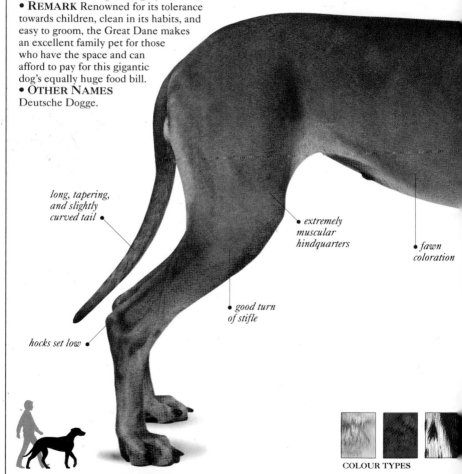

long, tapering, and slightly curved tail

extremely muscular hindquarters

fawn coloration

good turn of stifle

hocks set low

COLOUR TYPES

Height 76–81cm (30–32in)	Weight 45–55kg (100–120lb)	Temperament Alert, lively

long,
flat skull

ears set high
and folded
forwards

round, fairly
deep-set eyes

very deep chest
with well-sprung
ribs

short coat is
dense and sleek

harlequin
coloration

Country of origin Germany	First use Retrieving from water	Origins 1400s

STANDARD POODLE

This is the largest of the three breeds of poodle. An elegantly proportioned, squarely built dog, the Standard Poodle is a highly regarded retriever of game from rivers and marshland. The hair is clipped (as shown here), to provide warmth round its ankle joints, while the mane improves buoyancy.

• HISTORY Originating in Germany, the modern poodle is likely to have descended from the now rare French water dog, the Barbet (see p.95).

• REMARK As a working dog, its profuse coat used to hinder movement in the water, hence the need for clipping.

• OTHER NAMES Barbone, Caniche.

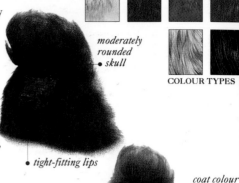

moderately rounded skull

COLOUR TYPES

tight-fitting lips

coat colour must be solid

long, straight muzzle

strong, well-proportioned neck

docked tail is set high and carried erect

muscular hindlegs

straight, parallel forelegs

deep chest with well-sprung ribs

Height 38cm (15in)	Weight 20.5–32kg (45–70lb)	Temperament Intelligent, lively

| Country of origin Germany | First use Baiting bulls, guard dog | Origins 1800s |

BOXER

This statuesque, mastiff-type dog has a boisterous and exuberant personality. However, the Boxer has a more refined appearance than many other mastiff breeds, with a less massive head and a leaner, more agile body.

• HISTORY The Boxer is the result of crossings between Bullenbeisser mastiffs and bulldogs in Munich, Germany, in the 1850s. It was first seen in Britain in the 1930s.

• REMARK Despite its pugnacious appearance and lively nature, it is responsive enough to be used as a guide dog in some countries.

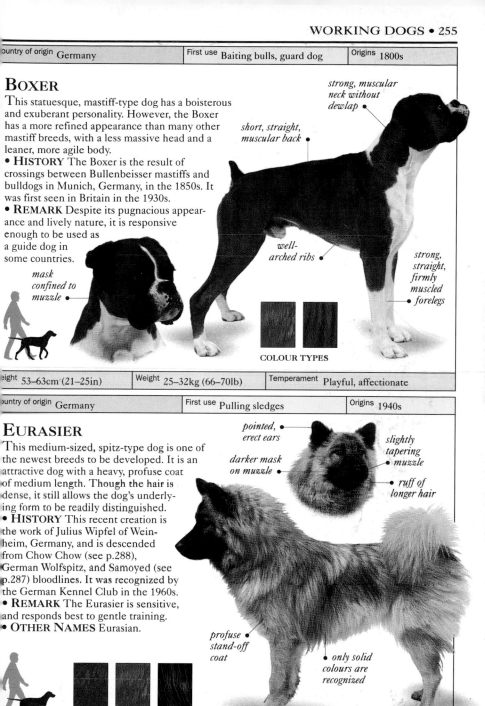

strong, muscular neck without dewlap

short, straight, muscular back

mask confined to muzzle

well-arched ribs

strong, straight, firmly muscled forelegs

COLOUR TYPES

| Height 53–63cm (21–25in) | Weight 25–32kg (66–70lb) | Temperament Playful, affectionate |

| Country of origin Germany | First use Pulling sledges | Origins 1940s |

EURASIER

This medium-sized, spitz-type dog is one of the newest breeds to be developed. It is an attractive dog with a heavy, profuse coat of medium length. Though the hair is dense, it still allows the dog's underlying form to be readily distinguished.

• HISTORY This recent creation is the work of Julius Wipfel of Weinheim, Germany, and is descended from Chow Chow (see p.288), German Wolfspitz, and Samoyed (see p.287) bloodlines. It was recognized by the German Kennel Club in the 1960s.

• REMARK The Eurasier is sensitive, and responds best to gentle training.

• OTHER NAMES Eurasian.

pointed, erect ears

darker mask on muzzle

slightly tapering muzzle

ruff of longer hair

profuse stand-off coat

only solid colours are recognized

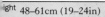

COLOUR TYPES

| Height 48–61cm (19–24in) | Weight 18–32kg (40–70lb) | Temperament Determined, alert |

Country of origin Germany	First use Helping fishermen	Origins 1800s

LANDSEER

This dog closely resembles the Newfoundland
(see pp.240–41), but differs most notably in its
coloration. Black areas should be prominent on
the back and rump, as well as the head, where
only a small white blaze is present. In some
countries, including Great Britain and the
USA, it is registered only as a colour form
of the Newfoundland.

- **HISTORY** In the early 1800s,
Newfoundlands varied a great
deal in appearance. Gradually,
two types evolved in mainland
Europe. The traditional form is larger,
with a short muzzle and a predominantly black
coat. The taller Landseer is lighter, has a longer
head, and a distinctive, slightly curly coat.
- **REMARK** The artist Sir Edwin Landseer
(1802–73) gave his name to the new breed.
Portraying contemporary Newfoundland dogs
in his painting *Off to the Rescue*, he established
the credentials for the Landseer.

*even, black
markings on
body*

*tail hangs
down, and
curves slightly
upwards when
dog stands
quietly*

*well-boned
limbs*

*medium-length,
dense coat*

Height 66–71cm (26–28in)	Weight 50–68kg (110–150lb)	Temperament Alert, friendly

massive head

strong, powerful
neck

short hair
on face

narrow, white
blaze

large feet for
swimming

huge, powerful
jaws

Country of origin Germany	First use Symbolic mascot	Origins 1800s

LEONBERGER

This large, friendly dog displays many of the characteristics of the breeds that contributed to its ancestry, most notably the New-foundland (see pp.240–41), from whom it inherited its love of water, and the St. Bernard (see p.273). Other breeds, such as the Great Swiss Mountain Dog (see p.272), were probably involved as well. Only very restricted areas of white are presently permitted in the Leonberger.

• **HISTORY** In the 1840s, Heinrich Essig, the Mayor of Leonberg, Germany, set out to create a breed of dog that resembled the dog featured on the town's crest. Not surprisingly it was named the Leonberger.

• **REMARK** This breed has a natural love of water and has proved outstanding as a water rescue dog. Its coat is waterproof and it has webs between its toes.

black mask on face is preferred

broad, square muzzle

distinctive mane at throat and chest

dark points permissible on coat

rounded feet with webbed toes

Height 65–80cm (26–31½in)	Weight 34–50kg (75–110lb)	Temperament Intelligent, friendly

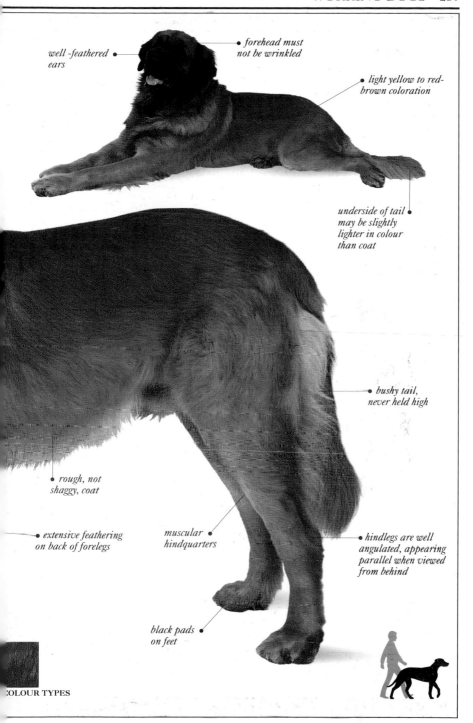

well-feathered ears

forehead must not be wrinkled

light yellow to red-brown coloration

underside of tail may be slightly lighter in colour than coat

bushy tail, never held high

rough, not shaggy, coat

extensive feathering on back of forelegs

muscular hindquarters

hindlegs are well angulated, appearing parallel when viewed from behind

black pads on feet

COLOUR TYPES

Country of origin Germany	First use Driving cattle, guard dog	Origins 1800s

ROTTWEILER

Enormously powerful and muscular, this breed has a calm, self-assured expression which reflects a tranquil temperament. Its coloration is black, with distinctive symmetrical tan markings. It is responsive to training and an enthusiastic worker.

• **HISTORY** The Rottweiler was developed in the German town of Rottweil, where it was used as a butcher's dog, for droving, and for guarding cattle. Now one of the top five most popular dogs in the USA, this breed came close to extinction in the early 19th century.

• **REMARK** The breed retains strong territorial instincts, and can be fierce if aroused.

relatively small, pendent ears, set wide apart

tan marking on muzzle

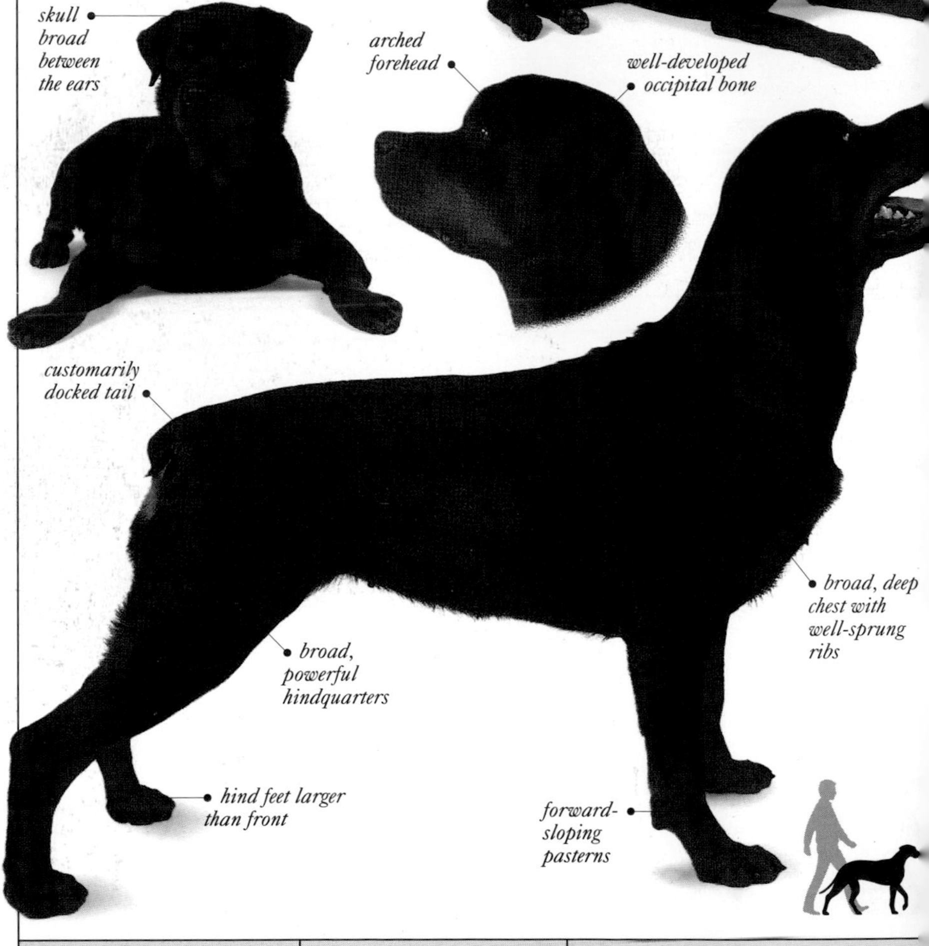

skull broad between the ears

arched forehead

well-developed occipital bone

customarily docked tail

broad, powerful hindquarters

broad, deep chest with well-sprung ribs

hind feet larger than front

forward-sloping pasterns

Height 58–69cm (23–27in)	Weight 41–50kg (90–110lb)	Temperament Protective, determined

Country of origin	Poland	First use	Guarding flocks	Origins	1700s

Owczarek Podhalanski

Although large and heavy, this sheepdog breed is surprisingly quick and agile. The usual coloration is solid white, although cream is also found, and both straight- and wavy-haired forms occur. This sturdy animal is well able to withstand the severe winter weather of its native Poland.

• **HISTORY** Received wisdom claims the Italian Bergamasco (see p.135) as this breed's ancestor, but its more likely forebears would seem to be the very similar sheepdog breeds of neighbouring Czechoslovakia and Hungary.

• **REMARK** A placid nature is one of the key characteristics of this breed, and individuals prone to irritability are likely to be disqualified from the show ring. The Owczarek has recently been adopted for military and police duties in North America.

• **OTHER NAMES** Tatra Mountain Sheepdog.

large, broad skull

dogs have shorter bodies than bitches

feathering on tail

hair on head and muzzle is shorter than body hair

strong neck

heavily boned forelegs

white- or cream-coloured, thick, dense coat

large, thick-soled feet

Height	61–86cm (24–34in)	Weight	45–68kg (100–150lb)	Temperament	Independent, friendly

Country of origin Belgium	First use Guard dog on barges	Origins 1500s

SCHIPPERKE

The Schipperke is relatively small for a member of the spitz family of dog breeds, but its attractive appearance has the distinctive features of this group. The outercoat is long, thick, and harsh, forming a ruff at the neck. According to the USA standard, solid black is the only acceptable colour, although in other countries other colours are also permitted.

- **HISTORY** The Schipperke has always been a small breed. It was used originally as a guard dog on barges and also perhaps to encourage barge ponies to renewed efforts. Its name is thought to derive from a corruption of the Flemish word for "little bargeman".
- **REMARK** Most Schipperke are born tailless. Individuals with tails must have them docked for showing.

very mobile, erect, triangular ears

fox-like head with pointed muzzle

short back

outer hair forms a ruff

fairly broad, flat skull with little stop

strong hindlegs

small, rounded, tight feet

short, strong neck

straight forelegs

COLOUR TYPES

Height 25–33cm (10–13in)	Weight 5.5–7.5kg (12–16lb)	Temperament Alert, loyal

Country of origin France	First use Baiting bulls	Origins 1800s

FRENCH BULLDOG

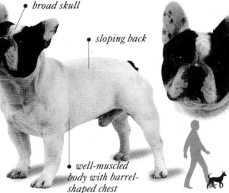

broad skull

sloping back

This small, compact breed has a large head and distinctive bat-like ears. It has suffered less from the breeding extremes that have afflicted its English relative.
• HISTORY These dogs are descended from the toy bulldogs of the 19th century, some of which were taken to France.
• REMARK Overweight individuals may have trouble with their breathing.
• OTHER NAMES Bouledogue Francais.

COLOUR TYPES

well-muscled body with barrel-shaped chest

Height 31cm (12in)	Weight 10–13kg (22–28lb)	Temperament Affectionate, playful

Country of origin France	First use Hunting game, guard dog	Origins 300s

DOGUE DE BORDEAUX

massive, broad skull

Descended from ancient mastiff stock, the Dogue de Bordeaux is a very powerful breed with a well-furrowed face and a head so massive it could be the largest in the canine world.
• HISTORY The sheer strength of this mastiff led to its being pitted against bulls in circus spectacles.
• REMARK Careful breeding has pacified these dogs. A special breeding programme was established in the 1960s.
• OTHER NAMES French Mastiff.

ears set well back on head

powerful hindquarters

COLOUR TYPES

undershot jaw with black or red muzzle

Height 58–69cm (23–27in)	Weight 36–45kg (80–100lb)	Temperament Determined, fearless

Country of origin France	First use Guarding sheep	Origins 2000BC

PYRENEAN MOUNTAIN DOG

Sometimes confused with the Pyrenean Mastiff (see p.278), this enormous yet elegant breed can be distinguished by the colour of its markings, which may be badger, wolf-grey, or pale yellow. Often, however, it is all white with distinctive black eye rims. The coarse coat enables it to withstand the severest climatic conditions.

• **HISTORY** Of ancient, French origin, this breed is thought to have descended from the old heavy shepherd dogs found in the Pyrenees.

• **REMARK** This giant takes three or four years to reach full maturity.

• **OTHER NAMES** Great Pyrenees, Chien des Pyrénées.

fairly small, triangular ears

mane of hair forms around neck

broad chest reaches just below elbows

straight, well-muscled forelegs

strong, slightly tapering muzzle

Height 65–81cm (26–32in)	Weight 41–57kg (90–125lb)	Temperament Watchful, loyal

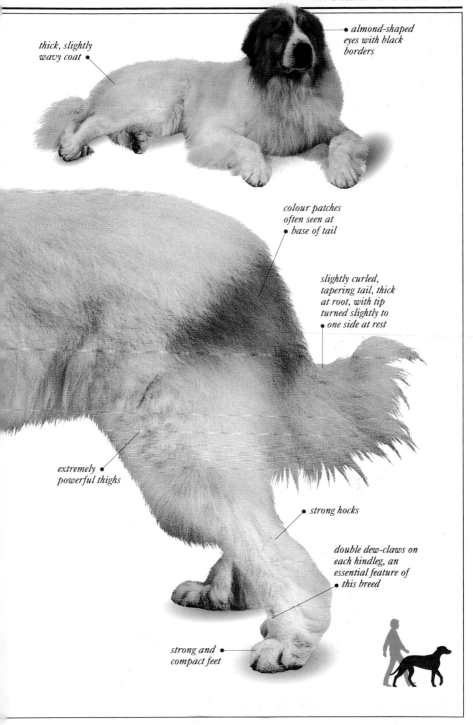

thick, slightly
wavy coat •

• almond-shaped
eyes with black
borders

colour patches
often seen at
• base of tail

slightly curled,
tapering tail, thick
at root, with tip
turned slightly to
• one side at rest

extremely •
powerful thighs

• strong hocks

double dew-claws on
each hindleg, an
essential feature of
• this breed

strong and •
compact feet

Country of origin Hungary	First use Guarding sheep	Origins 800s

KOMONDOR

The distinctive corded coat of the Komondor reaches down to the ground. The breed is similar in appearance to its Hungarian relative, the Puli (see p.133), although much larger and with a thick-boned skeleton.

• **HISTORY** The Komondor is well-suited to its traditional role as a flock guardian. Its coat helps it to blend in with the sheep, until it leaps out at unsuspecting predators. Its name may derive from *komondor kedvu*, which means "sombre" or "angry".

• **REMARK** The coat of the Komondor is particularly demanding. It must never be brushed or combed, for example; instead the hair is divided into cords and trimmed to suit.

corded coat with the • sensation of felt

• black nose

medium-sized • ears

• slightly arched profile to skull

• adult coat starts at six to nine months; coat may take two years to become fully corded

tail extends down to • hocks

• large, powerful feet

Height 66–81cm (26–32in)	Weight 36–61kg (80–135lb)	Temperament Protective, loyal

Country of origin Hungary	First use Guarding flocks	Origins 1200s

KUVASZ

A working dog developed specifically as a flock guardian, as opposed to herder, the Kuvasz is a sturdily built dog with a medium-boned frame of beautiful proportions. Its coat is dense and must be pure white or ivory in coloration. Its ears are folded and lie close to the head, which is large without being bulky and has a rounded stop.

• **HISTORY** The precise ancestry of the Kuvasz is not known. Its origins lie in Tibet, from where it travelled to Hungary via Turkey. In general appearance, it is similar to the Maremma Sheepdog (see p.275) and the Pyrenean Mountain Dog (see pp.264–65), and may share a common ancestry.

• **REMARK** The Kuvasz has a natural affinity with children, is very protective, and forms a strong bond with its owner.

elongated, but not pointed, head

straight muzzle

V-shaped ears with slightly rounded tips

large black nose with open nostrils

medium-length, muscular neck without dewlap

wavy hair on body and legs

deep chest and long, well-sprung ribs

cat-like feet with well-developed pads

Height 56–66cm (22–26in)	Weight 36–50kg (80–110lb)	Temperament Loyal, wary

Country of origin Hungary	First use Guarding flocks	Origins 1800s

MUDI

Less well known than its older and much better established countrymen, the Puli and Komondor (see pp.133 and 266), the Mudi is a versatile flock guardian and herder. It is both heavier and taller than the Puli, and the absence of the corded coat makes caring for the Mudi easier. The coat is usually black, but white is not uncommon, and a "pepita" form exists with an even distribution of both colours throughout its coat.

• **HISTORY** The development of the Mudi seems to have been unplanned. It is a versatile and favourable blend of the ancient sheep-herding dogs of its Hungarian homeland. The breed was unknown until about a hundred years ago.

• **REMARK** A good tracker and hunter, the Mudi also works well with livestock.

• **OTHER NAMES** Hungarian Mudi.

COLOUR TYPES

erect, triangular ears

straight, short back

coat length about 5cm (2in) on body

small, rounded feet

hair on muzzle and legs shorter than on body

Height 36–51cm (14–20in)	Weight 8–13kg (18–29lb)	Temperament Adaptable, friendly

Country of origin Switzerland	First use Herding goats	Origins 500s

APPENSELL MOUNTAIN DOG

One of four breeds of Swiss mountain dogs or sennenhunds, the Appenzeller is a hardy, well-built dog that can be distinguished from the other similar breeds by its tail, which is typically curled back over its thigh.
• **HISTORY** This dog is thought to be descended from the now-extinct Molussus.
• **REMARK** This dog has the unusual ability to both herd and guard livestock.
• **OTHER NAMES** Appenzeller Sennenhund.

tan markings above each eye

characteristic, curled tail

white area on chest

well-muscled hindquarters

blaze must be present on head

symmetrical facial markings

Height 48–58cm (19–23in)	Weight 23–25kg (50–55lb)	Temperament Lively, loyal

Country of origin Switzerland	First use Driving cattle	Origins 1800s

ENTELBUCH MOUNTAIN DOG

The smallest member of the sennenhund group, the Entelbuch is easily distinguished by the absence of a tail, which is docked at birth. All four sennenhunds share the same symmetrical coloration of black, tan, and white.
• **HISTORY** A native of the Swiss town of Entelbuch, this breed was traditionally used to drive cattle to market.
• **REMARK** Renowned for its gentle attitude to children, it makes a fine pet but must be exercised regularly to prevent it becoming obese.
• **OTHER NAMES** Entelbucher.

flat skull

V-shaped, pendent ears

powerful hindquarters

deep chest

strong hocks

white markings

Height 48–51cm (19–20in)	Weight 25–30kg (55–66lb)	Temperament Obedient, friendly

Country of origin Switzerland	First use Pulling weavers' carts	Origins 100BC

BERNESE MOUNTAIN DOG

This is the best known of the Swiss mountain dogs, or sennenhunds, and it can be readily distinguished from the other varieties by its coat. This is long and slightly wavy in appearance, without being curly. In terms of coloration and markings it is identical to the other forms. A white blaze on the head extending between the eyes, and a white chest marking known as a cross, are essential characteristics. White paws, ideally extending no farther than the pastern, are also preferred, as is a white tip to the tail. These affectionate and responsive dogs make good family pets if they have adequate exercise.

flat skull with slight furrow • apparent

• **HISTORY** It is possible that crosses between native Swiss herding dogs, and guard animals brought to Switzerland by the invading Roman legions, laid the early foundations for this breed. In more recent times, Bernese Mountain Dogs have worked on farms, notably in the canton of Berne, frequently acting as draught dogs on market days by pulling carts laden with produce.

• **REMARK** This breed has established a strong following in continental Europe, but is not so widely kept elsewhere in the world.

• **OTHER NAMES** Berner Sennenhund.

markings well defined, even in pups

rounded, compact feet •

• long sloping should

Height 58–70cm (23–27½in)	Weight 40–44kg (87–90lb)	Temperament Attentive, friendly

*soft, silky-
textured coat,
with good sheen*

*characteristic
white chest
marking*

*compact body
shape*

*medium-
length,
strong,
muscular
neck*

*broad, strong,
muscular
hindquarters*

*bushy tail can
extend to just
below hocks*

Country of origin Switzerland	First use Pulling farmers' carts	Origins 300s

GREAT SWISS MOUNTAIN DOG

This is the largest member of the four sennenhund breeds, and has a smooth coat and distinctively long tail, which is held below the level of the back. Like the other group members, its coloration is basically black and tan, the tan areas bordered by both black and white markings. White areas form a blaze, extending down to the chest, and are also present on the toes and on the tip of the tail.

- **HISTORY** This dog has a long history on Swiss farms. It declined during the mid-1800s, however, and by the turn of the century had almost vanished. The few pure-bred individuals left were crossed with smooth-coated St. Bernards. They are now once again well established and were introduced into the USA in 1968.
- **REMARK** Despite their size, grooming their coats is easy and straightforward.
- **OTHER NAMES** Grosser Schweizer Sennenhund.

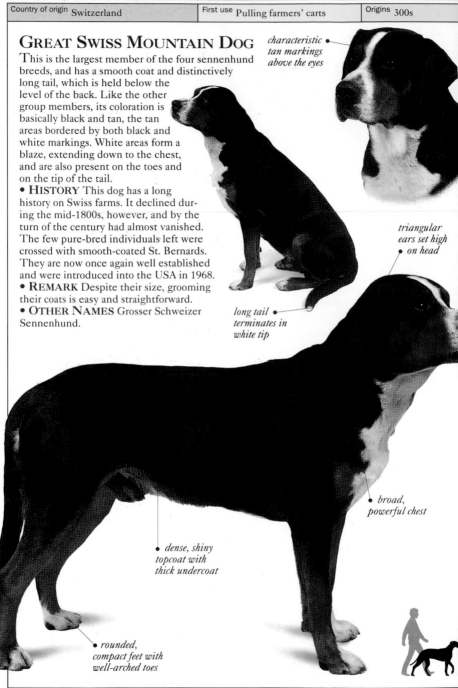

characteristic tan markings above the eyes

triangular ears set high on head

long tail terminates in white tip

broad, powerful chest

dense, shiny topcoat with thick undercoat

rounded, compact feet with well-arched toes

Height 60–72cm (23½–28½in)	Weight 59–61kg (130–135lb)	Temperament Active, calm

| untry of origin Switzerland | First use Searching and rescuing | Origins 1000s |

St. Bernard

The St. Bernard is a dog of imposing proportions – tall, broad, massively-boned, and
heavy – but it is always dignified in expression
and carriage. Both smooth- and rough-haired
forms of this breed exist, white and red, or red
and brownish yellow being the most favoured
colour combinations

• **HISTORY** The St. Bernard is descended
from the the Roman Molossus, which was the
original mastiff stock introduced into the Alps
by the Romans some 2,000 years ago. The
first St. Bernard was bred at the Hospice
of St. Bernard de Menthon about
1,000 years ago.

• **REMARK** This dog requires strong
handling when out walking on a lead.

• **OTHER NAMES**
St. Bernhardshund.

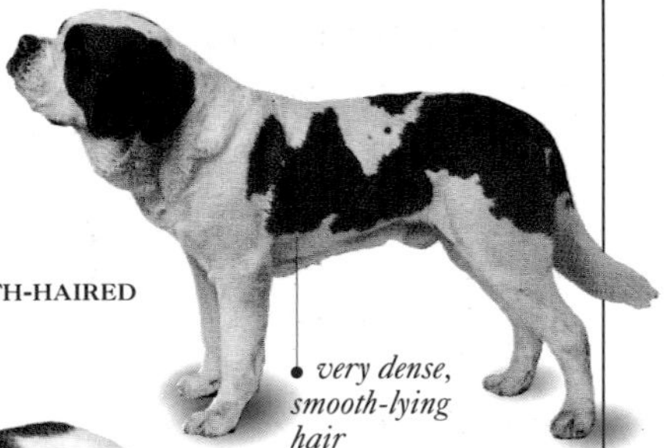

SMOOTH-HAIRED FORM

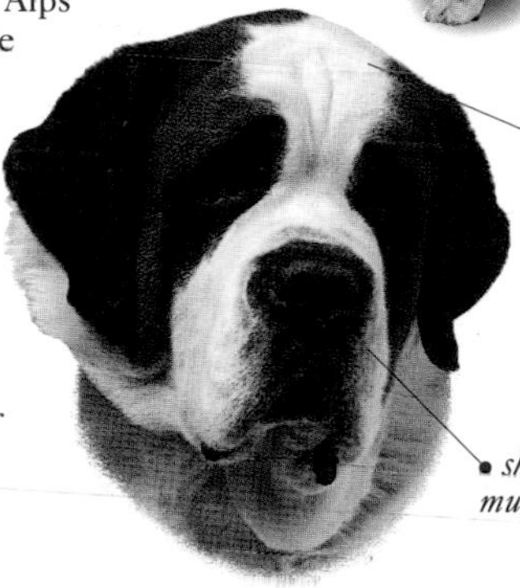

very dense, smooth-lying hair

slightly arched, massive skull

short, square muzzle

very muscular neck

deep chest

ROUGH-HAIRED FORM

dense, flat hair

large, compact feet with strong toes

| ght 61–71cm (24–28in) | Weight 50–91kg (110–200lb) | Temperature Tranquil, benevolent |

Country of origin Former Yugoslavia	First use Carriage dog	Origins 1400s

DALMATIAN

A bold, spotted patterning, offset against a clear, white background, makes this perhaps the most distinctive of all dog breeds. Black-spotted Dalmatians are far more common than their liver-coloured counterparts. The spots should be round in shape, clearly defined, and not overlapping. Those on the extremities should be smaller in size than elsewhere on the body. Dalmatian pups are pure white at birth and develop their spots only later.

• **HISTORY** This breed originated in Dalmatia, the region after which it is named, in what was formerly the country of Yugoslavia. It became very popular as a carriage dog in the 1800s, trotting alongside carriages and acting as a deterrent to highwaymen.

• **REMARK** The Dalmatian has attracted considerable attention through Dodie Smith's book *A Hundred and One Dalmatians*, which was later made into an extremely popular children's cartoon film by the Walt Disney Studios.

colour of eye rims matches that of spots

sleek, glossy coat

short, hard, dense hair

ears are set high on head and taper to a rounded point

rounded, well-arched, cat-like feet

markings on ears should be well-broken spots

tail should reach level of hocks

straight forelegs

elbows held close to body

rounded hindquarters

Height 56–61cm (22–24in)	Weight 23–25kg (50–55lb)	Temperament Quiet, alert

Country of origin Italy	First use Guarding flocks	Origins 100BC

MAREMMA SHEEPDOG

White is the predominant colour of this majestic sheepdog, sometimes with ivory or pale fawn shadings evident, notably on the ears. It is a muscular, powerful dog with a long, somewhat harsh coat. Its head is large and bear-like.

- **HISTORY** This breed may be descended from the earliest flock guardians, and may have been kept in the Maremma and Abruzzi regions of Italy since before Roman times.
- **REMARK** This majestic breed is highly intelligent but is not easy to train, having a rather independent and aloof character.
- **OTHER NAMES** Pastore Abruzzese.

large, conical head

thick ruff of hair

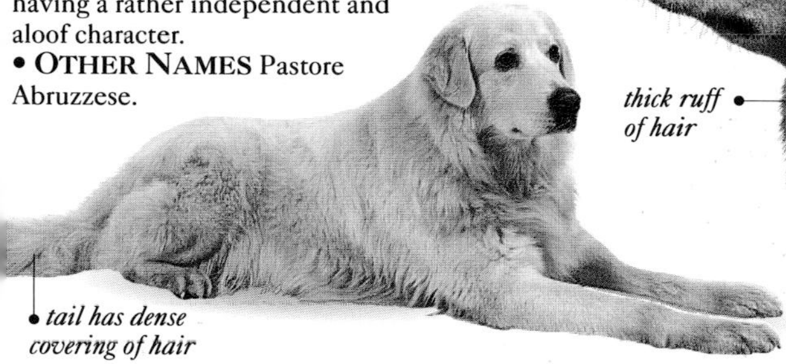

tail has dense covering of hair

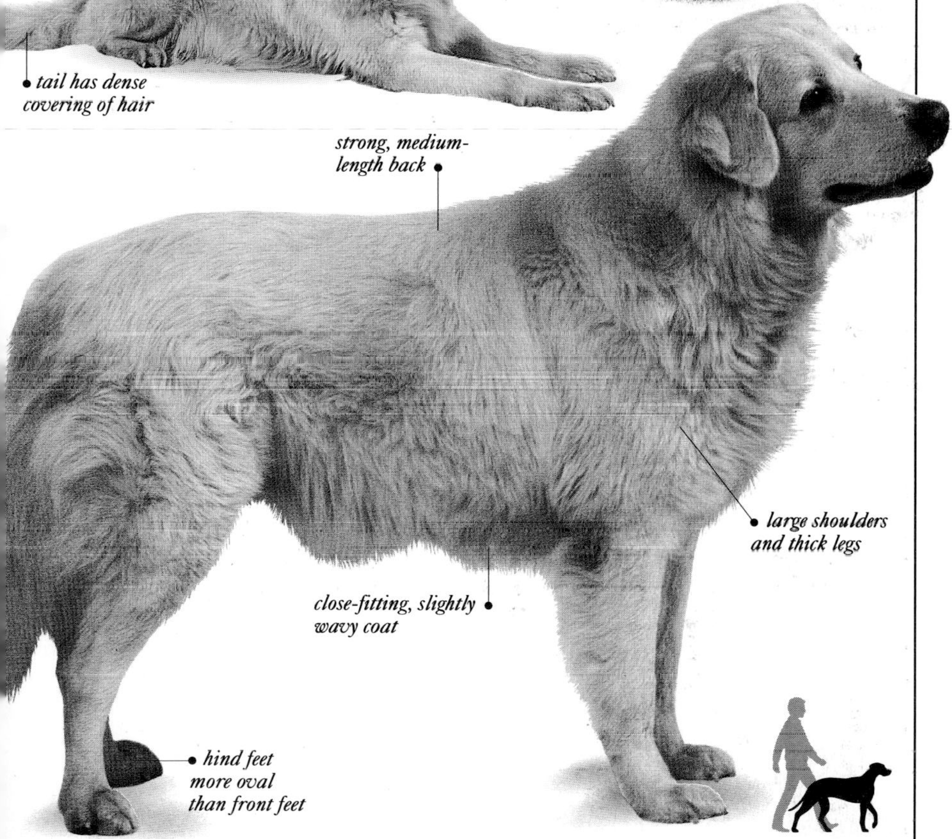

strong, medium-length back

large shoulders and thick legs

close-fitting, slightly wavy coat

hind feet more oval than front feet

Height 60–73cm (23½–28½in)	Weight 30–45kg (66–100lb)	Temperament Responsive, protective

Country of origin Italy	First use Guard dog, dog-fighting	Origins 100BC

NEAPOLITAN MASTIFF

This ancient breed of dog has a slow, ponderous, bear-like gait, in common with other mastiff-type breeds, and a very large head. From the head, prominent dewlaps of skin extend in folds down to the neck, thus producing a multi-chinned appearance. In spite of its aggressive history as a fighting dog, the Neapolitan Mastiff is generally a calm, placid, and friendly animal, especially with people whom it knows well.

- **HISTORY** The ancestry of the Neapolitan Mastiff may extend back to the Molossus breed of Roman times. Its enormous strength has seen it used for fighting, although it has also been a guard dog and a beast of burden, pulling carts. It was only in 1946 that steps were taken, by painter Piero Scanziani, to safeguard the breed's future. He established a kennel for the breed and did much to promote its survival.
- **REMARK** This huge dog is not aggressive by nature, although it will prove a loyal guardian, reflecting its mastiff ancestry.
- **OTHER NAMES** Mastino Napoletano.

small, well-spaced ears, positioned forwards on head

very muscular, short, stocky neck

in Italy the ears are cropped to the shape of an equilateral triangle

broad, well-muscled chest

dewlap hanging from lower jaw to mid-point of neck

forefeet slightly larger than hindfeet

Height 65–75cm (26–29in)	Weight 50–68kg (110–150lb)	Temperament Protective, alert

broad, flat skull

deep, spherical shape to the head

long, well-sprung ribs

broad, muscular croup with slight slope apparent

short, dense, fine coat, with hard texture and good sheen

tail is thick at root, may be docked by one-third length

oval feet with close-arched toes

COLOUR TYPES

Country of origin Spain	First use Guarding flocks	Origins 3000BC

PYRENEAN MASTIFF

Although the Pyrenean Mastiff is slightly smaller than the Pyrenean Mountain Dog (see pp.264–65), they share a common ancestry. The Mastiff is a robustly built, symmetrical dog with a large head, powerful neck (often with excessive dewlap), and a deep body, all supported on very sturdy legs.
• HISTORY Like the Pyrenean Mountain Dog, the Mastiff descended from dogs brought to Spain by early Mediterranean seafarers.
• REMARK For its enormous size, this breed has a small appetite and is light on its feet.
• OTHER NAMES Perro Mastin del Pireneo.

heavily boned,
• broad skull

pointed, pendulous
• ears

large, heavily
muscled chest

• thick,
powerful legs

broad, thick-
soled feet •

COLOUR TYPES

Height 72–86cm (28½–34in)	Weight 54.5–70kg (120–155lb)	Temperament Responsive, alert

Country of origin Spain	First use Guarding livestock	Origins 800s

SPANISH MASTIFF

This breed has the typical mastiff appearance: a broad head with a relatively short muzzle, a massive chest, and a characteristic dewlap on the neck. The ears are pointed and pendulous, but are not large.

• **HISTORY** These dogs have been used to guard farm stock in the hills of Spain for centuries. The origins of the breed may lie with ancient mastiff stock brought to the region by the Romans. It has only recently attracted attention from dog owners in northern Europe and in the USA.

• **REMARK** The Spanish Mastiff is essentially non-aggressive towards people, but may be combative with other dogs.

• **OTHER NAMES** Mastín Español.

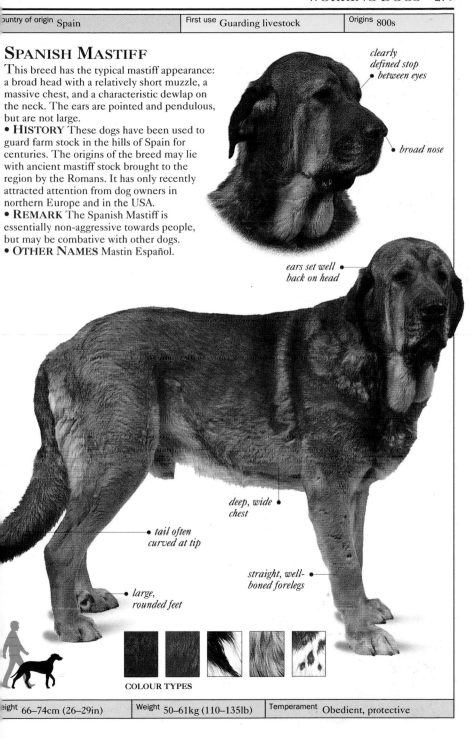

clearly defined stop between eyes

broad nose

ears set well back on head

deep, wide chest

tail often curved at tip

straight, well-boned forelegs

large, rounded feet

COLOUR TYPES

Height 66–74cm (26–29in)	Weight 50–61kg (110–135lb)	Temperament Obedient, protective

Country of origin Balearic Islands	First use Guarding farms	Origins 1700s

PERRO DE PASTOR MALLORQUIN

A well-defined head and a tapering muzzle give this breed a distinctive appearance. The tail is long and tapering towards the tip. Both long- and short-haired forms exist.

- **HISTORY** The Perro de Pastor Mallorquin is native to the Balearic Islands, off the coast of Spain, and is a utility animal.
- **REMARK** This dog was bred to withstand the heat of the Mediterranean sun, and can be fierce and aggressive.
- **OTHER NAMES** Ca de Bestiar.

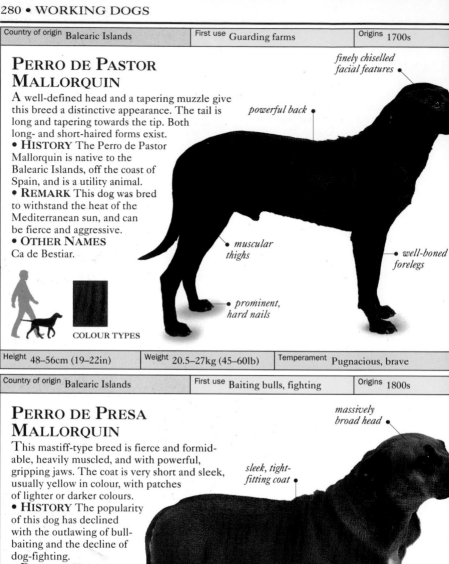

finely chiselled facial features

powerful back

muscular thighs

well-boned forelegs

prominent, hard nails

COLOUR TYPES

Height 48–56cm (19–22in)	Weight 20.5–27kg (45–60lb)	Temperament Pugnacious, brave

Country of origin Balearic Islands	First use Baiting bulls, fighting	Origins 1800s

PERRO DE PRESA MALLORQUIN

This mastiff-type breed is fierce and formidable, heavily muscled, and with powerful, gripping jaws. The coat is very short and sleek, usually yellow in colour, with patches of lighter or darker colours.

- **HISTORY** The popularity of this dog has declined with the outlawing of bull-baiting and the decline of dog-fighting.
- **REMARK** This breed needs firm discipline from a very early age.
- **OTHER NAMES** Ca de Bou.

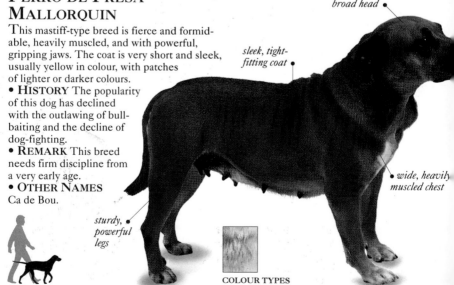

massively broad head

sleek, tight-fitting coat

wide, heavily muscled chest

sturdy, powerful legs

COLOUR TYPES

Height 58–61cm (23–24in)	Weight 55–68kg (121–150lb)	Temperament Independent, fierce

Country of origin Israel	First use Guarding livestock	Origins 2000BC

CANAAN DOG

This medium-sized, robustly made, spitz-type dog has been indigenous to the region encompassed by modern Israel for centuries. The ancestors of today's Canaan were pariah dogs, which have traditionally been domesticated to act as flock guardians, protecting the tribespeople's goats against jackals and other predators.

• **HISTORY** A programme to breed these dogs so that the puppies resembled their parents in appearance (breeding true) was begun in 1935 by a Dr. Menzel and her husband. Most of the stock seen around the world today originated in the Shaar Hagai Kennels in Jerusalem.

• **REMARK** In spite of its feral origins, this dog is easily trained.

• **OTHER NAMES** Kelef K'naani.

almond-shaped, dark brown rims

broad, erect ears with rounded tips

straight, strong forelegs

hard pads

muscular neck

thick, brush-like tail curves over back

short to medium-length coat

straight forelegs

rounded, strong feet

powerful nails

COLOUR TYPES

Height 48–61cm (19–24in)	Weight 16–25kg (35–55lb)	Temperament Intelligent, resourceful

Country of origin Portugal	First use Guarding flocks	Origins 1800s

ESTRELA MOUNTAIN DOG

Two distinct coat types are associated with this breed.
The longer-coated form displays more abundant
feathering than its smooth-coated counterpart, although
a double-layered coat affords both of them
excellent protection against the worst
of the elements. The large size and
loud bark could make them
formidable opponents, but
they are usually friendly dogs.

• HISTORY This breed is
named after the Estrela region
in central Portugal, where it was
traditionally used as a flock guardian.

• REMARK This is not a demonstra-
tive animal. Like all powerful dogs, it
requires thorough training.

• OTHER NAMES Cão da
Serra da Estrela.

COLOUR TYPES

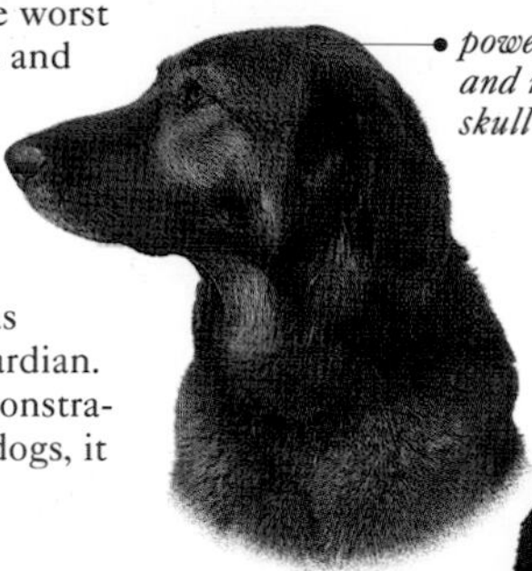

*powerful head
and rounded
skull*

SHORT-HAIRED
FORM

*long, well-
furnished tail*

*slightly sloping
croup*

*very
powerful
shoulders*

*solidly muscled,
straight legs*

*hind dew-
claws present*

LONG-
HAIRED
FORM

Height 62–72cm (24½–28½in)	Weight 30–50kg (66–110lb)	Temperament Loyal, active

Country of origin Portugal	First use Guard dog	Origins 1800s

RAFEIRO DO ALENTEJO

This powerful dog has a body not unlike that of a St. Bernard (see p.273), but has a head shaped like a bear's. This is the largest of the Portuguese breeds and is an imposing animal.
• **HISTORY** This breed originated in the Alentejo region of southern Portugal. The Spanish Mastiff (see p.279) may have contributed to its ancestry, along with the Estrela Mountain Dog (see p.282).
• **REMARK** This dog has an aggressive nature, as well as a strong independent streak.
• **OTHER NAMES** Portuguese Watchdog.

large head with broad muzzle

longer fur around neck

solid, muscular back

long, curved tail

short, stocky, powerful neck

distinctive markings, often spotted in appearance

well-boned, straight forelegs

smooth-coated legs

COLOUR TYPES

Height 76cm (30in)	Weight 43–50kg (95–110lb)	Temperament Alert, independent

Country of origin Portugal	First use Guarding and herding flocks	Origins 1500s

PORTUGUESE CATTLE DOG

This rugged, powerfully built dog has traditionally been used as a herding animal in the rocky, less accessible parts of Portugal. Its rather long body has a strong, weatherproof, coarse outercoat over a finer, thicker undercoat, making it ideal for the often harsh conditions of this region.
• **HISTORY** The isolated nature of the area of Portugal where this dog originated – Castro Laboreiro – makes it likely that only local breeds were used in its development.
• **REMARK** This breed is still widely employed in its homeland for herding and guarding stock.
• **OTHER NAMES** Cão de Castro Laboreiro.

large, narrow head

well-muscled body

wide, deep, powerful chest

straight, well-boned legs

COLOUR TYPES

Height 51–61cm (20–24in)	Weight 23–34kg (50–75lb)	Temperament Alert, brave

Country of origin Russia and Finland	First use Hunting big game	Origins 1700s

RUSSO-EUROPEAN LAIKA

This is a powerfully built dog, characterized by its black-and-white coloration and pricked ears. If present, its tail is distinctively curled, but this breed is often born without a tail.
• **HISTORY** The Russo-European Laika evolved near the border shared by Russia and Finland. Already an intrepid moose and wolf hunter, crossings with the fearless Utchak Sheepdog widened its role to encompass bear hunting.
• **REMARK** This breed cannot be regarded as a house dog or pet.
• **OTHER NAMES** Karelian Bear Laika, Lajka Ruissisch Europaisch.

conical head

large, prominent, upright ears

tail curled (if present)

broad, powerful chest

wide, thick-soled feet

Height 53–61cm (21–24in)	Weight 20.5–23kg (45–50lb)	Temperament Independent, brave

Country of origin Russia	First use Hunting bears	Origins 1800s

EAST SIBERIAN LAIKA

This member of the laika family is large, squarely built, and has a slightly spiky coat which stands away from the body. Its head is broad, its expression is alert, and its ears are large and erect.
• **HISTORY** This breed was used for pulling sledges, as well as for hunting such quarry as bear, elk, and reindeer.
• **REMARK** Laikas were used as test animals in the early Soviet space experiments.

shorter hair on head

well-spaced, erect ears

well-arched toes

COLOUR TYPES   *thickly muscled neck*

Height 56–64cm (22–25in)	Weight 18–23kg (40–50lb)	Temperament Obedient, loyal

Country of origin Russia	First use Hunting bears	Origins 1800s

WEST SIBERIAN LAIKA

The long legs and wolf-like face of the West Siberian Laika give it an apparent lightness of bearing which belies its power and immense endurance.
• **HISTORY** This breed is more firmly established than its East Siberian relative (above), and is certainly more numerous.
• **REMARK** The strenuous life of the West Siberian Laika means that its average working span is quite short.

erect ears

tightly curled tail

short, dense double coat

COLOUR TYPES   *prominent nostrils*

Height 53–61cm (21–24in)	Weight 18–23kg (40–50lb)	Temperament Active, lively

Country of origin Russia	First use Pulling sledges	Origins 1800s

SIBERIAN HUSKY

Although smaller and lighter than some other breeds of sledge dog, the
Siberian Husky is quick and athletic, agile and strong, as well as being
a tireless worker. This medium-sized dog has a dense and woolly
undercoat, well protected by a covering of tougher guard hairs, giving
the dog a fullness of form and providing excellent insulation against the
raw cold of its Siberian homeland.

medium-sized, triangular ears

• **HISTORY** Siberian Huskies were
developed by the Chukchi people
of northeast Asia as their only
means of transport.

almond-shaped eyes, sometimes blue

• **REMARK** Communal howling is a feature of this breed. An
amazing range of coat colours
and markings is permitted.

• **OTHER NAMES**
Arctic Husky.

medium-length muzzle

thick, bushy tail

strong, deep chest

shoulder fits tightly to ribcage

relatively long legs

well-furred, slightly webbed, oval feet

COLOUR TYPES

Height 51–60cm (20–23½in)	Weight 16–27kg (35–60lb)	Temperament Dependable, energetic

Country of origin Russia	First use Herding reindeer	Origins 1600s

SAMOYED

This far-northern breed has a very full coat, consisting of a long, weather-resistant outercoat covering an extremely dense and woolly undercoat. Samoyeds make popular and attractive pets, as well as being highly valued as sledge dogs.

- **HISTORY** Today's breed is said to derive from just 12 dogs brought out of the Arctic by explorers and travellers. The basic Samoyed was developed by the once-nomadic Samoyede tribe, who now live in the Antarctic region east of the Ural Mountains.
- **REMARK** Antarctic explorers Scott and Amundsen both used Samoyeds.
- **OTHER NAMES** Samoyedskaja.

thick, well-spaced, rounded ears

dark brown eyes

weather-resistant coat stands away from body

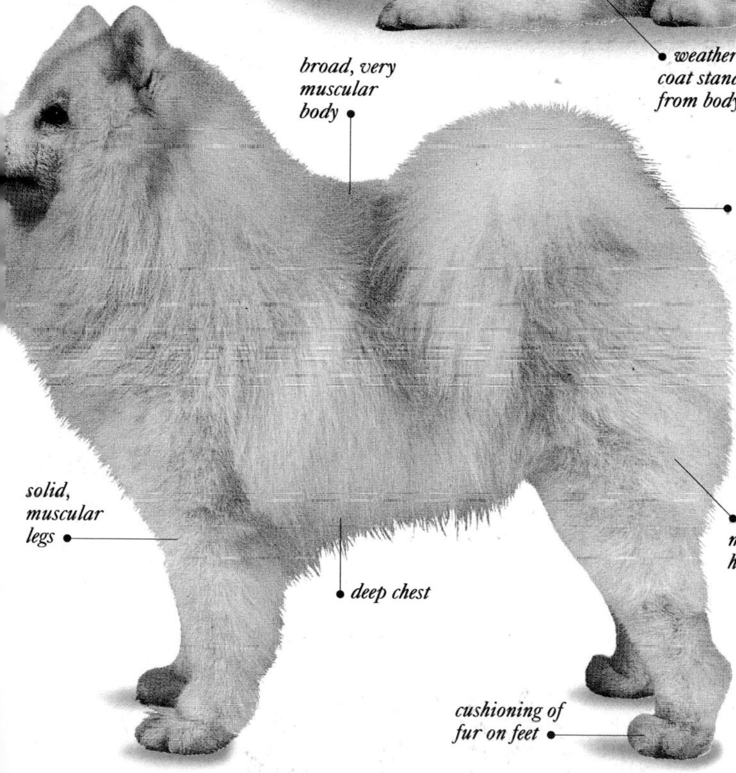

broad, very muscular body

long, well-covered tail is carried over the back and to one side

solid, muscular legs

exceedingly muscular hindquarters

deep chest

cushioning of fur on feet

Height 46–56cm (18–22 in)	Weight 23–29.5kg (50–65lb)	Temperament Companionable

Country of origin China	First use Guard dog, pulling carts	Origins 100s

CHOW CHOW

The rough-coated form (shown here) is most commonly seen; its coat is profuse, thick, and straight. The smooth-coated form reveals the squarely built, hugely muscled outline of this courageous and powerful dog. The Chow Chow is bred in solid colours from tan or red through to silver-grey or black, while white is rare.

• **HISTORY** Although popular in China for at least 2,000 years, the Chow first appeared in Britain only in the late 19th century. In its homeland it was used to pull carts and as a guard dog. Its fur was also a valuable commodity, as was its flesh for human consumption.

• **REMARK** The unusual tongue of the Chow Chow is, like that of the Shar Pei (opposite), blue-black in coloration.

broad, flat skull

small ears blend with the ruff

tail set high and curved over the back

broad, deep chest

small, rounded, cat-like feet

muzzle is broad along its length

COLOUR TYPES

Height 46–56cm (18–22in)	Weight 20–32kg (45–70lb)	Temperament Alert, independent

Country of origin China	First use Dog-fighting	Origins 1500s

SHAR PEI

The bristly coat of this dog is quite distinctive, but the folds of loose skin covering its body and especially its head, giving it a permanent frown, are by far its most striking feature.

• **HISTORY** This ancient breed is thought to result from crosses between mastiffs and certain Nordic breeds. It was in danger of extinction until a Hong Kong fancier established stock in the USA and elsewhere.

• **REMARK** The loose skin was originally developed for the gruesome purpose of making the animal impossible to pin down in a dog fight.

triangular, folded ears

dark, almond-shaped eyes

rounded tail set high on back

relatively long, broad muzzle

strong, short neck with loose skin

deep, broad chest

ear tips point towards eyes

abundant, loose folds of skin

SHAR PEI PUP

COLOUR TYPES

Height 46–51cm (18–20in)	Weight 16–20kg (35–45lb)	Temperament Independent, aloof

Country of origin Japan	First use Hunting big game	Origins 1600s

AKITA

The erect ears, and tail that curls forwards over its back, indicate that the powerful Akita dog is descended from spitz stock. The head is large and broad, with a very distinctive, bear-like expression.

- **HISTORY** The Akita was developed by a Japanese nobleman living in exile in the province of Akita, on Honshu island. Here the dogs were used in pairs to hunt such dangerous quarry as bears.
- **REMARK** The Akita was officially recognized as part of Japan's national heritage in 1931.
- **OTHER NAMES** Akita Inu, Japanese Akita.

strong, broad muzzle

erect ears carried over eyes in line with back of neck

tail is set high and curls forwards

thick, tight feet with broad pads

muscular hindquarters with well-developed thighs

clear, well-defined coloration

straight forelegs

COLOUR TYPES

Height 60–71cm (24–28in)	Weight 34–50kg (75–110lb)	Temperament Active, independent

| Country of origin | Japan | First use | Hunting small game | Origins | 1000BC |

SHIBA INU

This dog is similar to the Akita (opposite), but it is smaller in size, its name translating from the Japanese as "small dog". The keen and alert appearance results from the broad forehead, pointed muzzle, and triangular ears which incline slightly forwards.

• **HISTORY** The origins of the Shiba Inu breed go back more than 2,000 years in Japan, with the possibility of Chow Chow blood in its ancestry.

• **REMARK** The Shiba Inu is the most commonly kept of the native breeds in Japan.

• **OTHER NAMES** Brushwood Dog.

tapering muzzle

small, well-shaped oval eyes

short, level back

thick, sickle-shaped tail

harsh, double coat

COLOUR TYPES

| Height | 36–40cm (14–15½in) | Weight | 9–14kg (20–30lb) | Temperament | Independent, industrious |

| Country of origin | Japan | First use | Fighting dog | Origins | 1800s |

TOSA INU

A sturdy, very powerful frame and a well-muscled physique, coupled with capable jaws and solid teeth, combine to make the Tosa Inu a formidable combat dog in its native Japan.

• **HISTORY** Many of the Tosa's physical characteristics reflect its mastiff origins; it is, however, a modern fighting-dog breed dating only from about the 1860s.

• **REMARK** This potentially aggressive dog has been banned in the United Kingdom, but it is still kept in the USA.

• **OTHER NAMES** Tosa Fighting Dog.

well-developed cheek muscles

tail positioned high on back

short, close-lying coat

broad muzzle with powerful jaws

COLOUR TYPES

| Height | 62–65cm (24½–25½in) | Weight | 90kg (200lb) | Temperament | Stoic, relentless |

Country of origin Japan	First use Retrieving game, ratting	Origins 1700s

JAPANESE TERRIER

This terrier has a relatively small head and a tail that is traditionally docked quite close to the body. Its tricoloured coat is distinctive. It is predominantly white with black and tan areas of the coat proportionately small in size, creating an attractive, speckled appearance.

- **HISTORY** Descended from the Smooth Fox Terrier, which was introduced to Japan in 1702, the subsequent development of this breed centred on the cities of Kobe and Yokohama.
- **REMARK** In Japan this dog can be seen working as a water-fowl retriever.
- **OTHER NAMES** Nippon Terrier.

ears folded forwards and set high on head •

smooth, short coat with random speckling •

long, straight forelegs •

Height 33cm (13in)	Weight 4.5–6kg (10–13lb)	Temperament Affectionate, adaptable

Country of origin Japan	First use Hunting large game	Origins 1000BC

AINU

Resembling the Akita (see p.290), although smaller in size, the Ainu's fox-like head shape and curled tail carriage are typical spitz characteristics. This breed has an unusually fierce facial expression.

- **HISTORY** Developed in Japan by the Ainu people, this handsome breed is thought to be the oldest of all the Japanese dog breeds.
- **REMARK** Although not encouraged, a dark bluish tongue may occur, as with the Chow Chow and Shar Pei (see pp.288 and 289).
- **OTHER NAMES** Hokkaido Dog.

short, broad • muzzle

small, pricked • ears

broad, deep chest

short, thick coat standing off from the body

COLOUR TYPES

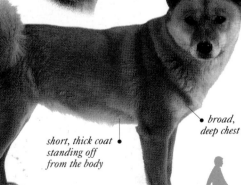

Height 46–56cm (18–22in)	Weight 20.5–29.5kg (45–65lb)	Temperament Brave, loyal

Country of origin Tibet	First use Guarding flocks	Origins 900s

TIBETAN MASTIFF

The formidable size of the Tibetan Mastiff makes it an excellent guard dog, yet it is responsive to training and usually proves gentle, even with children. Its distinctive, high-set tail curls to one side. In Tibet it is customary for the dog to wear a red yak's-hair collar as a sign of its status.

• **HISTORY** It is possible that many of today's European mastiff breeds are descended from the Tibetan Mastiff, which spread eastwards with the armies of Alexander the Great.

• **REMARK** The female Tibetan Mastiff may come into season only once rather than twice a year, as is usual with other breeds.

broad, massive head

high-set tail

fairly long, thick, double coat

sturdy legs

strong, muscular body

very large, powerful feet

COLOUR TYPES

Height 61–71cm (24–28in)	Weight 64–82kg (140–180lb)	Temperament Brave, loyal

Country of origin Canary Islands	First use Dog fighting	Origins 1800s

CANARY DOG

Bearing a strong likeness to the Perro de Presa Mallorquin (see p.280), the Canary Dog is a powerfully built, square-headed, mastiff-type dog. Fawn or brindle is the usual coloration, although white markings are also seen, and the coat itself is short and rough over slightly mobile skin.

- **HISTORY** The ancestry of the Canary Dog involved crosses between the extinct Bardino Majero and the Mastiff, the latter being developed in Great Britain and introduced into the Canaries in the 1800s. The Canary Dog was developed specifically for dog fighting.
- **REMARK** Now recovering in numbers, this breed was almost extinct by the 1960s due to the banning of dog-fighting in its homeland.
- **OTHER NAMES** Perro de Presa Canario.

large, powerful, square head

powerful, muscled back

slightly raised rump

blunt, broad muzzle

very broad, heavily muscled chest

short, coarse-textured coat

strong, heavily boned legs

COLOUR TYPES

Height 55–65cm (21½–25½in)	Weight 38–48kg (84–106lb)	Temperament Determined, forceful

Country of origin Morocco	First use Guard Dog	Origins 1000s

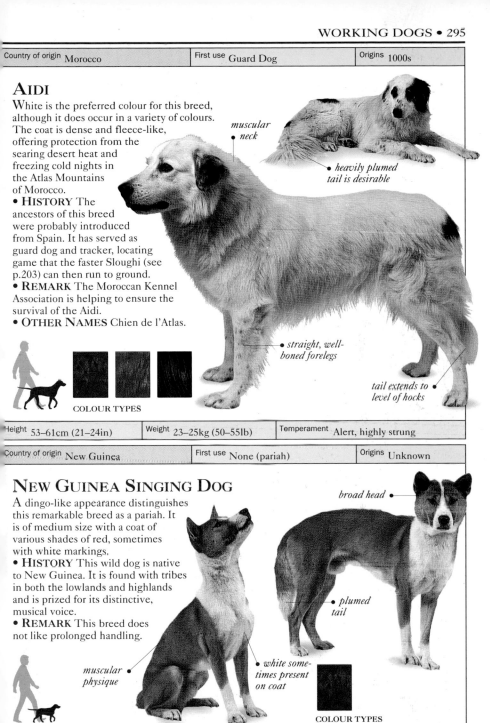

AIDI

White is the preferred colour for this breed, although it does occur in a variety of colours. The coat is dense and fleece-like, offering protection from the searing desert heat and freezing cold nights in the Atlas Mountains of Morocco.

• **HISTORY** The ancestors of this breed were probably introduced from Spain. It has served as guard dog and tracker, locating game that the faster Sloughi (see p.203) can then run to ground.

• **REMARK** The Moroccan Kennel Association is helping to ensure the survival of the Aidi.

• **OTHER NAMES** Chien de l'Atlas.

muscular neck

heavily plumed tail is desirable

straight, well-boned forelegs

tail extends to level of hocks

COLOUR TYPES

Height 53–61cm (21–24in)	Weight 23–25kg (50–55lb)	Temperament Alert, highly strung

Country of origin New Guinea	First use None (pariah)	Origins Unknown

NEW GUINEA SINGING DOG

A dingo-like appearance distinguishes this remarkable breed as a pariah. It is of medium size with a coat of various shades of red, sometimes with white markings.

• **HISTORY** This wild dog is native to New Guinea. It is found with tribes in both the lowlands and highlands and is prized for its distinctive, musical voice.

• **REMARK** This breed does not like prolonged handling.

broad head

plumed tail

muscular physique

white sometimes present on coat

COLOUR TYPES

Height 35–38cm (14–15in)	Weight 8–10kg (18–22lb)	Temperament Aloof, unpredictable

DOG CREDITS

Dorling Kindersley are greatly indebted to the many owners and breeders who allowed their dogs to be photographed for this book; without their help and enthusiastic cooperation, it could not have been produced. While every effort has been made to accredit all those involved, the publisher will gladly incorporate additional information in future editions. The dogs and the names of their owners are listed in page order.

COMPANION DOGS
• 38 *Kyi Leo* D. Weber
• 39 *Toy American Eskimo* (refer to publisher)
Bulldog C. Thomas & G. Godfrey
• 40 *Cavalier King Charles* T. Boardman; Hull; *King Charles Spaniel* D. Fry
• 41 *Chihuahua* S. Lee
• 42 *Mexican Hairless* S. Corrone; H. Hernandez; Terry; L. Woods
• 42 *Inca Hairless* C. & B. Christofferson; *Havanese* K. Olausson
• 44 *Giant German Spitz* A. Fiebich; M. Horhold; *German Spitz: Mittel* Bodimeade
• 45 *German Spitz: Klein* K. Hill & Trendle; *Pomeranian* Powell & Medcraft
• 46 *Keeshond* M.R. West; *Continental Toy Spaniel: Phalene* J. Meijer
• 47 *Continental Toy Spaniel: Papillon* Urquhart & Urquhart; *Toy Poodle* S. Riddett & Moody
• 48 *Miniature Poodle* Treagus
• 49 *Lowchen* K. Donovan
• 50 *Italian Greyhound* S. Dunning
• 51 *Bolognese* L. Stannard; *Volpino Italiano* A. Hammond
• 52 *Pekingese* Stannard

• 53 *Pug* N. Tarbitt; *Shih Tzu* J. Franks
• 54 *Chinese Crested Dog* (Hairless) Moon; (Powder Puff) S. Wrenn
• 55 *Tibetan Spaniel* J. Lilley; *Tibetan Terrier* T. & A. Medlow
• 56 *Lhasa Apso* L. Chamberlain; *Japanese Chin* J. Jolley
• 57 *Japanese Spitz* S. Jones; *Maltese* U. Campanis-Brockmann
• 58 *Bichon Frise* S.M. Dunger
• 59 *Basenji* J. Gostynska; *Coton de Tulear* P. Zinkstok & H. & R. Bonneveld

GUNDOGS
• 60 *American Cocker Spaniel* L. Pichard
• 61 *Chesapeake Bay Retriever* P. Taylor-Williams
• 62 *Clumber Spaniel* R. Furness
• 63 *Cocker Spaniel* (puppy) T. Morgan & N. Memery; (black and white) M. Robinson; (blue) P. & T. Read
• 64 *Curly-coated Retriever* A. Skingley
• 65 *English Setter* Grimsdell
• 66 *Gordon Setter* M. Justice; *English Springer Spaniel* D. & J. Miller
• 67 *Field Spaniel* G. Thwaites; *Flat-coated Retriever* A. Youens
• 68 *Golden Retriever* R.A. Strudwick; C. Carter
• 69 *Labrador Retriever* M. Prior; C. Coode
• 70–71 *Pointer* A. Morgan
• 72 *Welsh Springer Spaniel* J. Luckett-Roynon; *Sussex Spaniel* C. Mitchell
• 73 *Nova Scotia Duck Tolling Retriever* G. Flack
• 74 *Old Danish Pointer* E. Karlsson
• 75 *German Spaniel* L. Ahlsson
• 76–77 *Weimaraner* F. Thibaut
• 78 *German Wire-haired Pointer* M. J. Gorrissen-Sipos
• 79 *Small Münsterländer* G. Petterson
• 80–81 *Large Münsterländer* K. Groom
• 82 *Dutch Partridge Dog* S. Boersma; J.P.A. vd. Zanden; *Kooiker Dog* L.A. & B. Williams
• 83 *Stabyhoun* E. Vellenga; *Wetterhoun* J.P. Visser
• 84 *Irish Water Spaniel* G. Stirk
• 85 *Irish Red and White Setter* S.J. Humphreys
• 86 *Irish Setter* Napthine
• 87 *Braque St. Germain* J.P. Perdry
• 88–89 *Braque Francais: Gascogne* Y. Bassot
• 90 *Braque d'Auvergne* L. Ercole
• 91 *Braque du Bourbonnais* J. Regis
• 92 *Épagneul Francais* W. Klijn;

G. de Moustier; *Épagneul Picard* M. & P. Lempereur
• 93 *Épagneul Breton* E. Reeves
• 94 *Épagneul Pont-Audemer* Y. Fouquer; J.P. Tougard
• 95 *Barbet* J.C. Valée
• 96 *Épagneul Bleu de Picardie* M. Debacker
• 97 *Wire-haired Pointing Griffon* T. Schmeitz; *Czesky Fousek* M. Hahné
• 98 *Hungarian Vizsla* J. Perkins
• 99 *Wire-haired Vizsla* J. & L.V. Essen
• 100 *Spinone* S. Grief
• 101 *Bracco Italiano* J. & L. Shaw
• 102 *Perdiguero de Burgos* P. Moreira
• 103 *Portuguese Water Dog* J. & R. Bussell
• 104 *Perdiguero Portugueso* Canil do Casal das Grutas

HERDING DOGS
• 105 *Australian Shepherd* Macintyre
• 106 *Bearded Collie* J. Wiggins
• 107 *Border Collie* P. Haydock; *Lancashire Heeler* S. Whybrow
• 108 *Rough Collie* V. Tame
• 109 *Smooth Collie* P. Sewell; *Shetland Sheepdog* J. Moody
• 110 *Old English Sheepdog* (adult) J.P. & C. Smith; (puppy) Anderson
• 111 *Welsh Corgi: Cardigan* T. Maddox; *Welsh Corgi: Pembroke* Davies
• 112 *Australian Cattle Dog* (adult) S. & W. Huntingdon; (puppies) S. Smyth
• 113 *Australian Kelpie* P. Rönnquist; M. Nilsson
• 114 *Finnish Lapphund* S. Bolin; (youngest) S. Dunger; *Lapinporokoira* B. Schmitt
• 115 *Beauceron* M.V. Rie
• 116–17 *Briard* (fawn) Snelling; (black) R. Bumstead
• 118 *Berger de Picard* C.V. Doorn; (brindle) J.C.P. Bormans
• 119 *German Shepherd Dog* W. & J. Petrie
• 120–21 *Hovawart* (black) K. Stenhols; (golden) A. Göranson
• 122 *Giant Schnauzer* Wilberg
• 123 *Polish Lowland Sheepdog* M. de Groot; *Schapendoes* J. Wierda-Gorter; (head) C. Roux
• 124 *Dutch Shepherd Dog* J. Pijffers; M. Vermeeren
• 125 *Sarloos Wolfhound* C. Keizer
• 126 *Belgian Shepherd Dog: Groenendael* J. Luscott
• 127 *Belgian Shepherd Dog: Laekenois* Hogarty
• 128 *Belgian Shepherd Dog: Tervuren* K. Ellis & A. McLaren
• 129 *Belgian Shepherd Dog: Malinois* S. Hughes

130–31 *Bouvier des Flandres*
K.S. Wilberg
132 *Swedish Vallhund* J. Hammar;
Iceland Dog A.S. Andersson
133 *Puli* M. Crowther; Butler;
Pumi (black) P. Johansson; (grey
and cream) I. Svard
134 *Istrian Sheepdog*
M. Luttwitz; *Illyrian Sheepdog*
P. Gvozenovie
135 *Bergamasco* B. Saraber;
(puppy) M. Andreoli
136 *Catalan Sheepdog* M. Guasch
Roler
137 *Portuguese Sheepdog* Borges,
M. Loureiro; Canil do Magoito;
Canil da Valeira; Cunha,
M.L.N. Lopes; Gomez-Toldra
138 *Catahoula Leopard Dog*
M. Neal

IOUNDS
139 *Plott Hound* J. M. Koons;
B. L. Taylor & M. Seets; *Bluetick
Coonhound* D. McCormick;
R. Welch & B. Slaymon
140 *English Coonhound* M. Seets;
Mantanona
141 *Redbone Coonhound*
& C. Heck; C. Elburn
142–43 *Black and Tan Coonhound*
. & A. Shorter; D. Fentee &
R. Speer Jnr.
144 *Treeing Walker Coonhound*
E. Currens; J. Girnot & W. Haynes
145 *American Foxhound*
. Cannon
146 *Basset Hound* N. Frost;
Beagle M. Hunt
147 *Foxhound* The Berks and
Bucks Draghounds
148 *Deerhound* D. & J. Murray
149 *Otter Hound* Smith
150 *Greyhound* J. Baylis;
. Baudon
151 *Whippet* Oliver; S. Horsnell
152 *Dunker* Almerud
153 *Haldenstovare* G. Lerstad
154 *Hygenhund* R. Langland;
Finnish Hound T. Olkkonen;
Vilpula
155 *Drever* L. Jönsson;
Schillerstövare (refer to publisher)
156 *Hamiltonstövare* D. Cook
157 *Smålandsstövare* K. Skolmi
158–59 *Miniature Dachshund*
(long coat) L. Mears; (smooth
coat) B. Clark; (wire coat)
Seymour
160 *Hanoverian Mountain Hound*
Voegelen; *Bavarian Schweisshund*
Voegelen
161 *Polish Hound* A. Marculanis
162–63 *Irish Wolfhound* (grey)
Smith; A. Bennett
164 *Kerry Beagle* J. Sugrue;
O'Shea; M. O'Sullivan; P. Daly;
Kelly
165 *Lurcher* C. Labers
166–67 *Bloodhound* Richards
168 *Billy* A. Benoit
169 *Basset Fauve de Bretagne*
. Frost

• **170–71** *Grand Bleu de Gascogne*
Braddick
• **172** *Chien d'Artois* A. Lopez;
N.Bellet
• **173** *Basset Bleu de Gascogne*
J. Nenmann; *Basset Artésian
Normand* B. Hemmingsson
• **174** *Grand Gascon-Saintongeois*
(refer to publisher)
• **175** *Grand Basset Griffon Vendéen*
N. Frost & V. Philips
• **176** *Grand Griffon Vendéen*
G. Lamoureux; D. Boursier
• **177** *Briquet Griffon Vendéen*
D. Fabre; *Griffon Nivernais*
D. Duede
• **178** *Petit Bleu de Gascogne* (refer
to publisher)
• **179** *Petit Griffon Bleu de Gascogne*
(refer to publisher)
• **180** *Anglo-Francais de Petite
Vénerie* A. Dubois
• **181** *Griffon Fauve de Bretagne*
Cann
• **182** *Porcelaine* R. Lavergme
• **183** *Jura Laufhund: Bruno*
P. Guenole
• **184–85** *Jura Laufhund (St.
Hubert)* M. Aigret
• **186** *Hungarian Greyhound*
T. Christiansen; *Berner Laufhund*
R.J. Luchtmeijer
• **187** *Schweizer Laufhund*
O. Bonslet
• **188** *Luzerner Laufhund*
M.B. Mervaille
• **189** *Balkan Hound*
I. Vicentijevic; *Posavac Hound*
Z. Marinkovic
• **190** *Yugoslavian Mountain Hound*
D. Milosevic
• **191** *Yugoslavian Tricolored Hound*
R. Andelkovic
• **192** *Cirneco dell'Etna* D.H. Blom
• **193** *Pharaoh Hound* J. Gostynska
• **194** *Ibisan Hound* Carter &
Donnaby; F. Benecke
• **195** *Sabueso Español*
J.C. Palomo Romero
• **196** *Spanish Greyhound* J.F. Olij
& J.W. Luijken; L. Rapeport
• **197** *Podengo Portugueso Pequeño*
Macedo, L. Vaz; Reis,
A.S. Oliveira
• **198** *Podengo Portugueso Medio*
Canil G. Oleganense; Canil de
Veiros; Canil do Vale do Criz
• **199** *Saluki* (black) Ziman;
(grizzle) Spooner
• **200** *Borzoi* A.G.C. Simmonds
• **201** *Azawakh Hound* A.Hellblom
• **202** *Afghan Hound* R. Savage
• **203** *Sloughi* L. Vassalo
• **204** *Kai Dog* M. Malone
• **205** *Rhodesian Ridgeback*
M. & J. Morris

TERRIERS
• **206** *American Toy Fox Terrier*
A. Mauermann
• **207** *American Pit Bull Terrier*
P. Perdue; (orange and white)
T. Davis

• **208** *American Staffordshire Terrier*
M. & K. Slotboom; *Boston Terrier*
Barker
• **209** *Airedale Terrier* M. Swash &
O. Jackson; *Bedlington Terrier*
A. Yearley
• **210** *English Toy Terrier* T. Wright;
Manchester Terrier E. Eva
• **211** *Border Terrier* Dean;
Norwich Terrier R.W.J. Thomas
• **212** *Miniature Bull Terrier* Berry;
Staffordshire Bull Terrier
G. & B. McAuliffe
• **213** *Dandie Dinmont Terrier*
P. Keevil & S. Bullock; *Cairn
Terrier* K. Holmes
• **214** *Lakeland Terrier* J.C. Ruiz
Mogrera; Hedges; *Norfolk Terrier*
N. Kruger
• **215** *Parson Jack Russell Terrier*
J.P. Wood; *Wire Fox Terrier*
J. Palosaari; G. Düring
• **216** *Smooth Fox Terrier*
L. Bochese; *Welsh Terrier*
G. Aalderink
• **217** *Scottish Terrier* M.L. Daltrey;
Skye Terrier P. Bennett; (puppies)
D. & J. Miller
• **218** *Patterdale Terrier* B. Nuttall;
West Highland White Terrier
S. Thompson; J. Pastor &
M. Gonzalbo
• **219** *Yorkshire Terrier* H. Ridgwell
• **220** *Sealyham Terrier* D. Winsley;
Australian Terrier R. Buch-Jorgens
• **221** *Australian Silky Terrier*
I. Schmied; *German Hunting Terrier*
B. Andersson
• **222** *German Pinscher*
R. & M. Collicott; Boyer
• **223** *Affenpinscher* A.J. Teasdale;
Miniature Pinscher Gentle; A. Coull
• **224** *Miniature Schnauzer*
P. Gowlett
• **225** *Kromfohrländer* (short coat)
M. Schaub; (long coat) H. Hoppert
• **226** *Irish Terrier* A. Noonan &
Williamson
• **227** *Soft-coated Wheaten Terrier*
Hanton, Moyes, & Pettit
• **228** *Glen of Imaal Terrier*
J. Withers; *Kerry Blue Terrier*
Campbell
• **229** *Griffon Bruxellois* A.V. Fenn;
(black) H. Bleeker & J. den Otte
• **230** *Austrian Short-haired Pinscher*
I. Hartgers-Wagener; *Cesky Terrier*
D. Delplanque

WORKING DOGS
• **231** *American Bulldog* S. Leclerc
• **232** *Olde English Bulldogge* (refer
to publisher)
• **233** *Chinook* T.J. and G. Anderson; D. & C. Hendricks; *Carolina
Dog* S. McKenzie
• **234–35** *Alaskan Malamute* Lena-
Britt Egnell
• **236–37** *Mastiff* D. Blaxter; (dark
brindle) B. Stoffelen-Luyten
• **238** *Bull Mastiff* J. & A. Gunn
• **239** *Bull Terrier* Youatt; *Eskimo
Dog* E. & S. Hammond

- **240–41** *Newfoundland* Cutts & Galvin; (black and white) Cutts
- **242** *Dogo Argentino* Roelofs
- **243** *Fila Brasileiro* E.H. Vlietman
- **244** *Greenland Dog* M. Dragone; M. Demoor
- **245** *Norwegian Elkhound* A. Meijer; *Black Norwegian Elkhound* K. Bonaunet
- **246** *Lundehund* M. Jansson; *Norwegian Buhund* R.W.J. Thomas
- **247** *Finnish Spitz* Gatti; *Karelian Bear Dog* P. Gritsh
- **248** *Swedish Elkhound* A. Johansson
- **249** *Swedish Lapphund* R.A. Wind-Heuser; *Norbottenspets* A. Piltto
- **250–51** *Dobermann* K. le Mare; (head) B. Schellekens & S. Franquemont
- **252–53** *Great Dane* (fawn with black mask) D.J. Parish; (harlequin) N. Marriner
- **254** *Standard Poodle* E.A. Beswick
- **255** *Boxer* G. Nielsen & D. Spencer; *Eurasier* J. Bos Waaldijk
- **256–57** *Landseer* G. Cutts
- **258–59** *Leonberger* F. Inwood
- **260** *Rottweiler* Hine; T. Barnett

- **261** *Owczarek Podhalanski* G.V. Rijsewijk
- **262** *Schipperke* L. Wilson
- **263** *French Bulldog* J. Keates; *Dogue de Bordeaux* A.E. Neuteboom
- **264–65** *Pyrenean Mountain Dog* I. & W. Spencer-Brown
- **266** *Komondor* P. & M. Froome
- **267** *Kuvasz* J. Schelling; I. & H. Wallin
- **268** *Mudi* (refer to publisher)
- **269** *Appensell Mountain Dog* W. Glocker; *Entelbuch Mountain Dog* C. Fransson
- **270–71** *Bernese Mountain Dog* A. Hayden; (puppy) A. Hearne
- **272** *Great Swiss Mountain Dog* H. Hannberger
- **273** *St. Bernard* (short-haired) H. Golverdingen; (long-haired) T. Hansen
- **274** *Dalmatian* K. Goff
- **275** *Maremma Sheepdog* T. Barnes
- **276–77** *Neapolitan Mastiff* (black) A. E. Useletti; (grey) A.P. van Doremalen
- **278** *Pyrenean Mastiff* G. Marin
- **279** *Spanish Mastiff* Camps & Ritter
- **280** *Perro de Pastor Mallorquin* J. M. Martinez Alonso; *Perro de*

Presa Mallorquín J.J. Calderón Ruiz; E. Lurbe; M. Calvino Breijo
- **281** *Canaan Dog* M. Macphail
- **282** *Estrela Mountain Dog* P. Olsson; E. Bentzer
- **283** *Rafeiro do Alentejo* Gomes, J. Oliveira
- **284** *Portuguese Cattle Dog* Canil do Casal da Granja; Amorim, J.M.P. de Lima; Macedo, L. Vaz; *Russo-European Laika* S. Enochsson; B. Vujasinovic
- **285** *East Siberian Laika* L. Milic; *West Siberian Laika* S. Enochsson
- **286** *Siberian Husky* S. Hull
- **287** *Samoyed* C. Fox
- **288** *Chow Chow* P. Goedgezelschap; U. Berglöf
- **289** *Sharpei* B. & C. Lilley
- **290** *Akita Inu* A. Rickard
- **291** *Shiba Inu* M. Atkinson; *Tosa Inu* F. Kappe
- **292** *Japanese Terrier* M. Delaye; *Ainu* M.G. Schippers Hasselman
- **293** *Tibetan Mastiff.* P. Rees-Jones & E. Holliday
- **294** *Perro de Presa Canario* D. Kelly; Grupo los Enanos
- **295** *Aidi* M. Bouayad (Cluc Chien Atlas); *New Guinea Singing Dog* A. Riddle; P. & F. Persky

USEFUL ADDRESSES

The Kennel Club
1–5 Clarges Street, London W1Y 8AB, UK
www.the-kennel-club.org.uk

National Canine Defence League
17 Wakely Street, London EC1V 7LT, UK

The RSPCA
Causeway, Horsham, West Sussex RH12 1HG, UK
www.rspca.org.uk

Australian National Kennel Council
PO Box 285, Red Hill South, Vic 3937, Australia

New Zealand Kennel Club
Private Bag 50903, Porirua 6220, New Zealand
www.nzkc.org.nz

Irish Kennel Club
Fottrell House, Harold's Cross Bridge, Dublin 6W, Republic of Ireland
www.ikc.ie

Société Centrale Canine pour l'Amélioration des Races de Chiens en France
55, Avenue Jean Jaurès, F - 93535 Aubervilliers Cedex, France

Verband für das Deutsche Hundewesen
Westfalendamm 174,
Postfach 10 41 54,
D - 4600 - Dortmund 1, Germany

Clube Portuguès de Canicultura
Praça D. Joao Da Camara 4 - 3° Esq.
1200 - 147 Lisboa, Portugal
www.cpc.pt

Raad van Beheer op Kynologisch Gebied in Nederland, Postbus 75901
Nl - 1070 ax Amsterdam, Netherlands

GLOSSARY

• **ANGULATION**
Angle formed by the meeting of bones at a joint.

• **BARREL**
Rounded chest shape.

• **BAT EARS**
Erect ears, wide at the base and rounded at the tips, pointing out.

• **BAY**
Call of hounds in pursuit of quarry.

• **BEARD**
Long, thick hair around the jaws.

• **BELTON**
Blue-lemon flecked coloration associated with English Setters.

• **BITE**
The positioning of the upper and lower teeth relative to each other.

• **BLAZE**
White marking running down forehead to muzzle.

• **BOBTAIL**
Closely docked tail – or missing altogether on breeds born tail-less.

• **BRINDLE**
Combination of light and dark hairs, resulting in darker streaking.

• **BRISKET**
Area of the chest between the forelegs, including the breastbone.

• **BROKEN-COATED**
Rough, wire coat.

• **BRUSH**
Bushy tail.

• **BUTTERFLY NOSE**
Nose of two colours.

• **BUTTON EARS**
Semi-erect ears, folding over at their tips.

• **CLIP**
Type of trim, associated particularly with poodles.

• **COBBY**
Short-bodied and compact.

• **CONFORMATION**
Overall shape, resulting from combined relationship of all of a dog's physical parts.

• **COUPLING**
Region extending from the last rib to the pelvis.

• **COW-HOCKED**
Hocks point in towards each other.

• **CROP**
Removal of the tops of the ears, causing them to stand erect.

• **CROUP**
Area of back closest to tail.

• **CULOTTE**
Long hair at the back of the thighs.

• **DEW CLAW**
Claw on the inside of the legs, often removed in young puppies.

• **DEWLAP**
Pendulous, loose skin under the throat, as seen in the Bloodhound.

• **DOCK**
Shortening of the tail by cutting.

• **DOUBLE COAT**
Guard hairs protruding through softer, insulating layer beneath.

• **DROP EAR**
Ears that hang down, close to the sides of the head.

• **ELBOW**
Joint below shoulder.

• **ENTROPION**
Eye abnormality causing almost continual irritation.

• **FALL**
Hair hanging down over the face.

• **FEATHERING**
Long fringes of hair on the ears, body, legs, and tail.

• **FLEWS**
Pendulous upper lips.

• **FRILL**
Longer hair present on the lower neck and front of the chest.

• **GRIZZLE**
Bluish grey colour.

• **GUARD HAIRS**
Coarser outer hairs.

• **HACKLES**
Hair on the neck and back, raised to show aggression or fright.

• **HARE FEET**
Relatively long and narrow feet.

• **HARLEQUIN**
Black or blue patches set against white, as seen in the Great Dane.

• **HAUNCHES**
Back of thighs, in contact with the ground when the dog is sitting.

• **HOCK**
Hindleg joint – the dog's heels.

• **JOWLS**
The fleshy part of the lips and jaws.

• **LEATHER**
Ear flap.

• **LOBULAR**
Lobe shaped.

• **LOINS**
Region from last rib to back legs.

• **MANE**
Long hair on and around the neck.

• **MASK**
Dark, mask-like shading on head.

• **MERLE**
Marbled coat pattern, caused by darker patches on lighter background of same basic colour.

• **MUZZLE**
Portion of head in front of eyes.

• **OCCIPUT**
Highest part on back of skull.

• **PASTERN**
Lower part of leg, between wrist and foot.

• **PLUME**
Soft hair on the tail.

• **POINT**
Immovable stance of a hunting dog, indicating location of game.

• **POINTS**
Body extremities, usually referring to the coloration of ears, face, legs, and tail.

• **ROACHED**
Convex arching of the back.

• **ROAN**
Mixture of white and another colour, in even proportions.

• **ROSE-EARED**
Typically small ears, which fold down and show the inside.

• **RUFF**
Long, thick hair encircling neck.

• **SABLE**
White coat, shaded with black.

• **SABRE TAIL**
Tail in the shape of a semi-circle.

• **SADDLE**
Black markings in the shape and position of a saddle.

• **SOFT MOUTH**
A characteristic of hunting dogs, indicating ability to retrieve game without damaging it.

• **STAND-OFF COAT**
Long, heavy coat standing out from body, as in the Keeshond.

• **STIFLE**
Hindleg joint, the angle of which is important in breed standards.

• **STOP**
Depression between the eyes, where skull and nasal bone meet.

• **TICKING**
Coat pattern in which spots of colour stand out against the basic background colour.

• **TRIM**
Grooming that entails clipping or plucking.

• **WHELPING**
Giving birth to puppies.

• **WITHERS**
Highest point of the shoulders, behind the neck.

INDEX

A

Aberdeen Terrier 217
Affenpinscher 223
Afghan Hound 202
African Lion Hound 205
African Wild Dog 10
aggression 19
agility events 8
Aidi 295
Ainu 292
Airedale Terrier 209
Akita 290
Alaskan Malamute 234
Alopex lagopus 10
Alsatian 119
American Black and Tan Coonhound 142
American Bulldog 231
American Cocker Spaniel 60
American Foxhound 145
American Kennel Club 6
American Pit Bull 207
American Pit Bull Terrier 207
American Staffordshire Terrier 208
American Toy Terrier 206
anatomy 14
Anglo-Francais, de Petite
  Vénerie 180
Appensell Mountain Dog 269
Appenzeller Sennenhund 269
Arabian Greyhound 203
Arctic Fox 10
Arctic Husky 286
Argentinian Grey Fox 11
Argentinian Mastiff 242
Artesian Norman Basset 173
Atelocynus microtis 10
Australian Cattle Dog 112
Australian Kelpie 113
Australian Queensland Heeler 112
Australian Shepherd 105
Australian Silky Terrier 221
Australian Terrier 220
Austrian Pinscher 230
Auvergne Pointer 90
Azawakh Hound 201

B

Balkan Hound 189
Balkanski Gonic 189
Barb 113
Barbet 95
Barbone 48, 254
Basenji 59
Bas Rouge 115
Basset Artésian Normand 173
Basset Bleu de Gascogne 173
Basset Fauve de Bretagne 169
Basset Hound 146
Bat-eared Fox 10
bathing 26
Bavarian Mountain Hound 160
baying 18
Bayrischer Gebirgsschweisshund 160
Beagle 146

Bearded Collie 106
Beauceron 115
Bedlington Terrier 209
Belgian Cattle Dog 130
Belgian Griffon 229
Bergamasco 135
Berger de Beauce 115
Berger de Brie 116
Berger de Picard 118
Berner Laufhund 186
Berner Sennenhund 270
Bernese Hound 186
Bernese Mountain Dog 270
Bichon Bolognese 51
Bichon Frise 58
Bichon Havanais 43
Bichon Maltiase 57
Billy 168
Bingley Terrier 209
Björnhund 247
Black and Tan Coonhound 142
Black and Tan Terrier 210
Black Fell Terrier 218
Black Norwegian Elkhound 245
Bloodhound 166
Blue Gascony Basset 173
Blue Heeler 112
Blue Picardy Spaniel 96
Bluetick Coonhound 139
Bobtail 110
Bohemian Terrier 230
Bolognese 51
Border Collie 107
Border Terrier 211
Borzoi 200
Boston Terrier 208
Bouledogue Français 263
Bourbonnais Pointer 91
Bouvier des Flandres 130
Boxer 255
Bracco Italiano 101
Braque d'Auvergne 90
Braque du Bourbonnais 91
Braque Français de Grande Taille 88
Braque St. Germain 87
Brazilian Mastiff 243
breed standards 6
Briard 116
Briquet 172
Briquet Griffon Vendéen 177
Brittany 93
Broken-haired Scottish Terrier 219
brushing 24
Brushwood Dog 291
Brussels Griffon 229
Bulldog 39
Bullmastiff 238
Bull Terrier 239
Bush Dog 10

C

Ca de Bestiar 280
Ca de Bou 280
Cairn Terrier 213
Canaan Dog 281

Canadian Kennel Club 7
Canary Dog 294
Cane da Pastore Bergamasco 135
Cane de Quirinale 51
Caniche 47, 48, 254
Canidae 10
Canis adustus 10
Canis aureus 10
Canis dingo 10
Canis familiaris 10
Canis latrans 10
Canis lupus 10
Canis mesomelas 10
Canis rufus 10
Canis simensis 10
Cão da Serra de Aires 137
Cão da Serra da Estrela 282
Cão de Agua 103
Cão de Castro Laboreiro 284
Cape Fox 11
Cardigan Welsh Corgi 111
Carlin 53
Carolina Dog 233
Catahoula Hog Dog 138
Catahoula Leopard Dog 138
Catalan Sheepdog 136
Cavalier King Charles 40
Cerdocyon thous 10
Cesky Terrier 230
Chesapeake Bay Retriever 61
Chien d'Artois 172
Chien de Franche-Comte 182
Chien de l'Atlas 295
Chien de Pays 177
Chien des Pyrénées 264
Chien Loup 46
Chihuahua 41
Chin 56
Chinese Crested Dog 54
Chinook 233
choosing a dog 22
choosing a pup 23
Chow Chow 288
Chrysanthemum Dog 53
Chrysocyon brachyurus 10
Cirneco dell'Etna 192
clipping 26
Clumber Spaniel 62
coat colours 17
coat types 29
Cocker Spaniel 60, 63
Cocker Spaniel (American) 60
collars 25
Collie
  Bearded 106
  Border 107
  Rough 108
  Smooth 109
  Smooth-haired 109
colour types 17
Colpeo Fox 11
companion dogs 38
Congo Dog 59
Continental Phalene 46
Continental Toy Spaniel: Papillon 47
Continental Toy Spaniel: Phalene 46

Corgi
  Cardigan Welsh 111
  Pembroke Welsh 111
Corsac Fox 11
Coton de Tulear 59
Coyote 10
Crab-eating Fox 10
Cruft, Charles 7
Cuon alpinus 10
Curly-coated Retriever 64
Czesky 230
Czesky Fousek 97

D

Dalmatian 274
Dandie Dinmont Terrier 213
Deerhound 148
Deutsche Dogge 252
Deutscher Drahthaariger
  Vorstehhund 78
Deutscher Gross Spitz 44
Deutscher Jagdterrier 221
Deutscher Mittel Spitz 44
Deutscher Schäferhund 119
Deutscher Wachtelhund 75
Deutsche Spitz 45
dew claws 15
Dhokhi Apso 55
Dhole 10
Dingo 11
Dobermann 250
Doberman Pinscher 250
docked tail 29
dog beds 24
dog identification 28
Dogo Argentino 242
Dogue de Bordeaux 263
domestication 6
domestic dog 10
domestic dog groups 12
Drentse Partijshond 82
Drever 155
Drótszörü Magyar Vizsla 99
Dunker 152
Dusicyon culpaeus 11
Dusicyon griseus 11
Dusicyon gymnocercus 11
Dusicyon microtis 11
Dusicyon sechurae 11
Dusicyon thous 11
Dusicyon vetulus 11
Dutch Partridge Dog 82
Dutch Sheepdog 123
Dutch Shepherd Dog 124
Dutch Spaniel 83

E

ear cleaning 25
ear cropping 14
ear shape 29
East Siberian Laika 285
Elkhound 245
English Beagle 146
English Bull Terrier 239
English Cocker Spaniel 63
English Coonhound 140

English Foxhound 147
English Setter 65
English Springer Spaniel 66
English Toy Terrier 210
Entlebucher 269
Entlebuch Mountain Dog 269
Epagneul Bleu de Picardie 96
Epagneul Breton 93
Epagneul Français 92
Epagneul Nain 46, 47
Epagneul Picard 92
Epagneul Pont-Audemer 94
equipment 24
Eskimo Dog 239
Esquimaux 239
Estrela Mountain Dog 282
Eurasian 255
Eurasier 255
exercise 21

F

Fennec Fox 11
Field Spaniel 67
Fila Brasileiro 243
Finnish Hound 154
Finnish Lapphund 114
Finnish Spitz 247
Finsk Spets 247
Flat-coated Retriever 67
food bowls 25
Foxhound 147
French Bulldog 263
French Mastiff 263
French Spaniel 92
Friaar Dog 132

G

Galgo Español 196
Gammel Dansk Honsehund 74
Gazelle Hound 199
German Hunting Terrier 221
German Pinscher 222
German Shepherd Dog 119
German Spaniel 75
German Spitz: Klein 45
German Spitz: Mittel 44
German Wire-haired Pointer 78
gestation period 20
Giant German Spitz 44
Giant Schnauzer 122
Glen of Imaal Terrier 228
Golden Jackal 10
Golden Retriever 68
Gordon Setter 66
Gos d'Atura Catala 136
Grand Basset Griffon Vendéen 175
Grand Bleu de Gascogne 170
Grand Gascon Saintongeois 174
Grand Griffon Vendéen 176
Great Dane 252
Great Pyrenees 264
Great Swiss Mountain Dog 272
Greenland Dog 244
Grey Fox 11
Greyhound 150
Grey Wolf 10

Griffon Belge 229
Griffon Bruxellois 229
Griffon d'Arrêt à Poil Laineux 95
Griffon Fauve de Bretagne 181
Griffon Nivernais 177
Groenendael 126
Grønlandshund 244
grooming 16
Grosser Münsterländer Vorstehhund 80
Grosser Schweizer Sennenhund 272
Grünlandshund 244
guard dogs 23
gundogs 60

H

Halden Hound 153
Haldenstövare 153
Hamilton Hound 156
Hamiltonstövare 156
Hanoverian Mountain Hound 160
Hanoverian Schweisshund 160
Harrier 151
Havanese 43
head shape 28
hearing 18
heat 20
Heidewachtel 79
herding dogs 105
Hoary Fox 11
Hokkaido Dog 292
Hollandse Herdershond 124
hounds 138
Hovawart 120
howling 18
Hungarian Greyhound 186
Hungarian Mudi 268
Hungarian Puli 133
Hungarian Vizsla 98
Husky 239
Hygenhound 154
Hygenhund 154

I

Ibizan Hound 194
Iceland Dog 132
Icelandic Sheepdog 132
Illyrian Sheepdog 134

Inca Hairless 43
Indian Fox 11
instincts 18
Irish Red and White Setter 85
Irish Red Terrier 226
Irish Setter 86
Irish Terrier 226
Irish Water Spaniel 84
Irish Wolfhound 162
Island Grey Fox 11
Istrian Sheepdog 134
Italian Greyhound 50
Italian Hound 192
Italian Pointer 101
Italian Spinone 100

J

Jämthund 248
Japanese Akita 290
Japanese Chin 56
Japanese Small-sized Dog 291
Japanese Spaniel 56
Japanese Spitz 57
Japanese Terrier 292
Jugoslavenski Planinski Gonic 190
Jugoslavenski Tribarvni Gonic 191
Jura Hound 183, 184
Jura Laufhund: Bruno 183
Jura Laufhund: St. Hubert 184

K

Kai Dog 204
Karelian Bear Dog 247
Karelian Bear Laika 284
Karjalankarhukoira 247
Karst Sheepdog 134
Keeshond 46
Kelb Tal-fenek 193
Kelef K'naani 281
Kelpie 113
Kennel Club 6
Kerry Beagle 164
Kerry Blue Terrier 228
King Charles Spaniel 40
Kit Fox 11
Kleiner Münsterländer 79
Komondor 266
Kooiker Dog 82
Kooikerhondje 82
Korthals Griffon 97
Krasky Ovcar 134
Kromfohrländer 225
Kuvasz 267
Kyi Leo 38

L

Labrador Retriever 69
Lackense 127
Laekenois 127
Lakeland Terrier 214
Lancashire Heeler 107
Landseer 256
Lapinkoira 114
Lapinporokoira 114
Lapland Reindeer Dog 114

Lapplandska Spets 249
Large Blue Gascony Hound 170
large dogs 36
Large French Pointer 88
Large Münsterländer 80
Large Vendéen Griffon 175, 176
leashes 25
Leonberger 258
Lhasa Apso 56
Little Lion Dog 49
liver coat 17
Löwchen 49
Lucernese Hound 188
Lundehund 246
Lurcher 165
Luzerner Laufhund 188
Lycaon pictus 10

M

Magyar Agár 186
Magyar Vizsla 98
Malinois 129
Maltese 57
Manchester Terrier 210
Maned Wolf 10
Maremma Sheepdog 275
Mastiff 236
  Argentinian 242
  Brazilian 243
  French 263
  Neapolitan 276
  Pyrenean 278
  Spanish 279
  Tibetan 293
Mastin Español 279
Mastino Napoletano 276
medicine, administering 25
Medium Portuguese Hound 198
medium-sized dogs 32
Medium Vendéen Griffon 177
Mexican Hairless 42
Miniature Bull Terrier 212
Miniature Dachshund 158
Miniature Pinscher 223
Miniature Poodle 48
Miniature Schnauzer 224
mongrels 23
Mops 53
Mudi 268
mummified dogs 6

N

Neapolitan Mastiff 276
Newfoundland 240
New Guinea Singing Dog 295
Nordic Spitz 249
Norfolk Terrier 214
Norrbottenspets 249
Norsk Buhund 246
Norsk Elghund (Grå) 245
Norsk Elghund (Sort) 245
Norwegian Buhund 246
Norwegian Elkhound 245
Norwegian Hound 152
Norwegian Puffin Dog 246
Norwich Terrier 211

Nova Scotia Duck Tolling Retriever 73
nutritional care 25
Nyctereutes procyonoides 10

O

Ogar Polski 161
Old Country Bulldog 231
Old Danish Pointer 74
Olde English Bulldogge 232
Old English Sheepdog 110
open shows 8
Ormskirk Terrier 107
Österreichischer Kurzhaariger
  Pinscher 230
Otocyon megalotis 10
Otterhoun 83
Otter Hound 149
Owczarek Podhalanski 261

P

Pale Fox 11
Pampas Fox 11
Parson Jack Russell Terrier 215
Pastore Abruzzese 275
Patterdale Terrier 218
Pekingese 52
Pekingese Palasthund 52
Pembroke Welsh Corgi 111
Perdiguero de Burgos 102
Perdiguero Portugueso 104
Perro de Pastor Mallorquin 280
Perro de Presa Canario 294
Perro de Presa Mallorquin 280
Perro Mastin del Pireneo 278
Peruvian Hairless Dog 43
Petit Basset Griffon Vendéen 175
Petit Bleu de Gascogne 178
Petite Brabancon 229
Petit Griffon Bleu de Gascogne 179
pet care 24
pets 22
Pharaoh Hound 193
Picardy Shepherd 118
Picardy Spaniel 92
Piccolo Levrieri Italiani 50
Pinscher
  Austrian 230
  Doberman 250
  German 222
  Miniature 223
  Österreichischer Kurzhaariger 230
  Reh 223
  Standard 222
Pit Bull Terrier 207
play 25
Plott Hound 139
Pocadan 164
Podenco Ibicenco 194
Podengo Portugueso Medio 198
Podengo Portugueso Pequeño 197
Pohjanpystykorva 249
Pointer 70
  Auvergne 90
  Bourbonnais 91
  German Wire-haired 78
  Italian 101

Large French 88
Old Danish 74
Portuguese 104
St. Germain 87
Spanish 102
olish Hound 161
olish Lowland Sheepdog 123
olski Owczarek Nizinny 123
omeranian 45
ont-Audemer Spaniel 94
orcelaine 182
ortuguese Cattle Dog 284
ortuguese Pointer 104
ortuguese Sheepdog 137
ortuguese Watchdog 283
ortuguese Water Dog 103
osavac Hound 189
osavski Gonic 189
ug 53
uli 133
umi 133
uppies 20
yrenean Mastiff 278
yrenean Mountain Dog 264

R

accoon Dog 10
afeiro do Alentejo 283
edbone Coonhound 141
ed Fox 10
ed Setter 86
edtick Coonhound 140
ed Wolf 10
ch Pinscher 223
etriever
  Chesapeake Bay 61
  Curly-coated 64
  Flat-coated 67
  Golden 68
  Labrador 69
  Nova Scotia Duck Tolling 73
  Russian 68
  Yellow 68
hodesian Ridgeback 205
esenschnauzer 122
othbury Terrier 209
ottweiler 260
ough Collie 108
üppell's Fox 11
usso European Laika 284
ussian Retriever 68
ussian Wolfhound 200

S

arloos Wolfhound 125
bueso Español 195
. Bernard 273
  Bernhardshund 273
. Germain Pointer 87
. Hubert Hound 166
aluki 199
moyed 287
moyedskaja 287
r Planina 134
rplaninac 134
ent marking 19

Schapendoes 123
Schiller Hound 155
Schillerstövare 155
Schipperke 262
Schweizer Laufhund 187
Scottish Deerhound 148
Scottish Terrier 217
Sealyham Terrier 220
Sechura Fox 11
Segugio Italiano 192
senses 18
Shar Pei 289
Sheepdog
  Catalan 136
  Dutch 123
  Icelandic 132
  Illyrian 134
  Istrian 134
  Karst 134
  Maremma 275
  Old English 110
  Polish Lowland 123
  Portuguese 137
  Shetland 109
  Tatra Mountain 261
sheepdog trials 8
Shepherd Dog
  Dutch 124
  German 119
Shetland Sheepdog 109
Shiba Inu 291
Shih Tzu 53
short hair 29
showing 26–27
Siberian Husky 286
Sicilian Greyhound 192
Side-striped Jackal 10
sight 18
Silky Terrier 221
Silver-backed Jackal 10
Simien Jackal 10
size 28
skeleton 14
skull 15
Skye Terrier 217
sleeping quarters 24
Sloughi 203
Smålands Hound 157
Smålandsstövare 157
small dogs 30
Small-eared Dog 10
Small-eared Fox 11
Small French-English Hound 180
Small Münsterländer 79
Small Portuguese Hound 197
smell 18
Smooth Collie 109
Smooth Fox Terrier 216
Smooth-haired Collie 109
sociability 19
Soft-coated Wheaten Terrier 227
South American Fox 11
Spaniel
  American Cocker 60
  Blue Picardy 96
  Clumber 62
  Cocker 60, 63

Continental Toy 46
Dutch 83
English Cocker 63
English Springer 66
Field 67
French 92
German 75
Irish Water 84
Japanese 56
King Charles 40
Picardy 92
Pont-Audemer 94
Sussex 72
Tibetan 55
Welsh Springer 72
Spanish Greyhound 196
Spanish Hound 195
Spanish Mastiff 279
Spanish Pointer 102
Speothos venaticus 10
Spinone 100
Spion 79
Stabyhoun 83
Staffordshire Bull Terrier 212
Standard Pinscher 222
Standard Poodle 254
submission 19
Suomenajokoira 154
Suomenpystykorva 247
Sussex Spaniel 72
Swedish Dachsbracker 155
Swedish Elkhound 248
Swedish Lapphund 249
Swedish Vallhund 132
Swift Fox 11
Swiss Hound 187
Sydney Silky 221

T

tail docking 14
tail types 29
tan and white coat 17
Tatra Mountain Sheepdog 261
Tawny Brittany Basset 169
Tawny Britanny Griffon 181
Tazi 202
teeth care 25
Tenerife Dog 58
Tepeizeuintli 42
terriers 206
Tervuren 128

Tibetan Mastiff 293
Tibetan Sand Fox 11
Tibetan Spaniel 55
Tibetan Terrier 55
Tora Dog 204
Tosa Fighting Dog 291
Tosa Inu 291
Toy American Eskimo 39
Toy Fox Terrier 206
Toy Manchester Terrier 210
Toy Poodle 47
toys 25
training 21
Treeing Walker Coonhound 144
Tuareg Sloughi 201

V

Väsgötaspets 132
Virelade 174
Volpino Italiano 51
Vorstehhund 79

Vulpes bengalensis 11
Vulpes cana 11
Vulpes chama 11
Vulpes cinereoargenteus 11
Vulpes corsac 11
Vulpes ferrilata 11
Vulpes littoralis 11
Vulpes macrotis 11
Vulpes pallida 11
Vulpes ruepelli 11
Vulpes velox 11
Vulpes vulpes 10
Vulpes zerda 11

W

Waterside Terrier 209
weaning 20
Weimaraner 76
Weimaraner Vorstehhund 76
Welsh Springer Spaniel 72
Welsh Terrier 216

West Highland White Terrier 218
West Siberian Laika 285
Wetterhoun 83
Whippet 151
Wire Fox Terrier 215
wire hair 29
Wire-haired Pointing Griffon 97
Wire-haired Vizsla 99
wolf 6
Wolf Spitz 46
working dogs 231

XYZ

Xoloitzcuintli 42
Yellow Retriever 68
Yorkshire Terrier 219
Yugoslavian Mountain Hound 190
Yugoslavian Tricoloured Hound 191
Zwergpinscher 223
Zwergschnauzer 224
Zwergteckel 158

ACKNOWLEDGMENTS

THE AUTHOR AND PUBLISHER are indebted to a number of institutions and people, without whom this book could not have been produced: Mia Sandgren, Magnus Berglin, Thomas Miller, Maria Bruga, Steve Fielder, Jovan Serafin, Luis Isaac Barata, Luis Manuel Calado Catalan, Dr. J.L. Slack, Anita Bryant, Sergio Montesinos Vernetta, Ann Houdijk, Antonio Consta, Jose Carrera, Steven Boer, Egon Erdenbrecher, Mr. & Mrs. Lawlor, Mr. K. Bent, E. Vanherle, Dr. Herbert R. Axelrod, John Miller, M. Peonchon, Patrick Schwab, Mme. Dhetz, Stella Smyth, Mandy Hearne, Heather Head. Special thanks are also due to Sabine Weiss of SDK Verlags GmbH; Susanne Marlier of the Fédération Cynologigue Internationale; Susanne Lindberg of the norsk kennel klub; M. Noblet of the Société Centrale Canine; Mme Mila of the Fédération Cynologique de Yugoslavie; Mme. Durando of the Société Canine de Monaco, and Her Serene Highness, Princess Antoinette de Monaco.

Photography by Tracy Morgan, except for: p.6 (left) Bridgeman Art Library; p.7 (centre & bottom) The Kennel Club; p.8 (bottom), p.13 (top & bottom), p.151 (bottom) Animal Photography; p.8 (centre), p.174, p.178, p.179 Marc Henrie; p.152, p.153, p.154 (top), p.157, p.187, p.245 (bottom), p.268 Sandra Russell; p.155 (bottom), p.249 (bottom) Neil Fletcher; p.11 (right), p.12 (top), p.16 (top) Bruce Coleman Picture Library; p.145 (top right & centre) TFH Publications, Inc.; p.181 (top) Sunset NHPA.

The author would like to thank the many kind dog fanciers around the world who have allowed their dogs to be photographed. A particular debt is due to Tracy Morgan who, with the help of her husband, Neil, undertook the bulk of the photography, and to Andrea Fair who arranged the overseas trips. He would also like to thank Neil Fletcher, Marc and Fiona Henrie, James Harrison, Bob Gordon, and Jonathon Hilton for their input at various stages of the book. Thanks go to everyone at Dorling Kindersley, Richmond, who have contributed: in particular Jonathan Metcalf, Carole McGlynn, Constance Novis, Mary-Clare Jerram, Gill della Casa, Spencer Holbrook, Vicki James, Anne Thompson, and Sam Grimmer. Last, but not least, thanks to Rita Hemsley for her typing skills, and Les Crawley and John Mandeville for their invaluable contributions.

Dorling Kindersley would like to thank: Lemon Graphics, Alastair Wardle, Pauline Bayne, Elaine Hewson, and Sharon Moore for design assistance; Mike Darton and Amanda Ronan for proofreading; Michael Allaby for indexing; Julia Pashley for picture research; Helen Townsend, Angeles Gavira, and Lucinda Hawksley for editorial assistance.

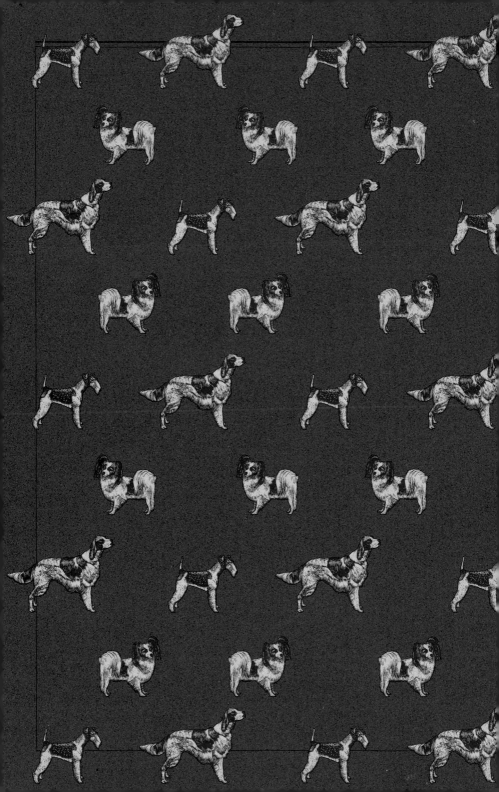